The Unity of Wittgenstein's Philosophy

SUNY SERIES IN PHILOSOPHY
George R. Lucas Jr., editor

The Unity of Wittgenstein's Philosophy

Necessity, Intelligibility, and Normativity

By
José Medina

STATE UNIVERSITY OF NEW YORK PRESS

Published by
State University of New York Press, Albany

Printed in the United States of America

For information, address State University of New York Press,
90 State Street, Suite 700, Albany, NY 12207

Production by Christine L. Hamel
Marketing by Michael Campochiaro

Library of Congress Cataloging in Publication Data

Medina, José, 1968–
The unity of Wittgenstein's philosophy : necessity, intelligibility, and normativity / by José Medina
p. cm. — (SUNY series in philosophy)
Includes bibliographical references and index.
ISBN 0-7914-5387-1 (alk. paper) — ISBN 0-7914-5388-X (pbk. : alk. paper)
1. Wittgenstein, Ludwig, 1889–1951. I. Title. II. Series.

B3376.W564.M42 2002
192—dc21 2002020780

10 9 8 7 6 5 4 3 2 1

For my parents:
Concha and Joaquin

CONTENTS

ACKNOWLEDGMENTS

This book began as a dissertation written in the philosophy department at Northwestern University from 1995 to 1998. Thanks are first due to the dissertation committee that supervised my work during those years: Meredith Williams, Michael Williams, Arthur Fine, and Joan Weiner. I am greatly indebted to all of them for their careful reading of my work and for being always both critical and supportive. But my greatest debt is to Meredith Williams, who chaired the dissertation from which this book originated and to whom I owe everything I know about Wittgenstein. Her work on Wittgenstein has always been and continues to be an inspiration for my own.

I could not have written this book without the support I have received from my colleagues at Vanderbilt University in the last two years. I am immensely grateful to the department of philosophy for providing the most stimulating intellectual environment one can hope for and to all its members for giving me their continued and enthusiastic support and for taking the time to read the manuscript. I am thankful for the comments of Professor Lenn Goodman on a draft of chapters 1 and 2 and for the careful critical remarks of Professor Jeffrey Tlumak on a complete draft of the manuscript (especialy his detailed criticisms of chapter 4). Special thanks go to Professor Michael Hodges, my colleague and chair, for numerous conversations on Wittgenstein, for attending my seminar on Wittgenstein in 1999, and for reading and commenting on drafts of the book (especially those of chapters 1 and 6). Finally, the person who is most directly responsible for the completion of this book is my mentor, Professor John Lachs, who has always been extremely enthusiastic about my work and has given me invaluable guidance. He was the first person to read a complete draft of the manuscript and had it not been for his encouragement, I would not have kept working on it. It was comforting to know that I could always count on his generous help. I am also grateful to John for suggesting that I submit the manuscript to the State University of New York Press.

Drafts of parts of the manuscript were read at professional meetings under the following titles: "The Role of the Community: Contextualism and Quietism in Wittgenstein's Later Philosophy" (*Pacific APA Meeting* in Albuquerque, 2000); "The Possibility of 'Logically Alien Thought' in Wittgenstein's Later Philosophy" (*Central APA Meeting* in Chicago, 2000); and "Verificationism and Inferentialism in Wittgenstein's Philosophy" (*Pacific APA Meeting* in San Francisco, 2001). I am thankful for the comments I received at these presentations.

On a personal note, I also want to express my gratitude to my family in Spain and to my friends both in Spain and here (they know who they are). Without their emotional support I would not have survived in exile. It is only thanks to them that I retained my sanity while writing this book.

ABBREVIATIONS

The following abbreviations are used to refer to Frege's and Wittgenstein's works, listed in chronological order. This list includes derivative primary sources and lecture notes taken by others. References to secondary literature will be provided in notes.

G. Frege

FA	*The Foundations of Arithmetic*, translated by J. L. Austin (Evanston: Northwestern University Press, 1980).
BLA	*The Basic Laws of Arithmetic*, in *Translations from the Philosophical Writings of Gottlob Frege*, edited and translated by P. Geach and M. Black (Oxford: Blackwell, 1952).

L. Wittgenstein

Tractatus	*Tractatus Logico-Philosophicus*, translated by D. F. Pears and B. F. McGuiness (London: Routledge and Kegan Paul, 1961).
SRLF	"Some Remarks on Logical Form," in J. Klagge and A. Nordmann (eds.), *Philosophical Occasions 1912–1951* (Indianapolis: Hackett, 1993), pp. 29–35.
WWK	*Wittgenstein and the Vienna Circle*, shorthand notes recorded by F. Waismann and edited by B. F. McGuiness (Oxford: Blackwell, 1979).

PR	*Philosophical Remarks*, edited by R. Rhees and translated by R. Hargreaves and R. White (Oxford: Blackwell, 1975).
Lectures 1930-32	*Wittgenstein's Lectures, Cambridge 1930–32*, from the notes of J. King and D. Lee, edited by D. Lee (Oxford: Blackwell, 1979).
PG	*Philosophical Grammar*, edited by R. Rhees and translated by A. Kenny (Oxford: Blackwell, 1974).
Lectures 1932–35	*Wittgenstein's Lectures, Cambridge 1932–35*, from the notes of A. Ambrose and M. MacDonald, edited by A. Ambrose (Oxford: Blackwell, 1979).
BLB & BRB	*The Blue and Brown Books* (Oxford: Blackwell, 1958).
RFM	*Remarks on the Foundations of Mathematics*, edited by G. H. von Wright, R. Rhees and G. E. M. Anscombe, and translated by G. E. M. Anscombe, revised edition (Oxford: Blackwell, 1978).
LFM	*Wittgenstein's Lectures on the Foundations of Mathematics, Cambridge 1939*, edited by C. Diamond (Chicago: University of Chicago Press, 1989).
PI	*Philosophical Investigations*, edited by G. E. M. Anscombe and R. Rhees, and translated by G. E. M. Anscombe, 2d edition (Oxford: Blackwell, 1958).
Z	*Zettel*, edited by G. E. M. Anscombe and G. H. von Wright, and translated by G. E. M. Anscombe (Oxford: Blackwell, 1967).

INTRODUCTION

Until recently it was almost universally[1] assumed in the literature on Wittgenstein that he developed two radically different philosophies, which found expression in his two main works, the *Tractatus* and the *Investigations*. Accordingly, the task for those interested in the evolution of Wittgenstein's thought was to explain the radical shift from his early to his later philosophy. Recent interpretations, however, have called into question the myth of the two Wittgensteins. Cora Diamond (1991), James Conant (1991b, 1998), and their followers (cf. A. Crary and R. Read [2000]) have argued persuasively that there is a unitary core in Wittgenstein's philosophy that runs from the *Tractatus* to the *Investigations*, a unique way of tackling philosophical problems and working toward their dissolution. But although of late many commentators have emphasized the unity of Wittgenstein's philosophy, this new line of interpretation still needs to be supported by a detailed account of the unity in the development of Wittgenstein's thought.[2] In this book I try to articulate such an account, examining how the stable core of Wittgenstein's philosophy is developed from the *Tractatus* to the *Investigations*.[3] The developmental story that I tell, however, is not the story of the unfolding of a single view,[4] but rather, the story of an ongoing philosophical conversation (or monologue) and its internal logic. As we shall see, Wittgenstein was an experimental philosopher who was always trying out new ways of thinking and resolving philosophical issues; and the different views that he elaborated at different stages in his career were always work in progress, transitional but never final sketches. I will argue that what gives unity and continuity to this experimental thinking is a set of themes and a particular way of approaching them. My developmental account will try to uncover both the *thematic* and the *methodological* unity of Wittgenstein's philosophy.

In the first place, I will try to show that what is at the core of Wittgenstein's philosophy in all its stages is a constant preoccupation with *two interrelated themes*—namely, *necessity* and *intelligibility*. Throughout his career Wittgenstein tried to dispel the metaphysical illusions concerning necessity that arise from the misguided attempt to find room for the necessary and the impossible in a world of contingency. Throughout his career he argued (in a variety of ways) that necessity does not concern the metaphysical structure of the world, but rather, the normative structure of language. He thought that all philosophical problems about necessity can be dissolved by means of an elucidation of ordinary language use. Thus, on Wittgenstein's view, the issue of necessity is bound up with the issue of the normativity of language, which concerns the distinction between sense and nonsense, between admissible and inadmissible combinations of signs. Throughout his career Wittgenstein tried to resist philosophical misconceptions concerning what *can* and *cannot* be said. Here too his primary aim was to debunk metaphysical illusions that arise when we depart from ordinary language, in this case by detaching the distinction between sense and nonsense from our ordinary ways of talking.

In the second place, I will argue that there is a strong *methodological* unity underlying the different treatments of these themes that Wittgenstein offered throughout his career. From the *Tractatus* to the *Investigations* Wittgenstein adopted a *deflationary* approach to tackle philosophical problems concerning necessity and intelligibility. More importantly yet, Wittgenstein's deflationary approach always relied on the same strategy—namely, *contextualism*. He identified decontextualization as the main source of philosophical confusions and argued that we can only achieve philosophical understanding by situating our ideas or concepts in the contexts in which they function. As we shall see, this is what his logical and grammatical elucidations of ordinary language try to achieve: to demystify concepts (such as "meaning" and "necessity") by viewing them against the background of our ordinary uses of language, that is, "to bring words back from their metaphysical to their everyday use" (PI §116). It was Wittgenstein's view throughout his career that this contextualist strategy is what enables us to deflate philosophical notions and dissolve the problems associated with them. However, the notion of *context* undergoes change in the development of Wittgenstein's thought. Initially Wittgenstein thought that the context that was the proper object of his philosophical elucidations was a *logical* context: what he called the "logical space" in which propositions signify, or the "logical scaffolding" surrounding our statements (cf. *Tractatus* 3.42). Later he contended that the context that needed to be examined in order to elucidate philosophical issues concerning necessity and intelligibility was the *grammatical* context provided by the system of rules or conventions underlying our *material* inferences. Finally, we will come across a third notion of context that includes not only words but also actions: the *pragmatic* context of our actual practices or "language games." So in my developmental account we will encounter three different versions of Wittgenstein's contextualism: an early, logical contextualism; an intermediate, conventionalist (or material-inferentialist) contextualism; and a later, pragmatic (or practice-based) contextualism.[5]

My developmental story will not be a neutral account of the adventurous life of Wittgenstein's contextualism, but rather, a critical reconstruction that examines the virtues and vices of these different versions of contextualism, criticizing its earlier logicist and inferentialist versions. It will be my thesis that—ultimately—it is only the pragmatic contextualism of Wittgenstein's later philosophy that actually provides a successful deflationary view of necessity, intelligibility, and the normativity of language. In this critical reconstruction I will try to identify the central challenges that Wittgenstein's various deflationary proposals face. In doing so, Frege will become a key character in my developmental story, for—I will argue—his views played a crucial role in setting the agenda of Wittgenstein's philosophy.

Until recently most commentators emphasized that Frege's views appear in Wittgenstein's philosophy *only* as a target of criticism.[6] The recent literature, however, underscores strong affinities between Frege's and Wittgenstein's philosophy. In particular, commentators have found an interesting convergence in the goals and methods shared by Frege and the early Wittgenstein.[7] Here too my interpretation is in line with the recent literature. I will argue that Frege's views exerted a strong positive influence not only on the *Tractatus*, but also on the intermediate and later periods of Wittgenstein's philosophy. My developmental account will underscore that Frege's twin critiques of formalism and psychologism play an important *positive* role in critically shaping Wittgenstein's thought from the 1920s on. On the one hand, the conventionalist view that Wittgenstein defended until the mid 1930s will have to meet the challenge raised by Frege's critique of formalism; namely, that normativity cannot spring from the mere stipulation of rules for the manipulation of signs. On the other hand, the practice-based view of normativity developed by the later Wittgenstein will have to meet the challenge raised by Frege's critique of psychologism; namely, that objective standards of correctness cannot be the product of a mere generalization of how things are done in actual practice. I will argue that Wittgenstein was unable to find a satisfactory answer to the challenge that Frege's critique of formalism posed to his conventionalist view and hence he abandoned this view. However, I will contend, the practice-based view of normativity that he went on to develop does avoid the pitfalls of psychologism underscored by Frege's critique. For this view does not reduce the normative to the empirical and psychological, and it does not conflate what is correct with what we happen to count as such. I will conclude my argument by defending Wittgenstein's pragmatic contextualism against some contemporary objections. In particular, I will try to show that this version of contextualism deflates necessity and normativity without falling into relativism.

The main goal of my developmental account of the unity of Wittgenstein's philosophy is to identify the key problems and arguments that structure the evolution of Wittgenstein's thought. But I hope that my critical reconstruction can shed some light on contemporary debates concerning necessity and intelligibility as well; for in this reconstruction we will encounter, diagnose, and criticize many philosophical accounts of necessity and intelligibility that are still influential today. Following Wittgenstein in trying to find a deflationary understanding of necessity free from philosophical illusions, a variety of views from metaphysical realism to radical conventionalism will be considered. On the other hand, my analysis of Wittgenstein's discussions of the distinction between sense and nonsense will lead us to examine different philosophical conceptions of language (esp. logicism, inferentialism, pragmatism, and their different construals of semantic holism). So I would like to think that the arguments I develop in what follows can be of some value not only to those interested in Wittgenstein's philosophy, but also to those interested in philosophical issues concerning necessity, intelligibility, and the normativity of language.

1

Necessity and Intelligibility in the *Tractatus*

> Wittgenstein's philosophy, throughout his life, is directed against certain ways of imagining necessity. Throughout his life, his treatment of logic aims at letting us see necessity where it does lie, in the use of ordinary sentences. The trouble with chickening out, or one trouble with it, is that it holds on to exactly the kind of imagination of necessity, necessity imagined as fact, that Wittgenstein aimed to free us from.
>
> —Cora Diamond 1991, p. 195

As many commentators have pointed out,[1] one of Wittgenstein's key concerns when he returned to philosophy in 1929 was the so-called color-exclusion problem; that is, the problem of how to account for the impossibility of attributing two colors to the same point in the visual field. However, although there are interesting analyses of this problem in the literature,[2] the questions of what is at stake in this problem and why it had the critical potential to destabilize the Tractarian framework have not yet been settled. What is so special about the mutual exclusion of colors? In the *Tractatus* the phenomenon of color exclusion appears as a very tangential problem, which is dealt with in a single section (6.3751). Color exclusion is one of the few examples that Wittgenstein gives in the *Tractatus* and, as such, it appears as a matter of detail without any special significance. So, one should think, Wittgenstein's dissatisfaction with the Tractarian treatment of the phenomenon of color exclusion should have called for no more than some tinkering within the Tractarian framework; and it would be quite surprising if this small problem could lead to a radical rethinking of the framework itself. In this chapter I will try to show that the color-exclusion problem is not as marginal as it seems at first sight. I will argue that this problem should be understood as a crucial test case of the new way of thinking about necessity that Wittgenstein proposes in the *Tractatus*, which is in turn a new way of thinking about how we manage to make sense as we do in ordinary language. So, if I am right, to miss the significance of the color-exclusion problem would be to miss the most original insights of Wittgenstein's early philosophy.

The argument that follows is both constructive and diagnostic. On the one hand, I provide an interpretation of the Tractarian notions of necessity and possibility (in 1.1) and an analysis of the color-exclusion problem and its far-reaching implications (in 1.2 and 1.3). On the other hand, I try to explain how and why this problem has been systematically misunderstood (in 1.2). As we shall see, what has precluded commentators from seeing the problem in the right light is a deep-seated philosophical way of conceptualizing necessity: namely, necessity conceived as constraining language from without; or as Diamond puts it, "necessity imagined as fact." Ironically, this philosophical picture of necessity is precisely what Wittgenstein was trying to subvert with his remarks on the phenomenon of color exclusion at 6.3751. Throughout his philosophical career, Wittgenstein held that it is a fatal mistake to think of necessity as grounded in the structure of reality. He repeatedly argued that it is pointless and ultimately nonsensical to look for the source of necessity outside language. He insisted that we can make no sense of a realm of ineffable necessities that exists independently of the realm of contingencies we ordinarily talk about. In the *Tractatus* Wittgenstein tried to deontologize and demystify the concept of necessity by showing that it is a logical concept that has to be clarified by means of logical elucidations of our ordinary ways of talking about what is the case. For the author of the *Tractatus*, the project of deontologizing necessity and the project of clarifying the logic of linguistic representation and showing how meaning is possible go hand in hand; they are, in fact, one and the same project. As Diamond suggests, on Wittgenstein's view, understanding the logical structure of language enables us to see that necessity lies "in the use of ordinary sentences"[3]; and conversely, understanding necessity as a symbolic phenomenon that originates in language use enables us to recognize the necessary features of our symbolisms—that is, the logical underpinnings of our ordinary ways of making sense. As we shall see, the Tractarian treatment of necessity and the Tractarian treatment of meaning are inextricably interwoven. It is this intimate connection between meaning and necessity that the color-exclusion problem brings to the fore; and this, I will argue, explains the special place that this problem occupies in the *Tractatus* and in the development of Wittgenstein's thought (cf. 1.3 and chapter 2). Finally, I will conclude by exploring the implications that my account of this seemingly marginal problem has for the interpretation of Wittgenstein's early philosophy. In particular, I will examine (in 1.4) how my account bears on the interpretative dispute between realist and deflationary readings of the *Tractatus*.

1.1. Possibility and Necessity in the *Tractatus*

The notions of *possibility* and *necessity* are central pillars of the pictorial account of meaning provided in the *Tractatus.* "A picture depicts reality by representing a *possibility* of existence and non-existence of states of affairs"; it "represents a *possible* situation" (2.201–2.202; my emphasis). A proposition, like a picture, depicts a *possible* state of affairs (cf. 3.11ff). On Wittgenstein's view, it is consubstantial to the pictoriality of a proposition that the proposition can be deemed "correct or incorrect, true or false" (2.21). The possible state of affairs represented by a proposition may or may not obtain, and accordingly the proposition may agree or fail to agree with reality. "In order to tell whether a picture is true or false we must compare it with reality. It is impossible to tell from the picture alone whether it is true or false" (2.223–2.224). But only what is *possible* is so evaluable; what is necessary or impossible cannot be symbolically represented ("There are no pictures that are true a priori"; 2.225). In short, the essence of a significant proposition is to give expression to a "truth-possibility" (cf. 4.3ff).

Wittgenstein distinguishes between two different kinds of truth-possibilities, simple and complex, and between two corresponding kinds of propositions. If the truth-possibility expressed by a proposition is logically dependent on other truth-possibilities, the proposition is complex and therefore analyzable into simpler propositions. There *must* be a last level of analysis where we reach propositions of "the simplest kind" (4.21): "It is *obvious* that the analysis of propositions *must* bring us to elementary propositions" (4.221; my emphasis). These propositions are concatenations of names (4.22), that is, combinations of logically simple signs that designate objects (cf. 3.202–3.203). Elementary propositions express *primitive* truth-possibilities. Their defining feature is that they are *logically independent* of one another ("It is a sign of a proposition's being elementary that there can be no elementary proposition contradicting it"; 4.211). Complex propositions are "truth-functions" of elementary propositions, which are their "truth-arguments" (5). The truth-functional composition of a proposition can be exhibited in a truth-table, which schematizes the truth-possibilities contained in the proposition (4.31). The truth-table analysis of language shows the possible truth-functional combinations of elementary propositions. If we were given "*all* elementary propositions," we could determine what propositions can be constructed out of them and hence fix the whole range of logical possibilities expressible in language (4.51–4.52).

However, there is a *special* class of propositions that do not express truth-*possibilities*, for they have a fixed truth-value: they are necessarily true or necessarily false. These are propositions that have a *tautological* or *contradictory* form. What is most characteristic about them is that their truth-value can be recognized "from the symbol alone,"[4] since they are true or false in virtue of their logical form. But, as we just saw, the correctness of a picture cannot be determined "from the picture alone" (2.224). So it follows that "tautologies and contradictions are *not pictures* of reality. They do not represent any *possible* situations. For the former admit all possible situations, the latter none" (4.462; my emphasis). And since they do not depict possible states of affairs, they have *no representational content*; they are entirely empty. By emphasizing the factual emptiness of tautologies and contradictions, Wittgenstein is trying to dissuade us from thinking about these peculiar symbolic constructions as expressions of a special kind of truth and falsehood about the world. As he remarks, a tautology is "unconditionally true" and "a contradiction is true on no condition," not because they have *special* truth conditions, but rather, because they have "*no truth-conditions*" at all (4.461; my emphasis). These symbolic constructions do not express *any* particular truth or *any* particular falsehood about the world because they do "not stand in any representational relation to reality" (4.462). Wittgenstein explains the factual emptiness of these constructions as follows:

> The truth-conditions of a proposition determine the range that it leaves open to the facts. [. . .] A tautology leaves open to reality the whole—the infinite whole—of logical space: a contradiction fills the whole of logical space leaving no point of it for reality. Thus neither of them can determine reality in any way. (4.463)

There are two crucial points that Wittgenstein's discussion of tautologies and contradictions brings out. The first one concerns the deontologization of necessity I alluded to in the introduction. According to Wittgenstein's discussion, there is no room in the world for necessities and impossibilities. For, on the Tractarian view, the world is composed of facts that can be depicted in language ("facts in logical space"; 1.13) but, as we just saw, necessities and impossibilities are not picturable facts. To imagine necessities and impossibilities as residing in the world would be to imagine facts of a special kind that are beyond the reach of our systems of representation. Wittgenstein tries to show that these elusive facts that we may be inclined to imagine vanish into thin air upon closer examination. For we have no model of these facts; the logic of factual discourse does not leave room for them. According to the *Tractatus*, when we talk about the world, we talk about contingencies; and when we talk about what is necessary and impossible, we are no longer talking about the world ("For example, I know nothing about the weather when I know that it is either raining or not raining."; 4.461). Thus Wittgenstein tries to convince us that, ultimately, given the logic of our ordinary ways of talking about the world, we cannot make sense of necessities and impossibilities imagined as facts.

However, the advocate of a metaphysical account of necessity may be unimpressed by these considerations, arguing that necessities constitute a factual domain that is simply not reachable by the logic of ordinary discourse. As Diamond has pointed out, it is characteristic of this kind of metaphysical account to appeal to a dual logic; that is, to argue that "what is necessary has got its own logic distinct from the logic of our ordinary descriptions of what is the case."[5] According to Diamond, this is the illusion underlying metaphysical accounts of necessity which Wittgenstein sets out to dispel. According to Wittgenstein's logical analysis, any attempt to separate the logic of what is necessary from the logic of what is merely possible falls into incoherence. For the logic of necessity and the logic of possibility define each other; they are not simply inseparable, but in fact one and the same logic. Thus, by embedding the logic of necessity in the logic of possibility that underlies ordinary discourse, Wittgenstein undercuts the misguided tendency to think of necessities as constituting an ontological realm that lies beyond the reach of our ordinary descriptions of the world. Necessities (and impossibilities) are neither intraworldly nor extraworldly facts; they are not facts at all.

The deflationary potential in Wittgenstein's discussion of tautologies and contradictions has already been emphasized by Diamond.[6] Where my analysis departs from her interpretation is in the second point contained in Wittgenstein's discussion: a point that concerns the *propositional status* of tautologies and contradictions. Once we accept the vacuity of these symbolic constructions, what are we supposed to do with them? Do they have any role to play in our symbolisms? Diamond argues that tautologies and contradictions do not turn out to be genuine sentences, but only "sentence-like constructions formulable from sentences": "We shall not be tempted to think of tautologies and contradictions as saying that something or other is the case. We shall not be tempted really to think of them as sentences."[7] But Wittgenstein does not say that tautologies and contradictions should be regarded as pseudopropositions. He is in fact rather stingy in the use of the term "pseudoproposition" (*Scheinsatz*). He reserves this term for those symbolic constructions that involve a misuse of the word "object" (4.1272) and those that contain the equality sign (5.534–5.535; 6.2). Pseudopropositions are symbolic creatures that have a deceitful nature: they are combinations of signs that have the appearance of saying something while they are in fact "nonsensical" (*unsinnig*; cf. 4.1272). We learn at the end of the book that all the "propositions" of the *Tractatus* are deceitful in this way: they have a propositional appearance but are in fact *unsinnig* (6.54). But tautologies and contradictions are not deceitful. On the contrary, they make their emptiness perspicuous: they "show that they say nothing" (4.461). Given their lack of representational content, tautologies and contradictions are certainly not *significant* propositions: they are "senseless" (*sinnlos*; 4.461). But Wittgenstein is quick to point out that they "are not, however, nonsensical [*unsinnig*]. They are part of the symbolism" (4.4611).

To think that the emptiness of tautologies and contradictions is tantamount to their lack of propositional status is to overlook the distinction between *sinnlos* and *unsinnig*. On Wittgenstein's view, a string of signs is nonsense, plain nonsense, and therefore a pseudoproposition only when it lacks logical form altogether (and not just pictorial form and representational content). Pseudopropositions are strings of signs which, strictly speaking, are uncombined since they have not been combined according to the rules of logical syntax. Tautologies and contradictions do not fall into this category, for, as Wittgenstein remarks, "signs are still combined with one another even in tautologies and contradictions" (4.4661). These nonpictorial propositions are very peculiar indeed, but they are not illicit combinations of signs. They are "the *limiting cases*—indeed the *disintegration*—of the combinations of signs" (4.466; my emphasis). They have logical form, albeit an aberrant one.[8] And it is in virtue of their aberrant logical form that tautologies and contradictions play a fundamental role in language: they show the limits of significance, the points at which logical form disintegrates; they constitute the boundary stones of what is expressible. The logical space for meaningful discourse is the realm of logical possibilities that lies between tautologies and contradictions: "A tautology's truth is certain, a proposition's possible, a contradiction's impossible" (4.464).

But why does Diamond want to banish tautologies and contradictions from our symbolisms? There are two different arguments one can draw from her discussion that speak against granting propositional status to tautologies and contradictions. First, one might think that keeping these symbolic constructions as genuine propositions would be what Diamond calls "chickening out," that is, holding on to the "ladder" that we are supposed to let go. But I don't see why this warranted worry about "chickening out" should apply here. What Wittgenstein and Diamond refer to as the "ladder" that has to be thrown away is supposed to encompass the propositions of the *Tractatus* and, more generally, all philosophical propositions. But there is no reason why we should treat tautologies and contradictions as Tractarian propositions or as philosophical propositions. The propositions of the *Tractatus* are certainly not tautological or contradictory. More importantly, unlike Tractarian propositions, tautologies and contradictions are not attempts to say anything philosophical, since (as Diamond herself shows) they are not attempts to say anything *at all*. The Tractarian remarks about necessity have to be ultimately discarded, not because they are empty, but because they are *unsinnig* (cf. 6.54).[9] On the other hand, tautologies and contradictions are not *about* anything and a fortiori they are not about necessity either. They have to be granted propositional status precisely because of their emptiness, not in spite of it. For it is their emptiness that makes them harmless as well as useful. Without saying anything at all tautologies and contradictions show where logical form disintegrates and thus they demarcate the limits of language from within.

There is another, more technical argument that Diamond offers for disqualifying tautologies and contradictions as genuine propositions. This argument has to do with the logical atomism of the *Tractatus*. According to Diamond, the logical independence that defines elementary propositions would be untenable if we were to allow logical truths and logical falsehoods to be expressed in propositions. An elementary proposition "p" cannot have a determinate truth-value unless it presupposes the truth of tautologies such as "p or not p" and the falsity of contradictions such as "p and not p." But then it appears that no proposition can be a candidate for truth or falsity independently of the truth-value of all other propositions, for the truth of tautologies and the falsity of contradictions must always be presupposed. Diamond argues that the only way out of this difficulty is to deny propositional status to tautologies and contradictions: "If tautologies and contradictions are genuine sentences, the idea of sentences as [. . .] capable of truth or falsity regardless of the truth or falsity of any sentence [. . .] has to go."[10] This ad hoc solution really smells like a dirty trick: "To avoid trouble let's not consider these peculiar constructions as part of the symbolism." This is a solution that flies in the face of Wittgenstein's words ("Tautologies and contradictions [. . .] are part of the symbolism"; 4.4611). But, at any rate, it is a solution that is not needed, for it answers an artificial problem. The difficulty that Diamond discusses is an artifact of an overly strong reading of the logical atomism of the *Tractatus*. The idea that "sentences must be capable of truth or falsity regardless of the truth or falsity of *any* sentence," which she attributes to Wittgenstein,[11] is nowhere to be found in the *Tractatus*. Elementary propositions are said to be logically independent only *from each other*, but not from every other proposition (cf. 4.211). An elementary proposition certainly enters into logical relations with *complex* propositions in which it figures as a component; and it is always logically related to all those propositions that have a tautological or contradictory form (since their logical truth or falsity is entailed by the truth-valuedness of *any* proposition). However, this does not present a problem. An elementary proposition expresses a primitive truth-possibility, a simple determination of reality, and it cannot presuppose any other simple determination of reality. But, as we saw, tautologies and contradictions do not "determine reality in any way" (4.463). Therefore, the fact that the truth of tautologies and the falsity of contradictions are presupposed by all propositions does not undermine the logical independence that elementary propositions are supposed to have.

Commentators have often regarded the atomistic and the holistic strands in the *Tractatus* as being in conflict.[12] However, when we recognize that the Tractarian atomism has a very limited scope, that it concerns only the relations among elementary propositions, the alleged conflict disappears. The truth-possibilities of elementary propositions are said to be logically independent from each other (4.3ff), but they are not supposed to be independent from necessities and impossibilities. On the contrary, on the Tractarian view, something is a possibility only against the background of what is necessary and impossible. Logical truths and falsehoods provide the *logical space* in which possibilities can be pictured. As Wittgenstein observes, a proposition cannot picture a truth-possibility all by itself, but only against a background: "A proposition can determine only one place in logical space: nevertheless *the whole of logical* space must already be given by it. [. . .] (The logical scaffolding surrounding a picture determines logical space. The force of the proposition reaches through *the whole of logical space*)" (3.42; my emphasis). The whole of logic (all logical truths and falsehoods) must already be given when a truth-possibility is depicted in an elementary proposition. (Hence Wittgenstein's remark: "An elementary proposition really contains all logical operations in itself"; in it "we already have all the logical constants"; 5.47.) This logical dependence of elementary propositions on tautologies and contradictions is not an unwelcome result of the Tractarian analysis but the core idea that drives the analysis. This dependence is as should be and it could not be otherwise; for, as we saw, the logic of possibility and the logic of necessity (and impossibility) are inextricably intertwined and their separation is neither desirable nor possible.

So, according to the logical holism of the *Tractatus*, the linguistic representation of what is possible can only take place against the background of logical necessities and impossibilities. One might be suspicious of this conception of necessities and impossibilities as the requisite background of symbolic representation, for it is reminiscent of what Diamond takes to be the principal sign of "chickening out"—namely, "the idea of a realm of necessities underlying our capacity to make sense as we do."[13] However, as Diamond points out, we chicken out only when we think of necessities as constituting an *ontological realm*, that is, as grounded in "ontological categories, objectively fixed and independent of language, which the logical syntax of language is then required to mirror."[14] But when we appreciate the emptiness of tautologies and contradictions and we no longer imagine necessities and impossibilities as facts, then we can see that they are *nothing* to be afraid of, for we learn that necessities and impossibilities cannot be thought of as *things* that are beyond the reach of language. What the emptiness of tautologies and contradictions shows is precisely that necessities and impossibilities do not reside in an ontological realm that logical syntax has to mirror, but rather, that they reside in the logical form of our symbolisms, in the "logical scaffolding" surrounding our symbolic representations (cf. 3.42). So to say that the significance of a proposition presupposes the necessary truths and falsehoods of tautologies and contradictions is just to say that it presupposes logical syntax. It is in this way that Wittgenstein's views of necessity and logical composition mutually support each other.[15]

1.2. What's Color Got to Do with It?

The logical account of necessity that Wittgenstein develops in the 6s draws on the truth-functional account of logical composition offered in the 4s and 5s. According to this account, necessarily true and necessarily false propositions cannot be elementary: they must have a complex logical structure in which elementary propositions are truth-functionally combined in such a way that the last column of the proposition's truth-table admits only one value (only T's or only F's), whatever the values of its truth-arguments happen to be. That certain combinations of truth-possibilities are either necessary or impossible can only be shown by complex propositions whose logical form is either tautological or contradictory. What is necessary and impossible is exhibited in the logical form of our symbolisms and is determined by the logical syntax of truth-functionality. Therefore, Wittgenstein concludes: "The only necessity that exists is *logical* necessity" (6.37); and, correspondingly, "the only impossibility that exists is *logical* impossibility" (6.375). This last remark precedes the introduction of the color-exclusion problem.

The phenomenon of color exclusion is presented as an illustration of the idea that whatever is impossible must be logically impossible: "For example, the simultaneous presence of two colours at the same place in the visual field is impossible, in fact logically impossible" (6.3751). Wittgenstein's choice of example is indeed peculiar. The mutual exclusion of colors does not seem to be the most appropriate example to convince someone of the logical nature of necessity. For, prima facie, color incompatibility appears to be a brute fact of nature, rather than a phenomenon patently derived from logical laws. However, Wittgenstein's remark that color incompatibility is a matter of logical impossibility is not meant as an obvious illustration of the hegemony of logical necessity, but rather, as a counterintuitive (but unavoidable) corollary of his thesis that there is only logical necessity and impossibility. The contentious claim is that even this seemingly physical impossibility must, in the end, be reducible to a logical impossibility. And, given Wittgenstein's truth-functional account of necessity and impossibility, what this means is that a statement that attributes two colors to the same point in the visual field must be a complex proposition which has the aberrant logical form of a *contradiction*: "The statement that a point in the visual field has two different colours at the same time is a contradiction" (6.3751).

Now, if a proposition is contradictory, we must be able to recognize from its notational features—*from the symbol alone*—that the proposition is necessarily false: "If two propositions contradict one another, then their structure shows it" (4.1211). On Wittgenstein's view, the aberrant logical form of contradictory statements is to be brought to light by means of truth-functional analysis. The truth-functional analysis of a contradictory statement must show that there is no truth-value assignment that can make the statement true, and therefore no combination of states of affairs that can correspond to it. According to 6.3751, the statement "A (a point in the visual field) is both red and blue at the same time" is a logically impossible combination of elementary propositions and it must have the aberrant logical form of a contradiction. However, this aberrant logical form is in no way reflected in the surface form of the statement. On the contrary, the statement has the deceiving appearance of a simple conjunction ("P & Q"), and we are inclined to think that its truth-functional analysis must yield the truth-table for conjunction (TFFF). This is precisely why it is hard to see that color incompatibility is a *logical* impossibility: because we cannot recognize the necessary falsity of statements such as "A is both red and blue at the same time" *from the symbol alone*. So these statements seem to be necessarily false propositions that are not reducible to truth-functional contradictions. However, Wittgenstein's contention is that they *must* be so reducible. But how?

The statement "A is both red and blue at the same time" cannot be the logical product of two elementary propositions, for, if it were, it could "neither be a tautology nor a contradiction" (6.3751). In his review of the *Tractatus*, Ramsey drew the following conclusion from Wittgenstein's remarks at 6.3751: "That 'This is both red and blue' is a contradiction [. . .] implies that the apparently simple concepts red, blue (supposing us to mean by those words absolutely specific shades) are really complex and formally incompatible."[16] Ramsey's thought seems to be that since "This is red" and "This is blue" cannot be elementary propositions, that is, concatenations of names, some of their component terms must be complex expressions susceptible of further analysis. And Ramsey assumes that the only candidates for further analysis are the terms "red" and "blue." So he concludes that color terms cannot be logically simple expressions, that elementary propositions must be curled up in them somehow. For if "red" and "blue" were not complex predicates but unanalyzable names, their concatenation could not possibly yield a contradiction. So on Ramsey's reading of 6.3751, the color-exclusion problem is, at bottom, a problem about *simplicity and elementariness*: a problem about which signs qualify as logically simple, and which combinations of signs as elementary propositions. Following Ramsey's interpretation, Shanker contends that the immediate implications of the claim that "A is both red and blue" is a contradiction are "that 'red' cannot be the name of a simple, and thus that 'A is red' is not fully analysed."[17]

But we must proceed with caution in drawing these conclusions, for the contradiction discussed in 6.3751 is not between 'A is red' and 'A is blue' *simpliciter*, but rather, between 'A is red at time t' and 'A is blue at time t'. The contradiction arises when a point in the visual field is said to have "two different colours *at the same time*." This is what Wittgenstein's analogy with statements about velocity emphasizes: "a particle cannot have two velocities at the same time; that is to say, it cannot be in two places at the same time" (6.3751). The phenomenon of exclusion only occurs when a temporal element is introduced. Nothing in Wittgenstein's discussion suggests that a statement about a particle (A) being in a particular place (P^1, P^2, P^3 . . .) cannot be elementary. Strictly speaking, the propositions "AP^1," "AP^2," "AP^3," . . . , are logically independent; any one of them makes a simple determination that does not exclude any other unless we introduce the idea of simultaneity. The logical product of any two of these propositions is not a contradiction. The contradiction that Wittgenstein alludes to is not "AP^1 & AP^2" (objects can change place!), but rather, "AP^1T^1 & AP^2T^1." So it follows that "AP^1T^1" and "AP^2T^1" cannot be elementary. But nothing follows about "AP^1" and "AP^2." Similarly, it is not statements *about color* as such that are deemed complex in the argument of 6.3751. A proposition ascribing two colors, say red (R) and blue (B), to a point in the visual field ("RP^1 & BP^1") is not a contradiction if the element of simultaneity is not introduced (points in the visual field can change color!). The propositions that are mutually exclusive and therefore complex are "RP^1T^1" and "BP^1T^1." Nothing follows about "RP^1" and "BP^1."

At 6.3751 Wittgenstein does not address the issue of whether or not colors are primitive simples. His claim is that statements ascribing colors to spatiotemporal points in the visual field cannot be elementary propositions. But he does not try to determine whether the logical complexity of these statements stems from the spatiotemporal individuation of points in the visual field, or from the ascription of colors to these points. Wittgenstein's point is simply that "A is both red and blue at the same time" *must* turn out to be a more complex logical product than it seems at first sight, that its full analysis *must* reveal that it is in fact a truth-functional combination of elementary propositions that cannot be true under any assignment of truth-values. This conclusion is established on a priori grounds; it is presented as a direct consequence of the truth-functional account of logical composition and logical necessity developed previously. But Wittgenstein does not attempt to specify exactly how we are supposed to transform incompatible color attributions into truth-functional contradictions. In fact, it would be very surprising if he did. It would be surprising if Wittgenstein made the attempt to identify elementary propositions and the logically simple names of which they are composed in a few parenthetical remarks in the 6s, after carefully avoiding the issue throughout the *Tractatus*. Moreover, he explicitly states in the *Tractatus* that it is not possible to identify the names of objects a priori and, therefore, "we are also unable to give the composition of elementary propositions" (5.55).

But why cannot we specify the names of objects a priori? One might think that the reason is that we need to carry out an investigation of the world in order to determine what its most basic components are. But Wittgenstein remarks that the objects that names designate are utterly independent of what is the case (cf. 2.024). According to the *Tractatus*, objects are not specifiable either a priori or a posteriori; they simply are not specifiable at all (cf. 3.26–3.261). On a realist reading of the *Tractatus*, this is regarded as an indication that objects belong to the ineffable metaphysical structure of reality: they subsist *necessarily*, they are the building blocks, not just of this contingently developed world, but of all possible worlds; and this special metaphysical status makes them ineffable. However, in the *Tractatus* the claim that objects cannot be specified is suggested by logical and semantic considerations, not by ontological ones. To say that the meanings of names are specifiable would be to say that names are definable; but names belong to the last level of analysis, they are "primitive signs," and there is no further level in which they can be "dissected" (3.26). Every complex sign is definable—that is, reducible to names—but the names themselves "*cannot* be anatomized by means of definitions" (3.261). Names are the building blocks of all linguistic representations and, therefore, their meanings cannot be captured in descriptions, for these would have to be linguistic representations without names. But the claim that names are indefinable does not indicate anything mysterious about their meanings. As Wittgenstein remarks, the meanings of primitive signs cannot be described, but they can be *elucidated* by means of "propositions that contain the primitive signs" (3.263). The meanings of names are exhibited in how they are *used* in propositions, for as Wittgenstein puts it, echoing Frege, "only in the nexus of a proposition does a name have meaning" (3.3).

As Hidé Ishiguro has observed,[18] we do not have to wait until the *Investigations* to find the idea that meaning (*Bedeutung*) is determined by use. Ishiguro has argued persuasively that the Tractarian notion of *meaning* is not a purely extensional notion. On her interpretation, the meaning of a name, the object (*Gegenstand*) it designates, is a function of the semantic contribution the name makes to the sense of the propositions in which it figures: "We settle the identity of the object referred to by coming to understand the sense, i.e. the truth conditions, of the proposition in which [the name] occurs."[19] Thus Ishiguro's interpretation suggests that the Tractarian notion of *object* is not an ontological notion, but a semantic notion that can be fully explicated in terms of the interchangeability or semantic equivalence of names: "Two names refer to the same object if the names are mutually substitutable in all propositions in which they occur without affecting the truth-value of the propositions."[20] This interpretation has been further elaborated by Brian McGuinness, who argues that Tractarian objects are to be viewed as the "truth-value potential" or "semantic role" of names.[21] What the Ishiguro-McGuinness interpretation calls into question is the realist view of objects as entities that exist independently of language and determine (from without, as it were) how we can talk about them.[22] The upshot of this interpretation is that objects, the meanings of names, are not mysterious *things* that we may or may not be lucky enough to bump into; but rather, that they should be thought of as discourse entities, that is, as entities whose profile is configured by the semantic features exhibited in the use of simple signs in our symbolism.[23]

On a realist reading, the objects of the *Tractatus* are said to be independent of what is the case because they have a special kind of existence, a necessary existence that is ineffable.[24] By contrast, McGuinness suggests that the reason why the existence of Tractarian objects cannot be either asserted or denied is not that they have a special kind of being, but rather, that they are "beyond being" altogether.[25] This deflationary interpretation suggests that Tractarian objects should be conceived as logical entities, as possibilities for language and thought, not as *things* that actually exist (whether contingently or necessarily). These objects are given independently of what happens in the world, not because they constitute the metaphysical furniture of all possible worlds, but because they are *possible* objects of discourse and their possibility is already contained in the logical structure of language and thought. The reason why most commentators have interpreted the Tractarian notion of *object* as an ontological notion is because it is first introduced in the ontological remarks that open the book (cf. 2.01ff and 2.02ff). However, there is a way of reading these opening sections that is consistent with the Ishiguro-McGuinness interpretation: they can be read as offering an "ontological myth" that ultimately cancels itself, leaving us only with certain logical insights into the structure of language and thought. As McGuinness suggests, this "ontological myth" erases itself, since it is used to help us attain a particular view of language and "one of the chief results of the view of language so attained is the rejection of all such myths."[26] In a similar vein, Diamond argues that "object" is one of those inflated philosophical words that Wittgenstein ultimately wants to eliminate by means of logical analysis.[27]

However, in his review of the *Tractatus* Ramsey assumed that this was first and foremost a metaphysical treatise and that the view of language presented in it was based on an ontological doctrine. It is this assumption that led Ramsey to misunderstand the nature of the color-exclusion problem, which he took to be, at bottom, an ontological problem. According to Ramsey, what makes this problem particularly interesting is that the logical issues raised in it give way to a fundamental ontological issue. Ramsey seems to reason as follows: in order to analyze the truth-functional composition of statements of color attribution we need to determine how they can be resolved into elementary propositions; and this in turn requires that we be able to identify the names of which these propositions are composed and thereby also the simple objects that these names designate. We are thus led from a logical problem about elementariness and simplicity to a metaphysical problem about the structure of reality. On Ramsey's reading, the solution to the problem of color exclusion calls for the identification of the fundamental structure of reality that corresponds to the logical structure of language. But is there any textual evidence for this reading? Does Wittgenstein make any attempt to solve the problem along these lines? Ramsey thinks that he does. According to Ramsey, the middle paragraph of 6.3751 offers a hint as to how we can carry out the analysis of statements of color attribution. He interprets the excursus about velocity and the logical impossibility of a particle being in two places at the same time, not as an analogy, as yet another phenomenon of exclusion, but rather, as the actual explanation of the phenomenon of color exclusion. According to Ramsey, Wittgenstein was trying to explain colors "in terms of vibrations."[28] And this explanation suggests that color terms are in fact descriptions of the movement of particles. On Ramsey's reading of 6.3751, Wittgenstein's solution to the color-exclusion problem is an attempt to reduce colors to the physical properties of particles. But by appealing to a physicalistic reduction, Ramsey replies, Wittgenstein does not show that the phenomenon of color exclusion involves a *logical* impossibility. On the contrary, such a reduction strongly suggests that color exclusion is a matter of *physical* necessity. As Ramsey puts the objection:

> Even supposing that the physicist thus provides an analysis of what we mean by "red" Mr. Wittgenstein is only reducing the dif-

> ficulty to that of the *necessary* properties of space, time, and matter, or the ether. He explicitly makes it depend on the *impossibility* of a particle being in two places at the same time. These necessary properties of space and time are hardly capable of a further reduction of this kind.[29]

So what is achieved by reducing colors to the movement of particles? Nothing. And this should be taken as an indication that Wittgenstein did not cite the impossibility of a particle being in two places at the same time as a physicalistic explanation of the phenomenon of color exclusion. (How could he, if 6.3751 is a corollary of the principle that there are only *logical* impossibilities?) Rather, the excursus about velocity simply offers another example of the phenomenon of exclusion. As Hintikka and Hintikka have noted, "the middle paragraph of 6.3751 is not an explanation of the *physical basis* of color incompatibility, as most interpreters have taken it to be. Instead, it presents a solvable (Wittgenstein thinks) *analogue* to the problem from the field of particle mechanics."[30] However, Wittgenstein does not give us a hint of how to carry out the analysis that would transform the phenomenon of exclusion in the field of particle mechanics into a logical impossibility. So what is gained by the analogy? How is it supposed to shed light on the color-exclusion problem? The point of the analogy seems to be to give plausibility to the conclusion, established a priori, that colors exclude one another as a matter of *logical* necessity. This reading is supported by a passage in the *Notebooks* (from August 16, 1916):

> A point cannot be red and green at the same time: at first sight there seems to be no need for this to be a logical impossibility. (. . .) The fact that a particle cannot be in two places at the same time *does look more like a logical impossibility*.[31]

But why is it more plausible to say of the latter incompatibility that it is a logical impossibility? Presumably because the surface form of statements about the position of particles in *space and time* shows more perspicuously their complexity. Logical relations of exclusion are clearly displayed by the purely notational features of the symbolisms we use for the spatiotemporal individuation of particles. (Think, for instance, of how the trajectory of a particle is represented in a system of coordinates.) Wittgenstein's analogy underscores that statements of color attribution are as complex as statements about the spatiotemporal individuation of particles. In both cases it is the element of *simultaneity* that gives rise to the phenomenon of exclusion. Admittedly, it is still unclear how the analysis of statements that attribute mutually exclusive properties can yield truth-functional contradictions. But Wittgenstein's aim is simply to make plausible the claim that in the full analysis we *must* find logically impossible combinations of elementary propositions underlying such statements, whatever those propositions turn out to be.

Ramsey's physicalistic reading of 6.3751 has not had a noticeable impact in the literature, but unfortunately his metaphysical interpretation of the color-exclusion problem has determined the way this problem has been perceived by commentators. Thus while Hintikka and Hintikka reject the idea that 6.3751 contains the sketch of a physicalist account of color, they still follow Ramsey in thinking that what is at stake in the color-exclusion problem is the ontological issue of the identification of simples. To Ramsey's physicalistic interpretation Hintikka and Hintikka oppose a phenomenalistic one, suggesting that colors can be Tractarian simples after all. They emphasize that the *Notebooks* attest to Wittgenstein's leanings towards phenomenalism, and that in the *Tractatus* he held that the analysis of ordinary-language statements can be carried out "in a purely phenomenalistic language."[32] According to Hintikka and Hintikka's interpretation of the *Tractatus*, experiential terms are the names of simples, and sense-data propositions are elementary.[33] However, even if Wittgenstein flirted with phenomenalism in the early 1910s, there is no evidence that he held this view in the *Tractatus*. Moreover, there is textual evidence that suggests that he *could not* hold this view. As indicated above, Wittgenstein did not think that it was possible to specify the nature of elementary propositions and their component terms (cf. 5.55). In the *Tractatus* the existence of elementary propositions and logically simple terms is required by Wittgenstein's a priori argument concerning the conditions of possibility of significance. As he puts it: "The requirement that simple signs be possible is the requirement that sense be determinate" (3.23). For sense to be determinate there must be a last level of analysis; our logical analysis of propositions must reach primitive units of significance that cannot be analyzed any further (cf. 4.221). But *nothing* in the general argument of the *Tractatus* depends on what these units might turn out to be. Not even the claim that the mutual exclusion of colors is a logical impossibility. The problem that this claim poses does not concern, as Ramsey thought, whether or not colors can be counted as primitive simples, as irreducible particulars. Whether or not colors are amenable to a physicalistic reduction is in fact quite immaterial for the logical problem of exclusion. Even on Ramsey's reading, the exclusion problem is left untouched by explaining color incompatibilities as the surface expression of some other (deeper) nonlogical incompatibilities, such as the impossibility of a particle being in two places at the same time. For, since the latter is not a *logical* impossibility, it cannot be the last level of analysis. This seems to be Wittgenstein's central point at 6.3751. Ironically, this very point is also Ramsey's objection.

Pace Ramsey, the color-exclusion problem is not a problem about metaphysical simples at all. It is a *general* problem about the logical form and the truth-functional analysis of the statements of *ordinary language.* What makes 6.3751 so special is that it is one of the few places where the abstract argument of the *Tractatus* touches on ordinary language directly. In the argument of 6.375–6.3751 Wittgenstein draws a specific conclusion about statements of ordinary language; namely, that statements that assert color incompatibilities *must* contain a truth-functional contradiction. The core of the color-exclusion problem is, I contend, whether or not we can make sense of the idea of a *hidden contradiction.* What is at stake in this problem is not whether or not phenomenal predicates like "red" and "blue" can represent Tractarian objects. What is really at stake is whether or not the notions of *logical form* and *logical analysis* can actually play the role assigned to them in the *Tractatus.*

1.3. The Myth of "Hidden Bodies"

The general significance of the color-exclusion problem and its crucial role in the development of Wittgenstein's thought are missed if the problem is understood to be about whether color is a primitive dimension of reality. That the color-exclusion problem concerns the identification of simples has been a very influential interpretation (endorsed by G. E. M. Anscombe[34] and Max Black,[35] among others). Shanker has suggested that Ramsey's objection about the futility of a physicalistic analysis of color terms was probably what moved Wittgenstein to come back to the exclusion problem in 1929. He writes: "Ramsey would undoubtedly have pressed home this point when Wittgenstein returned to Cambridge, and it thus seems likely that 'Some Remarks on Logical Form' reflects Ramsey's success in persuading Wittgenstein that the argument at 6.375–6.3751 needed emendation."[36] However, as we shall see, in Wittgenstein's discussions of that argument in 1929–30 there is no mention of the issue of whether or not colors are genuine simples, or of whether a physicalistic reduction of sensory qualities is needed—neither in "Some Remarks on Logical Form"[37] nor anywhere else where Wittgenstein discusses the color-exclusion problem. Instead, what Wittgenstein seems to find problematic in the argument of *Tractatus* 6.375–6.3751 is the idea that statements that assert color incompatibilities must contain a *hidden* contradiction.[38] He began to doubt that a truth-functional analysis can solve the color-exclusion problem; and this led him to lose faith in logical analysis as conceived in the *Tractatus.* So let's examine more closely what is involved in the claim that a hidden contradiction can be uncovered by means of logical analysis.

As noted above, the contradiction underlying a statement that asserts color incompatibility is not displayed by its surface form. But it follows from the Tractarian account of logical composition that a contradiction must be contained or *hidden* in the aberrant combination of elementary propositions in which the statement consists. Now, why is this a problem? After all, on the Tractarian view, every statement of ordinary language is supposed to have a *hidden* logical form. So the aberrant logical form underlying a contradictory attribution of colors is no more hidden than the customary logical form of any factual statement of ordinary language. The logical form of ordinary statements does not lie on the surface; it resides in a calculus of propositions that is not open to view. Behind each well-formed sentence of ordinary language there lies a logical body composed of truth-functional combinations of elementary propositions. The shape of this *hidden body* is what Wittgenstein calls *logical form.* Diamond explains this picture of language as follows: "We have to think of lifting up an ordinary sentence, and noticing, attached to it, like little wires, all the sentences which entail that it is true or that it is not. The ordinary sentence, together with all its little wires, is the same sentence as the fully analyzed one."[39]

The Tractarian view of language demands that every statement be decomposable into a truth-functional combination of elementary propositions. But notice that this is a *logical*, not an epistemic, requirement. Speakers are not required to know the truth-functional decomposition of the statements they utter: "Man possesses the ability to construct languages capable of expressing every sense, without having any idea how each word has meaning or what its meaning is—just as people speak without knowing how the individual sounds are produced" (4.002). Statements signify, not through the knowledge of the speakers who utter them, but through their own underlying logical structure. So what is so problematic about the idea of a "hidden contradiction"? Isn't it just to be expected that in the truth-functional analysis of ordinary statements we will find tautologies and contradictions as well as combinations of elementary propositions that express truth-possibilities?

The possibility that a statement of ordinary language whose *form* seems to be in order can contain a contradiction is less innocent than it may seem. The sentence "A is red and blue at the same time" has the same form as "A is red and round at the same time." However, while the latter expresses a significant proposition, the former is entirely empty. But we cannot distinguish between these two statements as instances of two different logical types on the basis of their surface form alone. Logical analysis must uncover the combination of elementary propositions *hidden* in the visible signs and determine, for each statement of ordinary language, whether *or not* it is a factual proposition, a proposition that pictures a *possible* state of affairs. In the light of 6.3751 it appears that the surface form of the statements of ordinary language is not a good guide for the statements' meaningfulness. This has led some commentators to conclude that, according to the *Tractatus*, ordinary language is logically defective and needs to be replaced by a logically perfect notation that can *show* perspicuously the logical form of propositions. In such notation, statements containing incompatible color attributions would be distinguished, *by their very form*, from statements about color with factual content. This is the conclusion that Hintikka and Hintikka draw from their interpretation of *Tractatus* 6.3751. They contend that Wittgenstein "thought he could in principle devise a notation to *reflect* the necessities of color concepts and thereby to show how the appropriate structures (forms) are built into the objects we are dealing with in color attributions."[40] According to Hintikka & Hintikka's reading, 6.3751 reveals that the Tractarian view of language applies first and foremost to ideal languages, to logically perfect notations, and only approximately and derivatively to ordinary languages.

According to this interpretation of the implications of the color-exclusion problem, there is a close relationship between 6.3751 and sections 3.323–3.325, which are usually interpreted as stressing the logical flaws of ordinary language and the need for a perfect notation. In these sections Wittgenstein notes that in ordinary language different words are employed "in what is superficially the same way" and the same word is used to convey different meanings (3.323). He remarks that this has led to "the most fundamental confusions" (3.24), and that in order to avoid these confusions, we must construct "a sign-language that excludes them" (3.325). In the light of these sections, 6.3751 could be read as suggesting that the statements of ordinary language are just as logically defective as the words of which they are composed. However, this interpretation of 3.323–3.325 and 6.3751 flies in the face of a long-standing view of Wittgenstein that runs from the *Tractatus* to the *Investigations*, namely, the view that ordinary language has no *logical* flaws: "*all* the propositions of our everyday language, just as they stand, are *in perfect logical order*" (5.5563; my emphasis).[41] And how can Wittgenstein state what seem to be clearly contradictory theses about ordinary language in a book as carefully drafted as the *Tractatus*?

There is indeed a close analogy between sections 3.323–3.325 and 6.3751. But this analogy does not have the revisionistic implications that Hintikka and Hintikka suggest. The common point of these sections is that the surface forms of the statements of ordinary language are not a good guide to their logical structure: in ordinary language superficial uniformity frequently *hides* logical diversity. However, from the fact that the expressions of ordinary language are "superficially" ambiguous (cf. 3.323 and

3.325), Wittgenstein does not conclude that ordinary language lacks logically simple signs with definite meaning. On the contrary, the upshot of Wittgenstein's argument is that simple names must be somehow contained in ordinary language; otherwise we would not be able to communicate at all. Similarly, although the surface form of ordinary-language statements gives no indication of how these statements can be constructed out of elementary propositions, Wittgenstein still holds that their logical analysis "must bring us to elementary propositions" (4.221). So the point is that the surface structures of ordinary language *hide, but do not contravene*, the underlying logical structure that a meaningful language must have. As Wittgenstein puts it: "The outward form of the clothing is not designed to reveal the form of the body" (4.002).

It is also important to notice that the "fundamental confusions" that, according to Wittgenstein, result from the ambiguous surface forms of ordinary language are not linguistic confusions that obstruct communication and preclude meaningful discourse; they are, rather, philosophical mistakes: they constitute "the whole of philosophy" (3.24). So Wittgenstein's claim that we need to construct "a sign-language" that prevents these confusions (3.325) should not be understood as the claim that ordinary language must be *replaced* by a perfect notation. For the purpose of this "sign-language" is not to correct the logical flaws of ordinary language, but to prevent *philosophical* misunderstandings. The kind of "language" that Wittgenstein has in mind is something like the T-F notation that he goes on to propose in the 4s, that is, a notation that *shows* "what is common to all notations for truth-functions" (3.3441). But a logical notation of this kind could not possibly be meant as a perfect language that can replace ordinary language. For, strictly speaking, a logical notation is not a language (a representational system) at all, since its propositions do not picture facts: "the propositions of logic say nothing" (6.11); they show "the formal—logical—properties of language and the world" (6.12). Logical notations have a special status because they are the *tools* of logical analysis (3.3441–3.3442), not because they are perfect *languages*. They are not intended to improve ordinary languages, but to bring them to their bare bones. They are supposed to display on the surface what already lies in the hidden structure of ordinary languages. The target of logical analysis is to dissect complex sentences and to resolve them into "completely analysed" propositions (3.201); that is, to exhume the hidden bodies of propositions that lie beneath the statements of ordinary language. The spirit of this analysis is nonrevisionary. According to the *Tractatus*, there is no privileged symbolism or "perfect" notation; every language or system of representation stands on a par: every notation is a truth-functional calculus of elementary propositions with the same logical structure. Admittedly, logical form is not identified with the surface forms of ordinary language; it is rather something that only a suitable logical notation can bring out. But these hidden structures that logical analysis is supposed to reveal are not structures to be imposed on ordinary language; they are, instead, the logical structures that are required to be already *there*, underlying meaningful discourse. So the general approach to ordinary language that we find in the *Tractatus* does not seem to leave room for drawing revisionistic conclusions from the color-exclusion problem.[42]

As discussed above, tautologies and contradictions, being "the limiting cases of the combinations of signs," show where logical form "disintegrates" (cf. 4.466), thus constituting the boundary stones that separate what is significant from what is pure nonsense. According to the *Tractatus*, every symbolism must have definite limits which are marked by the "disintegration" of logical form. In order to identify the domain of significance of a symbolism we must be able to recognize its limits, which are displayed by tautologies and contradictions. In the language of color attribution, for example, we must be able to recognize which combinations of signs are tautological (e.g., "A is not both red and blue at T") and which ones contradictory (e.g., "A is both red and blue at T"), in order to see the domain of factual discourse that lies between them. But the problem is precisely that statements of color attribution containing tautologies and contradictions are in fact indistinguishable, by their surface form alone, from factual statements. Fortunately, the formalist requirement that logical form be displayed in the permissible combinations of signs, and its dissolution in the limiting cases of those combinations, does not apply to the surface form of statements but to their underlying structure.

The thesis that the statements of ordinary language are "in perfect logical order" is thus maintained in the *Tractatus* by appealing to their *hidden* logical composition. However, the possibility that ordinary language can contain tautologies and contradictions that are not recognizable from the surface form of its signs is still disquieting. To be sure, given the a priori argument of the *Tractatus*, we can rest confident that the *meaningful* statements of ordinary language are "in perfect logical order." But which statements of ordinary language are *meaningful*? A statement is meaningful if it contains a logically *possible* combination of elementary propositions. But this is not something open to view; rather, it is something that requires logical analysis. We must await logical analysis to tell us which statements of ordinary language express significant propositions. This is brought to light by the claim at 6.3751 that statements of color incompatibility are contradictions. This claim is presented as a harmless corollary about the logical nature of necessity and impossibility that does not deserve further elaboration. But, in fact, it is crucial to determine *exactly how* statements of color incompatibility can be transformed into truth-functional contradictions by logical analysis. This is not just a matter of detail peripheral to the argument of the *Tractatus*, as it seems to have appeared to Wittgenstein before 1929.

In order to demarcate the logical space for meaningful discourse in ordinary language, we need a *method* of logical analysis that can enable us to unmask tautologies and contradictions—that is, to identify the "limiting cases of the combinations of signs." Since no such method is provided in the *Tractatus*, the idea that logical analysis will bring out combinations of elementary propositions contained or *hidden* in complex statements is not given a precise meaning. As Wittgenstein put it in the early 1930s, "the only way in which something like a logical product can be hidden in a proposition is the way in which a quotient like 753/3 is hidden until the division has been carried out."[43] The problem is that we have a precise method for determining quotients, but we do not have a method for bringing elementary propositions out into the open! This is the criticism that Wittgenstein posed to the Tractarian notion of logical analysis in the 1930s: "Can a logical product be hidden in a proposition? And if so, how does one tell, and what methods do we have of bringing the hidden element of a proposition to light? If we haven't yet got a method, then we can't speak of something being hidden or possibly hidden."[44]

As Diane Gottlieb, for one, has pointed out, in the *Tractatus* Wittgenstein talks about the "complete analysis" of statements "as if there were a calculus according to which the analysis could be carried out"; but he does not provide a precise method for resolving complex statements into elementary propositions.[45] One might reply: How about the truth-functional analysis of statements that Wittgenstein proposes? Don't the rules of truth-functionality provide a method of logical analysis? The problem is that truth-functional analysis is presented and used in the *Tractatus* as a method of logical *composition*, not as a method of decomposition. The rules for truth-functional compounding enable us to *construct* complex propositions out of elementary ones (cf. 4.51). But we cannot decompose statements according to these rules *unless* we are given their elementary constituents. Hence it is not surprising that we find ourselves at a loss when we want to transform incompatible color attributions into truth-functional contradictions.

But by demanding the availability of a method of logical decomposition, are we not turning the *logical* requirement that every sentence be analyzable into a truth-functional combination of elementary propositions into an *epistemic* requirement? We cannot demand that speakers have knowledge about the logical composition of the sentences they utter. As we have seen, there is a strong *externalist* element in the Tractarian view of meaning. It is not the case that if I make sense I must know that I do, and how I do it. In order to make sense one only needs to use signs according to the rules of logical syntax. Speakers do not need to have access to a precise method of logical analysis in order to speak meaningfully. However, *Wittgenstein* does need such a method for his a priori argument in the *Tractatus* to honor the thesis that the statements of ordinary language are "in perfect logical order." In order to show that ordinary language meets the conditions that the *Tractatus* imposes on any representational system, we would have to be able to uncover a truth-functional calculus of elementary propositions beneath the statements of ordinary language. And this can only be done by means of a precise method of logical decomposition.

Wittgenstein remarks that our ignorance about the truth-functional composition of statements does not affect our capacity to make sense. He illustrates this point with an analogy between our capacity to produce meaningful statements and our capacity to produce sounds. The analogy suggests that we can separate the products of these capacities from their processes of production: We speak meaningfully "without having any idea *how*," just as we emit sounds "without knowing *how* [these] sounds are produced" (4.002; my emphasis). But this analogy is misleading. For *how* the sounds of our vocalizations are produced does not determine *what* these sounds are (or *whether* they are sounds). And the reason is that the identity of sounds is independent of their genesis. We have independent (acoustic) criteria for the individuation of phonemes that do not rest on their processes of production. However, according to the *Tractatus*, we do *not* have independent criteria for what counts as a meaningful statement apart from its truth-functional composition. What determines the identity of a statement is how its constituents are put together. The hidden logical composition of statements is *constitutive* of what those statements are: significant propositions, tautologies, contradictions, or pure nonsense. The investigation of the processes of sound production is extraneous to the individuation of sounds; it is merely a matter of empirical detail. But the examination of the internal constitution of statements is *not* a peripheral question of detail, as the analogy with sounds suggests. What is at stake in the logical analysis of statements is not simply *how* they signify, but also *whether* they do. In order to ascertain whether a statement has sense or only contains an appearance of meaning, we need a method of analysis that can determine whether the statement contains a *possible* combination of elementary propositions. Of course speakers need not have knowledge of the underlying structure of their statements. But Wittgenstein needs to specify how the logical composition of statements is to be determined, how the hidden bodies of propositions that lie beneath them are to be exhumed. Otherwise, his a priori argument about the conditions of possibility of significance would fail to show that ordinary language is "in perfect logical order."

Given the abstract account of logical composition offered in the *Tractatus*, Wittgenstein concluded that a statement that is necessarily false *must* contain a hidden contradiction. But his *modus ponens* in the *Tractatus* will be his *modus tollens* in the late 1920s. In 1929 he came to the conclusion that no hidden contradiction is to be found in the logical analysis of incompatible color attributions and that, therefore, something must be wrong with the abstract account of logical composition given in the *Tractatus*. However, he did not think that what was wrong was any metaphysical doctrine about the nature of elementary propositions and their component terms. In a conversation with the Vienna Circle in 1931 Wittgenstein remarked that the *Tractatus* is a "*dogmatic*" book, and he went on to explain that its dogmatism consists not in any unwarranted view about elementary propositions, but rather in the unwarranted assumption that elementary propositions must be there, that there must be a calculus of elementary propositions hidden in the statements of ordinary language.[46]

1.4. Deflationism and Realism in the *Tractatus*

The interpretation of the Tractarian notions of possibility and necessity articulated in section 1.1 and the account of the color-exclusion problem developed in sections 1.2 and 1.3 cast doubt on the traditional realist reading of the *Tractatus* as a metaphysical treatise that erects a view of language on the basis of an ontological doctrine. By the same token, my arguments in those sections give support to the deflationary interpretations of Ishiguro, McGuinness, and Diamond. As these interpretations suggest,[47] the *Tractatus* offers a view of language that helps us overcome metaphysical problems by bringing about a perspective in which these problems cannot even be formulated. This is a perspective that leaves no room for metaphysical realism or antirealism, a perspective from which all metaphysical positions appear as one and the same (cf. 5.64) because they are all equally nonsensical.[48] The attainment of this deflationary perspective is the primary goal of the Tractarian elucidation of the logical underpinnings of language. As argued above, too much of the *Tractatus* is left in the dark if we ignore its deflationary moves—if, for example, we continue to imagine necessity as fact or to think of objects as the metaphysical joints of reality. However, this metaphysical deflationism is achieved at a high price, for the view of language that makes it possible rests on substantive assumptions about logical form and logical analysis. The a priori argument of the *Tractatus* brings with it very strict demands concerning the logical structure of language. In particular, as McGuinness observes, it "demands that every proposition be capable of a full analysis in just one form, whether or not such analysis has ever been reached."[49] This involves a peculiar *realism* and *monism* concerning logical form. According to the *Tractatus*, it is possible to give a unified account of the logical form of everything that can be expressed (cf. 4.5), for there is a *single* logical structure underlying all possible symbolisms. For every proposition, there is one and only one complete analysis that can uncover its logical form; and this underlying logical form is something that a proposition has *in itself*, whether or not it is recognized by any speaker: it is the shape of a truth-functional calculus of elementary propositions hidden in the unanalyzed proposition. This is what I have called "the myth of *hidden bodies*": the idea that beneath every significant statement there lies a hidden body of propositions attached to it "like little wires." As Diamond puts it, in the *Tractatus* Wittgenstein assumed that "the little wires are all there, all fixed by the logical structure of language."[50]

So, despite the strong metaphysical deflationism of the *Tractatus*, Wittgenstein's early philosophy still contains a residual realism, albeit a deflated one: a *logical* realism without ontological commitments. This logical realism has to do, not with a special realm of objects, but with the necessary features of symbolic representation. Therefore, it does not involve ineffable truths about reality[51] but only certain insights into the underlying logical structure of language. The *Tractatus* promotes a realist attitude with respect to the limits of intelligibility by presenting them as fixed, not by the metaphysical structure of reality, but by the logical form of any possible symbolism. Wittgenstein does say that the possible combinations of objects set the limits to what can be symbolically represented (cf. 2.0123–2.0124). However, as suggested above (cf. 1.2), when Wittgenstein talks about objects and their "internal properties" (2.01231), he is not talking about the denizens of an ontological realm and their inner natures; rather, he is talking about the *possible* objects of language and thought and their logical properties. According to the *Tractatus*, all the *possible* objects that we can think of and talk about are already contained in the logical structure of any system of representation. An examination of the logical form of language can reveal all the logical possibilities that can be symbolically represented. As Wittgenstein remarks: "Logic deals with every possibility and all possibilities are its facts" (2.0121). "There cannot be a proposition whose form could not have been foreseen" (4.5).

So the logical realism of the *Tractatus* is a realism about *possibilia*.[52] On the Tractarian view, logic determines *sub specie aeternitatis* the range of possibilities that are thinkable and expressible in language. This grid of logical possibilities that constitutes the domain of significance of any symbolism is the *logical space* that lies between the logical truths of tautologies and the logical falsehoods of contradictions (cf. section 1.1). According to the *Tractatus*, propositions can make sense only against the background of this logical space (3.42). In his later view, however, Wittgenstein rejects the idea that what sustains the significance of our statements is an invisible logical background (cf. esp. PI §102). In the *Investigations* he describes this idea as a philosophical illusion that arises when we abstract from our actual practices of language use and ask "How do sentences manage to represent?" (PI §435), as if this were something that sentences could do by themselves. Under the spell of this illusion we are inclined to think that there must be a "logical scaffolding" surrounding every significant proposition[53] (cf. *Tractatus* 3.42), that there must be hidden logical bodies that support the significance of our statements: we proceed "as if our usual forms of expression were, essentially, unanalyzed; as if there were *something hidden* in them that had to be brought to light" (PI §91; my emphasis). But now Wittgenstein insists that "nothing is hidden" (PI §435), that "everything lies open to view" and "what is hidden [. . .] is of no interest to us" (PI §126). As we shall see, the rejection of the myth of *hidden bodies* is one of the main points of evolution from the *Tractatus* to the *Investigations*.[54] And this explains the crucial role that the color-exclusion problem played in the development of Wittgenstein's thought. For, as I have argued, this problem calls into question the Tractarian assumption that ordinary statements contain hidden bodies of propositions that logical analysis must dig up.

2

From Pictures to Yardsticks

THE COLORFUL TRANSFORMATIONS OF THE TRACTARIAN VIEW OF LANGUAGE

In 1929 the reexamination of the color-exclusion problem led Wittgenstein to rethink the notions of logical form and logical analysis. A new version of these core Tractarian notions together with a new analysis of the color-exclusion problem appeared in "Some Remarks on Logical Form" (hereafter SRLF), the paper that Wittgenstein wrote for the 1929 Joint Session of the Aristotelian Society. The arguments of this paper did not leave Wittgenstein satisfied for very long. Though it was published in the proceedings, he had already rejected it before the session, where he spoke on an entirely different topic.[55] However, despite its short-lived arguments, SRLF constitutes a decisive turning point and it contains crucial ideas that determined the subsequent development of Wittgenstein's thought.

In the opening page of SRLF Wittgenstein gives a brief summary of the central ideas of the Tractarian account of logical composition. But he goes on to introduce modifications into this account that result in substantial transformations of the Tractarian view of language. He first states the thesis that complex propositions are "logical sums, products or other truth-functions of simpler propositions" (p. 29). As in the *Tractatus*, Wittgenstein claims that "analysis, if carried far enough, must come to the point where it reaches [. . .] atomic propositions," which are "the kernels of every proposition" (p. 29). He emphasizes that finding these propositional "kernels" is an extremely difficult task, and that "philosophy has hardly yet begun to tackle it" (p. 29). He then poses the crucial question: "What method have we for tackling it?" (p. 29). This question serves as a preface to the first important departure from the Tractarian view. Wittgenstein now contends that there is no method of logical analysis that can lead us from the statements of ordinary language to the simplest propositional forms (pp. 30–31). He argues that "we can only arrive at a correct analysis by what might be called *the logical investigation of the phenomena themselves*" (p. 30; my emphasis). In order to elucidate the logical form of a representational system, we must begin, not by examining "our particular language," but "by inspecting the phenomena which we want to describe, thus trying to understand their logical multiplicity" (p. 30). This move away from language and toward "the phenomena" is motivated by the color-exclusion problem. In what follows I will first examine the new analysis of the color-exclusion problem offered in SRLF, and then come back to the idea that logical form is to be determined by "the logical investigation of the phenomena themselves."[56]

2.1. Let the Phenomena Speak for Themselves!

In SRLF Wittgenstein argues that he made a mistake in the *Tractatus* by trying to reduce the relation of *exclusion* between two propositions to a truth-functional *contradiction*, "for there is a difference between these two notions" (p. 33). The color-exclusion problem is brought up to explain where the difference lies. When we attribute a color to a point in the visual field at a particular time, say red ("RPT") or blue ("BPT"), our color attribution excludes any other. That's why we find no place in our speech for the conjunction "RPT & BPT." Although this conjunction is an admissible combination of signs in our language, it is clear "to all of us in ordinary life" that "RPT & BPT" is "not merely a false proposition" but "some sort of contradiction" (p. 33). However, Wittgenstein goes on to argue, it is a mistake to think that the inadmissibility of "RPT & BPT" can be explained through a truth-functional analysis that will reveal a *hidden contradiction*. For "RPT & BPT" to be a contradiction, it would have to be a logical product whose truth-table contains only F's. But the mistake is to think that "RPT & BPT" is a permissible logical product at all, even if a contradictory one. "RPT" and "BPT" do not express two independent possibilities that, when combined, cancel each other; each of them expresses a *complete* possibility, a determination that saturates the logical space for color attribution: "The mutual exclusion of RPT and BPT [. . .] consists in the fact that RPT as well as BPT are in a certain sense *complete*. That which corresponds in reality to the function '()PT' leaves room only for one entity" (p. 33). This is the reason why there cannot be a contradiction between one statement of color attribution and another: because when one is asserted there is no room to assert another, there cannot be.

For Wittgenstein, a complex statement is the logical product of two propositions if and only if it expresses the combination of possibilities specified by the last column of the truth-table for conjunction ("TFFF"). But the truth-table for "RPT & BPT" cannot be "TFFF": "In this case the top line 'TTT' must disappear, as it represents an impossible combination" (p. 34). In this case only the other three lines of the truth-table for conjunction represent genuine possibilities (when either one or both of the conjuncts are false). But this is to say, Wittgenstein notes, that "RPT & BPT" is not really a conjunction properly so called. And if it is not a conjunction, it cannot be, a fortiori, a contradictory logical product. As Wittgenstein puts it:

> There *is* no logical product of RPT and BPT [. . .] and herein lies the exclusion as opposed to a contradiction. The contradiction, if it existed, would have to be written—
>
> | RPT | BPT | |
> |---|---|---|
> | T | T | F |
> | T | F | F |
> | F | T | F |
> | F | F | F |
>
> but this is nonsense, as the top line, 'TTF', gives the proposition *a greater logical multiplicity than that of the actual possibilities.* (SRLF, p. 35; emphasis preserved and added)

For there to be a contradiction between two propositions, there must exist the possibility of their conjunction. But this is precisely what the propositions of color attribution lack. This criticism of the Tractarian treatment of the color-exclusion problem may seem curiously ineffective. For, after all, the contradiction that Wittgenstein appealed to in *Tractatus* 6.3751 was not between "RPT" and "BPT"; it was, rather, a contradiction to be found in the combination of elementary propositions *hidden* in the statement "RPT & BPT." So it should come as no surprise that the truth-functional analysis of "RPT & BPT" does not even yield a consistent assignment of truth-values. This analysis was to be applied to the statement *in its fully analyzed form*: it was there where a truth-functional contradiction was supposed to be found. However, Wittgenstein now thinks that statements of color attribution are *unanalyzable* and, therefore, their exclusion relations cannot be truth-functionally explained by appealing to their internal logical structure. The argument for the elementary character of color statements is to be found in the discussion of quantitative statements about properties that admit of gradation (e.g., temperature). The analogy between color statements and statements of degree underscores that what is at stake in the color-exclusion problem is not something specific about the dimension of color. The exclusion problem is a general problem that can also be illustrated by statements about the individuation of particles (*Tractatus* 6.3751) or by statements of degree (SRLF, pp. 32–33). What is at stake in this problem is the status of the logical relations among propositions, whether these relations are primitive and constitutive or derivative and emergent from the internal structure of propositions.

Wittgenstein remarks that the commonality between a statement of color attribution and a statement of degree is that they both are "a *complete* description which needs no supplementation" (p. 32). A statement of degree picks out one value in the appropriate scale and excludes all others. This we know intuitively, and it is for this reason that when we say that the temperature is eighty degrees, if we are asked "And is it ninety degrees?" we should answer "I told you it was eighty" (p. 32). One might think that the completeness of a statement of degree and its exclusion relations with any other such statement are to be explained in terms of the underlying logical structure of the statement. From a logical point of view, it may seem that a statement of degree is a complex description in need of analysis, that it has to be broken down into an enumeration of units of degree and a completing clause that brings the description to an end and makes it exhaustive:

> One might think—and I thought so not long ago—that a statement expressing the degree of a quality could be analyzed into a logical product of single statements of quantity and a completing supplementary statement. As I could describe the contents of my pocket by saying "It contains a penny, a shilling, two keys, and nothing else." (SRLF, p. 32)

However, Wittgenstein argues that the enumerative analysis of statements of degree does not work. For example, "the proposition E(2b), which says that E has two degrees of brightness," cannot be analyzed into the logical product "E(b) & E(b)" because "this is equal to E(b)" (p. 33). Alternatively, "E(2b)" cannot be analyzed into "E(b') & E(b")" either, because this analysis assumes "two different units of brightness; and then, if an entity possesses one unit, the question could arise, which of the two—b' or b"—it is; which is obviously absurd" (p. 33). We could say that this last version of the analysis manages to distinguish between the individual units of the scale by assigning a proper name to each unit. This analysis would enable us to resolve the proposition into a concatenation of names, very much in the spirit of the *Tractatus*. But, as David Pears points out, "it is of the essence of units that they are not distinguished in this way or in any other way."[57] The units of a scale are not individual building blocks that make an independent contribution to the scale and can, accordingly, be independently identified. A scale is not simply a collection of objects; it is a relational structure whose elements are essentially interdependent. The units of a scale can only be identified as relative positions within the scale; that is, the identity of each unit presupposes *the whole scale*. There is, therefore, an unavoidable *holistic* aspect in the attribution of a degree to a quality. The holism underscored in this discussion signals a crucial point in the development of Wittgenstein's thought. As discussed in chapter 1, a strong holistic element was already present in the Tractarian view of language. But the holism of the *Tractatus* coexisted with the separatism of elementary propositions, for the compositional account of language developed there required semantic building blocks that were logically independent from each other. In 1929 this requirement is given up and, thus, the separatism of elementary propositions is abandoned and the holistic strand of the *Tractatus* is fully developed.

Wittgenstein's discussion of statements of degree in SRLF makes two crucial points. First, Wittgenstein argues that these statements "cannot further be analyzed" (p. 33): they are not the logical product of more elementary propositions; they themselves are atomic propositions. And second, Wittgenstein contends that it is an essential feature of these propositions that they exclude each other: the exclusion relations between these statements cannot be eliminated by means of analysis; they subsist at the atomic level. Thus Wittgenstein explicitly rejects the Tractarian thesis of the logical independence of elementary propositions: "The mutual exclusion of unanalyzable statements of degree contradicts an opinion which was published by me several years ago and which necessitated that atomic propositions could not exclude one another" (p. 33). Wittgenstein emphasizes that there is "an internal relation" between a proposition that attributes a degree to a quality and every other proposition that attributes a different degree to the same quality (p. 33). That these propositions are *internally related* is disclosed by the relations of mutual exclusion that hold between them. These relations bring the propositions together into a holistically structured system for the description of the same quality.

According to SRLF, it is not the underlying logical structure of color statements and statements of degree that makes them mutually exclusive. So what is it? The mutual exclusion of unanalyzable statements consists in their "collision" in the *logical form of the phenomena* they describe (p. 34). Wittgenstein now thinks that we could not have discovered that "RPT & BPT" is an impossible combination of signs by inspecting the underlying logical structure of the statement, for it is the "logical multiplicity" of the phenomena described by the statement that precludes such a combination (p. 35). But this is in no way *shown* in the logical form of "RPT & BPT." The statement neither says nor shows anything; it is not just senseless but "nonsensical" (p. 35). Statements that attribute incompatible colors to a point in the visual field are now compared to "nonsensical pseudopropositions [. . .] such as 'red is higher than green'" (p. 29). These statements have no role to play in language. They do not show the limits of significance, they are beyond these limits. They contain only the *appearance* of meaning: they are well-formed statements that do not in fact express genuine propositions at all.

According to SRLF, those statements that clash with the logical form of the phenomena such as "RPT & BPT" have to be banished from language by the rules of logical syntax. These rules are supposed to "tell us in which connections only a word gives sense, thus excluding nonsensical structures" (p. 29). As before, Wittgenstein thinks that the rules of logical syntax cannot be read off the surface forms of ordinary language. For "the syntax of ordinary language [. . .] does not in all cases prevent the construction of nonsensical pseudopropositions" (p. 29). According to the *Tractatus*, however, this did not constitute a logical flaw of ordinary language, for the underlying structure of ordinary-language statements was thought to comply with the rules of logical syntax. In SRLF, by contrast, the inadequacy of the syntactic structure of ordinary-language statements cannot be redeemed by appealing to their hidden logical structure, for Wittgenstein now thinks that there is no underlying calculus of elementary propositions lurking beneath these statements. And therefore, the fact that the syntax of ordinary language does not prevent the construction of nonsensical combinations of signs becomes *a real logical flaw*: "It is, of course, a *deficiency* of our notation that it does not prevent the formation of such nonsensical constructions, and *a perfect notation* will have to exclude such structures by *definite rules of syntax*" (p. 35; my emphasis). According to SRLF, the syntax of ordinary language *not only hides, but actually contravenes* the rules of logical syntax. Now logical analysis takes up a *revisionary* role: it is supposed to unmask the logical deficiencies of our language. Accordingly, artificial notations are not simply invoked to eliminate philosophical misunderstandings, they are called for to "replace" ordinary language wherever a logical flaw is found (pp. 29–30).

From his examination of the color-exclusion problem in SRLF, Wittgenstein concludes that the rules of logical syntax cannot be derived from the logical analysis of the statements of ordinary language. Logical analysis must take a different direction if it is to yield "definite rules of syntax" that exclude all "nonsensical constructions" (p. 35). Wittgenstein argues that, in order to obtain rules of syntax that are faithful to the logical form of the phenomena that we want to describe, what is needed is a logical analysis of the phenomena themselves: "Such rules [. . .] cannot be laid down until we have actually reached the ultimate analysis of the phenomena in question" (p. 35). Only the actual phenomena can teach us what is possible and what is necessary and impossible. For instance, from a logical examination of the phenomenon of color exclusion we learn the truth-possibilities that can be expressed in a language for the description of color: we learn that "in the case of certain kinds of atomic propositions [. . .] certain combinations of the T's and F's must be left out" (p. 35).

As in the *Tractatus*, in SRLF Wittgenstein argues that logical form fixes the range of logical possibilities expressible in language. But this realism about *possibilia* is not maintained by appealing to the logical structure of every symbolism or the metaphysical structure of the world. Rather, what now fixes the range of significant possibilities is the logical form of *the phenomena*. This retreat to the phenomena is not surprising if we remember what was needed for an adequate solution to the color-exclusion problem; namely, a method of logical analysis that could bring logical form into the open. According to the *Tractatus*, logical form was supposed to be hidden in the underlying structure shared by statements and the facts they depict. But Wittgenstein provided no method of analysis according to which this hidden logical form could be disclosed. He now claims that the objects of logical analysis must be accessible to us: logical form is to be found in the contents of our experience, in what appears to us. Thus in the opening page of SRLF Wittgenstein remarks that the discovery of "the kernels of every proposition" is "the task of the theory of knowledge" (p. 29). The adoption of a certain phenomenalism[58] probably became attractive to Wittgenstein as a way of fleshing out the Tractarian notion of logical analysis. At the same time, this revised notion of logical analysis directed toward the experienceable becomes a channel of transformation for central ideas of the *Tractatus*.

In the first place, the new direction that logical analysis takes in SRLF transforms the Tractarian notion of *logical form*. Wittgenstein argues that logical analysis must direct its attention to each *kind* of phenomenon that we want to describe, for different kinds of phenomena have different logical forms. Logical form thus becomes *plural and content specific*. This plurality of logical forms is concealed by the uniform syntactic structures of ordinary language "into which we project in *ever so many different* ways *ever so many different* logical forms" (pp. 30–31). But in the "actual analysis" of the phenomena, "we meet with the forms of space and time, with the whole manifold of spatial and temporal objects, as colours, sounds, etc., etc., with their gradations, continuous transitions, and combinations in various proportions, all of which we cannot seize by our ordinary means of expression" (p. 31). This pluralism of logical form contrasts with the monism of the *Tractatus*: "The general form of a proposition is: This is how things stand" (4.5). Wittgenstein now thinks that the idea that there is a logical form shared by every proposition is an empty generalization. There is no such thing as one general logical form that can capture the logical multiplicity of every phenomenon. And since logical form is content specific, so must be the rules of logical syntax that fix the range of admissible propositions within a given symbolism. In order to prevent the construction of nonsensical combinations of signs, we need not only general logical laws that apply to all propositions but also content-specific rules of syntax that determine the logical form of particular *kinds* of propositions. For example, in the language of color attribution, we need not only a logical rule that prohibits the construction of propositions such as "p & not-p", but also a logical rule that bans propositions such as "RPT & BPT." The repertoire of logical rules is thus substantially widened.

In the second place, the new view of logical analysis espoused in SRLF transforms Wittgenstein's view concerning the status that our *knowledge* of logical form has. Knowledge of logical form, he contends, is not a matter of speculation: it cannot be attained "by conjecturing about *a priori* possibilities"; it requires an investigation which is "in a certain sense *a posteriori*" (p. 30). This idea constitutes an important departure from the Tractarian view, according to which we have "*a priori* knowledge of the possibility of a logical form" (6.33; my emphasis); and "there cannot be a proposition whose form could not have been foreseen" (4.5). By contrast, Wittgenstein now argues that we must avoid the temptation "to ask from an *a priori* standpoint: What, after all, *can* be the only forms of atomic propositions" (p. 30). For the diversity of logical forms that our propositions can display cannot be determined a priori. Which logical forms are admissible in language depends on the logical multiplicity of the *actual* phenomena, and this is something that we cannot foresee: "An atomic form cannot be foreseen. And it would be surprising if the actual phenomena had nothing more to teach us about their structure" (p. 30).

But the *actual* phenomena belong to the realm of the contingent, while logical form belongs to the realm of the necessary, of what cannot be otherwise. So how can an examination of the actual phenomena serve to establish logical form? How can we derive what is logically possible from what is actually the case? For instance, does the impossibility that two colors cannot be in the same place at the same time consist simply in the fact that we have never seen them combined in this way? According to Wittgenstein, what is *possible* can only be established through a very peculiar kind of investigation of the actual phenomena, a *logical* one. In this investigation we have to determine what belongs to the logical form of the phenomena and what does not. Any given feature that we find in a phenomenon is part of the logical form of that phenomenon if it contributes to fix its *identity*, that is, if it is a feature that is criterial for being a phenomenon of that *kind*. So in SRLF "logical form" designates the identity criteria of our experiential contents. Logical features are defining or constitutive features, as opposed to accidental ones. Thus, for instance, Wittgenstein argues that it is a constitutive feature of colors that they cannot coexist in the same point of the visual field and, therefore, the rule that prescribes the mutual exclusion of color attributions is a *necessary* law. But we learn this rule of logical syntax a posteriori, from an examination of color phenomena. And it would be a mistake to think that this rule has the status of an a priori truth: the logical structure of the phenomena could have been otherwise, and then the logical rules for their description would have been different. But given that color phenomena have the logical structure that they do, the coexistence of two colors in the same point of the visual field is not just unprecedented, but impossible. It is in fact *logically* impossible, for it is the logical form of the phenomena and not any fact of physics that prevents it. Thus Wittgenstein's view of logical form and logical analysis in SRLF gives a new twist to the Tractarian view of necessity: it allows for necessity to remain logical[59] without thereby being a priori.

According to SRLF, although the logical forms of the different kinds of phenomena (e.g., colors, sounds, etc.) can only be determined a posteriori, it is not simply a contingent fact that these phenomena have the forms that they do. To say that the phenomena could have had a different logical form is to say that they could have been phenomena of a different kind, for being a phenomenon of a certain kind just is having a particular logical form. Thus Wittgenstein emphasizes that the rules of logical syntax that he derives from the logical analysis of "the actual phenomena" are a posteriori (p. 30) and yet necessary (p. 32). The idea of *a posteriori necessity* is very familiar to a contemporary audience. It is the core idea of Kripke's account of identity statements in *Naming and Necessity*.

In fact, there is a striking similarity between Kripke's account of identity statements concerning natural kinds and Wittgenstein's remarks on logical form. Kripke argues that identity statements such as 'Water is H_2O' or 'Heat is the motion of molecules' express "necessary *a posteriori* truths."[60] These statements are the product of empirical investigations and yet their truth is necessary: "such statements representing scientific discoveries about what this stuff *is* are not contingent truths but necessary truths in the strictest possible sense."[61] Kripke emphasizes that the peculiarity of identity statements is that they are such that if true, they must be necessarily true, for they pick out their referents by specifying their *essential* properties—properties without which they wouldn't be what they are. The necessity of identity statements is utterly independent of the way in which we came to establish the truth of these statements. According to Kripke, it is a mistake to think that what is necessary and what is known a priori must go together. This seems to be also Wittgenstein's thought in

SRLF. The logical forms of the phenomena play in Wittgenstein's view the same metaphysical role that the essential properties of natural kinds play in Kripke's. And although Wittgenstein's remarks on logical form are a posteriori, he emphasizes that "the important point here is that these remarks do not express an experience but are *in some sense* tautologies" (p. 32; my emphasis). They are very peculiar tautologies indeed, since they are derived from experience.[62] What they really are is Kripke's necessary a posteriori truths about identity.

I have tried to show what Wittgenstein means by calling certain features of the phenomena "logical" and hence "necessary": these are identity-fixing features. But now a further question arises: *How* does one tell whether a particular feature of a phenomenon is *essential or accidental* to its identity? The features that Wittgenstein cites as belonging to the logical form of the phenomena are features that can be *intuitively* recognized as necessary (e.g., that a point in the visual field cannot have two different colors at the same time, or that a quality cannot have two different degrees simultaneously). But he provides no hint as to how we form these intuitions and no method to unravel them. In SRLF Wittgenstein took the logical analysis of the actual phenomena to be a promising path for the study of logical form. But in the absence of a method according to which we can distinguish between the logical and the nonlogical aspects of the phenomena, the idea of a "logical investigation of the phenomena" remains hopelessly underdescribed. One would expect that Wittgenstein's next step should have been to specify such method. But he never took this step. He became very quickly disenchanted with the idea of a "logical investigation of the actual phenomena." In the next section I will examine the reasons for this disenchantment. For now, it suffices to point out that the logical phenomenalism of SRLF was simply a tentative experiment, an exploratory attempt to improve the Tractarian treatment of the color-exclusion problem by giving epistemic content to the notions of logical form and logical analysis. The life of this attempt in Wittgenstein's philosophy was as ephemeral as that of its revisionistic implications. Immediately after he wrote SRLF Wittgenstein returned to the Tractarian view that ordinary language is "in perfect logical order"[63] and that logical form is immanent in our symbolisms, not in the phenomena we describe with them.

As we shall see, in 1929–30 Wittgenstein will emphasize that we cannot simply let the phenomena speak for themselves, for they are mute, we speak for them. But although Wittgenstein rejected the general argument of SRLF in the very same year in which he wrote it, some of the central ideas there put forth had a decisive influence on the subsequent development of his thought. In particular, much of Wittgenstein's efforts in 1929–1930 will be devoted to developing two ideas already formulated in SRLF: first, the idea that there is an irreducible *plurality* of logical forms corresponding to different *kinds* of propositions; and second, the idea that there are *holistic* relations among propositions of the same kind that bring them together into a unified *system* of description. The holistic and pluralistic view of language that emerged from the ideas espoused in SRLF is what Wittgenstein referred to as his "conception of a *system of propositions*" (WWK, p. 64; my emphasis).

2.2. The Emergence of the Satzsystem Conception of Language

According to the *Tractatus*, the significance of a proposition springs from its internal logical complexity. It is in virtue of having a certain logical structure that a proposition pictures a possible state of affairs: "That is how a picture is attached to reality; it *reaches right out* to it. It is laid against reality *like a measure*" (2.1511–2.1512; my emphasis). When we utter a significant proposition, we set it against reality "like a measure" and the proposition is true if "the measure" fits—that is, if the logical structure of the proposition coincides with that of the facts. In 1929–30 Wittgenstein remarks that although the analogy between speaking and measuring contains a deep insight about language, this analogy was ill-posed in the *Tractatus* and its basic insight was obscured. Wittgenstein now argues that describing reality is like taking a measurement in that any particular description presupposes an entire *system* of description just like any particular measurement presupposes a whole scale of measurement: "I now prefer to say that a *system of propositions* is laid against reality like a ruler" (WWK, p. 63); "It isn't a proposition which I put against reality as a yardstick, it's a *system* of propositions" (PR §82). The Tractarian formulation of the analogy was misleading because we don't describe reality by comparing isolated propositions with isolated facts, one by one, just as we don't take measurements by applying isolated graduation marks:

> If I lay a ruler against a spatial object, I lay *all the graduating lines* against it at the same time. It is not the individual graduating lines that are laid against it, but the entire scale. [. . .] The statements describing for me the length of an object form a system, a system of propositions. Now it is such an entire system of propositions that is compared with reality, not a single proposition. (WWK, pp. 63–64)

> Propositions turn out to be even more like yardsticks than I previously believed. [. . .] just as all the graduation marks are on *one* rod, the propositions corresponding to the graduation marks similarly belong together, and we can't measure with one of them without simultaneously measuring with all the others. (PR §82)

Propositions come in clusters; they form systems. The upshot of the analogy with yardsticks is that the significant use of a proposition presupposes an entire propositional system. However, although we know what it means for a measure to belong to a system of measurement, it is not entirely clear what it means for a proposition to belong to a propositional system. It may be obvious how a single graduation mark presupposes all the other marks of the scale, but in what sense does a single proposition presuppose all the others propositions of the system to which it belongs? Both in *Philosophical Remarks* (§§76ff) and in his conversations with the Vienna Circle (WWK, pp. 64ff), Wittgenstein appeals to the mutual relations of exclusion among statements of color attribution to explain how propositions are brought together into systems. What we have to learn from the phenomenon of mutual exclusion among propositions, Wittgenstein now argues, is that propositions are glued together into unified systems through *inferential* connections: "If I say, for example, that this or that point in the visual field is *blue*, then I know not merely that, but also that this point is not green, not red, not yellow, etc. I have laid the entire colour-scale against it at one go" (WWK, p. 64).

On Wittgenstein's view, what is most characteristic of a proposition is that it is tightly connected to other propositions through inferential relations. This is why propositions form systems. The Satzsystem view of language that Wittgenstein developed in 1929–30 is an attempt to elaborate this inferentialist insight. On this view, the interrelations that bring propositions together into systems are not *formal* inferential relations, but relations of *material* inference: inferential relations that are based on the *content* of the propositions involved. This inferentialist view constitutes a radical departure from the formalism of the *Tractatus*. According to the *Tractatus*, every inference is based on the logical form of the propositions involved. On this formalist view, the logical structure of a proposition determines the inferential relations into which the proposition can enter. Inferential relations ultimately depend on content-independent rules of logical syntax that specify how a proposition is truth-functionally related to other propositions. Valid inferences are licensed by the necessary truths of logic: for instance, the inference from "P & Q" to "P" is valid; and its validity is shown by the tautological form of the truth-function "P & Q —> P". On this view, material inferences constitute a derivative category. Inferences whose validity is not based on the logical form of the propositions involved are enthymemes: if an inference from "P" to "Q" is valid, we must be able to derive "Q" from "P" according to formal rules of inference when the statements are resolved into truth-functional combinations of elementary propositions. Thus, on the Tractarian view, all inferential relations among propositions result from their truth-functional composition out of logically independent elementary propositions. The validity of inferring one statement of color attribution (e.g., "Not-RPT") from another (e.g., "BPT") demands that these statements have the internal logical complexity required to ground the inference. As Wittgenstein explains to Schlick and Waismann, it was the Tractarian formalist approach to inference that precluded the emergence of the inferentialist view of language he now endorses:

> All this I did not yet know when I was writing my work: at that time I thought that *all inference was based on tautological form.* At that time I had not yet seen that an inference can also have the form: This man is 2m tall, therefore he is not 3m tall. [. . .] But if my present conception of a system of propositions is correct, it will actually be the rule that from the existence of one state of affairs the non-existence of all the other states of affairs described by this system of propositions can be inferred. (WWK, p. 64; my emphasis)

Through the examination of the color-exclusion problem provided in SRLF Wittgenstein recognized that there are relations among propositions that cannot be captured by the formal rules of logical syntax of the *Tractatus.* He concluded that these rules must be supplemented by content-specific rules of syntax. But now Wittgenstein goes a step further: in the Satzsystem view the Tractarian notion of logical syntax is not simply stretched; it is substantially transformed. As in SRLF, in his conversations with the Vienna Circle and in *Philosophical Remarks* Wittgenstein emphasizes that the conjunction of mutually exclusive propositions has a truncated truth-table ("FFF" instead of "TFFF"). But he now draws very different conclusions from this analysis. In SRLF Wittgenstein claimed that the truncated truth-table of "RPT & BPT" shows that it lacks *the* logical form that every conjunction must have and is, therefore, a pseudoproposition. The incipient pluralism of logical form of SRLF did not go so far as to affect the logical connectives; their logical form was assumed to remain fixed for the description of all phenomena. This assumption is precisely what Wittgenstein criticizes in Book VIII of *Philosophical Remarks* (§§76–86). There he argues that the logical connectives do not have just *one* inviolable logical form that must remain fixed across different propositional systems. And, of course, when the assumption of the unitary meaning of conjunction is given up, there is nothing that prevents us from granting propositional status to "RPT & BPT". Wittgenstein argues that by banishing this combination of signs from language "RPT & BPT" has been done "an injustice" in the name of the logical form of the proposition; it has "been cheated of its rights as a proposition" (PR §86). So again, as in the *Tractatus*, "RPT & BPT" is not a nonsensical proposition but a necessary falsehood, though now this falsehood is not claimed to be reducible to a truth-functional contradiction.

Wittgenstein remarks that in the conjunction of mutually exclusive propositions "not *all* truth possibilities disappear, even if they are all rejected" (PR §79). The conjunction sign still has some meaning here, although not the usual one: "'&' has a different meaning here, since 'x & y' usually means (TFFF); here, on the other hand, it means (FFF)" (PR §79). Against SRLF Wittgenstein argues that conjunction does not have a fixed meaning to which every logical product must conform. "TFFF" may be the general form of conjunction, but it is not *the* logical form of every conjunction. Wittgenstein now thinks that what this shows is that the meaning of the conjunction sign is sensitive to the meaning of the propositions conjoined by it. So he concludes that, contrary to what he previously thought, even the most general rules of syntax, the rules for logical connectives, are in fact content sensitive: "What was wrong about my conception was that I believed that the syntax of logical constants could be laid down without paying attention to the inner connection of propositions. That is not how things actually are. [. . .] Rather, the rules for the logical constants form only a part of a more comprehensive syntax about which I did not yet know anything at the time" (WWK, p. 74). The truth-functional rules of the *Tractatus*, Wittgenstein argues, give us only a partial account of the meaning of the logical connectives: "The rules for 'and', 'or', 'not' etc., which I represented by means of the T-F notation, are *a part* of the grammar of these words, but not *the whole*" (PR §83).

The relations of material inference that hold among the statements of color attribution constituted an *anomaly* for the formalist account of logical composition and inference of the *Tractatus*. Now these inferential relations that cannot be derived from formal rules of logical composition become the *paradigm* for the interconnections among propositions: "it really is the same as this everywhere" (WWK, p. 74). Wittgenstein now thinks that the moral to be drawn from the analysis of color statements is that we need "a more comprehensive syntax" (WWK, p. 74). This transformed notion of "syntax" is what Wittgestein will soon start referring to as "grammar" in the 1930–32 Lectures (e.g., p. 9) and in *Philosophical Remarks* (e.g., §6). This is a "syntax" which is not simply an account of the logical composition of complex propositions, but a "syntax" that is first and foremost an account of the inferential relations into which propositions of all kinds can enter. According to this new view of "syntax," the inferential relations among propositions are not to be explained in terms of their internal logical structure. On the contrary, the logical composition of propositions is to be explained in terms of the inferential relations that hold between them. And this is the key point of evolution. The crucial move from the formalism of the *Tractatus* to the inferentialism of the Satzsystem view is a radical *reversal of the order of explanation*: inferential relations take priority over logical composition. Of course this does not mean that, for Wittgenstein, the logical complexity of propositions is no longer an important feature of language. It is. But this feature no longer comes first in the order of explanation.

The shift of emphasis from logical composition to inferential relations is illustrated by the different analogies that Wittgenstein uses to explain what is most characteristic of propositions. The metaphor of the picture is now replaced with the metaphor of the yardstick: the former calls attention to the internal structure of propositions, the latter to their interrelations within a system of propositions. However, the pictorial metaphor is not entirely abandoned in 1929–30. Interestingly enough, it is still used *precisely* to emphasize the "composite" nature of propositions: "It is the essential feature of a proposition that it is *a picture* and has compositeness" (WWK, p. 90). More interestingly yet, the fact that a linguistic representation of reality has the compositeness of a picture is no longer considered a fact that, by itself, has explanatory value; it becomes a fact to be explained. Why is compositeness an essential feature of a proposition such as 'Fa'? Wittgenstein answers that it is essential that the proposition 'Fa' have different component parts related in a certain way only when and because 'Fa' *presupposes* other propositions of similar structure such as 'Fb', 'Fc', etc., and 'Ga', 'Ha', etc. (WWK, p. 90). Compositeness is an essential feature of a proposition because by virtue of having a composite structure, the proposition becomes inferentially related to other propositions. If a seemingly complex proposition such as 'Fa' were not in this way related to other propositions, "the propositional sign would be simple and not composite"; for instance, "if there were only the proposition 'Fa' but not 'Fb', it would be superfluous to mention 'a'. It would suffice to write just 'F'" (WWK, p. 90). The logical composition of the proposition is now holistically explained; it is explained in terms of the inferential relations into which the proposition can enter: the symbols 'F' and 'a' make distinct contributions to the meaning of the proposition 'Fa' because each of them connects the proposition with a whole range of propositions.

In *Philosophical Remarks* (§§24ff) Wittgenstein warns us that the analogy between propositions and pictures can be misleading, for the pictorial metaphor may suggest that it is the internal structure of the proposition that bears all the weight of the representational relation between language and the world. What can lead us astray is the idea that a picture must have *in itself* the right logical multiplicity required to represent reality. Of course it never escaped Wittgenstein's attention that a picture cannot represent anything unless it is understood according to a particular *method of projection* (cf. *Tractatus* 3.11). But our familiarity with the method of projection can lead us to think that its application can be taken for granted as something unproblematic, while in fact a method of projection *can always be applied in many different ways*. Wittgenstein emphasizes that the multiple applicability of the method of projection makes "the transition from the picture to what is depicted" indeterminate (PR §27). He thinks, however, that the problem of multiple applicability disappears when propositions are viewed as parts of a larger whole, as members of a propositional system. For the "grammatical conventions" (PR §§4ff) of a Satzsystem fix how each individual proposition within the system is to be projected onto reality, just as the conventions of a calculus of measurement fix the application of a yarstick. A yardstick does not have any intrinsic representational value; its capacity to describe reality is crucially dependent on the system of representation to which it belongs. Thus the metaphor of the yardstick underscores the holistic nature of linguistic representations obscured by the pictorial metaphor. On the Satzsystem view, a proposition still reaches right out to reality, but only against the background of the entire propositional system to which it belongs, like a yardstick: "You cannot compare a picture with reality, unless you can set it against it as a yardstick" (PR §43).

The holistic point that the simile of the yardstick is supposed to convey is that the most basic units of significance in language are not propositions, but systems of interrelated propositions. This holistic point constitutes a substantial extension of the so-called *context principle*[64] formulated by Frege. Just as Frege argued that only in the context of a proposition does a word have meaning,[65] Wittgenstein now argues that only in the context of a propositional system does a proposition have sense: We must "understand a proposition as *a* member of a system of propositions" (PR §15); "Understanding p means understanding its system" (PR §153). On this holistic view, the distinction between elementary and complex propositions can no longer be drawn. Since now logical composition is not to be explained in terms of logically independent semantic atoms and the rules for their combination, but in terms of the inferential relations among propositions, there is no longer need for primitive building blocks of meaning and inference: "The concept of an 'elementary proposition' now loses all of its earlier significance" (PR §83).

It is important to notice that it is not until inferential relations take priority over logical composition that the Tractarian idea of a propositional unit "of the simplest kind" (cf. *Tractatus* 4.21) is abandoned. This idea was still maintained in "Some Remarks on Logical Form" despite the fact that Wittgenstein explicitly rejected the thesis of the logical independence of elementary propositions. In 1929 elementary propositions had still a role to play in Wittgenstein's view because no reversal in the order of explanation had yet taken place. As the opening page of the 1929 paper makes clear, Wittgenstein was still trying to give an account of *logical composition* that could identify "the kernels of every proposition" (SRLF p. 29). Wittgenstein recognized that elementary propositions can be holistically interrelated and he argued that these holistic relations call for special rules of syntax. But this holistic insight did not immediately lead Wittgenstein to consider the logical form of propositions in a new light. He still held that the task of the logical analysis of propositions was to determine how propositions are to be constructed out of simpler elements. At the end of 1929, however, Wittgenstein started to argue that in order to determine the logical form of *any* proposition, we need to analyze its inferential connections with other propositions: we need to examine what the proposition follows from and what follows from it (cf. WWK, pp. 64ff).

On the Satzsystem view, what determines the logical form of a proposition is its place within a network of propositions. A combination of signs can only have the logical form of a proposition within a particular Satzsystem: "A proposition is not a proposition unless it occurs within a grammatical system" (Lectures 1930–32, p. 37). What this extended version of the context principle underscores is that the very notion of "proposition" is Satzsystem-specific. In the *Tractatus* Wittgenstein tried to establish a general criterion for what counts as a genuine proposition by appealing to the notion of truth. He argued that a combination of signs is a proposition if it expresses a truth-possibility, if it can be true or false. Now he contends that it is the grammar of each propositional system that determines what we can call "true" and "false" and what we can call "a proposition": "A proposition is simply characterised by the grammatical rules which apply to it. So to say that a proposition is what can be true or false is to say that a proposition is anything which grammar allows me to call true or false" (Lectures 1930–32, p. 47). There are as many ways in which a proposition can be true or false as there are Satzsysteme. The terms "true" and "false" can only be predicated of propositions, but it is a mistake to think that we have an independent grasp of the meaning of these terms that enables us to determine what is and is not a proposition. As Peter Winch puts it, in the early 1930s Wittgenstein realizes that the meaning of the predicates 'true' and 'false' "varies *pari passu* with our understanding of the propositions to which we apply them, and they cannot be used as points of reference for fixing the sense of the propositions."[66]

In the *Tractatus* Wittgenstein offered a logical elucidation of language that delimited the bounds of sense for all possible symbolisms: logical form was supposed to establish, *sub specie aeternitatis*, the whole range of possible significant propositions. But according to the Satzsystem view, there is no prospect for such a general account, for there is no standpoint from which we can establish universal requirements that all possible symbolisms have to meet. As he puts it, there is no single "logical space" where language signifies, each propositional system has its own "logical space": "Systems are certainly not all in *one* space" (PR §162). On this pluralistic view of language, there is no privileged way of drawing the distinction between sense and nonsense; the permissible propositional forms are *autonomously* determined by the grammatical rules of each Satzsystem.

A central tenet of the Satzsystem view of language is the so-called thesis of *the autonomy of grammar.*[67] According to this thesis, the grammar of a propositional system is "self-contained," "complete in itself" (cf. Lectures 1930–32, pp. 30, 45–46; also PR §158). Wittgenstein appeals to the "autonomy" of grammar to emphasize two distinct claims: first, the claim that grammar is not determined by facts of any kind and that it is, therefore, *arbitrary* (cf. Lectures 1930–32, pp. 44–47, 57–59, 91–103; PR §4, §109); and second, the claim that the grammar of one propositional system cannot be justified or refuted by the grammar of another and that, therefore, Satzsysteme are *logically independent* from one another (cf. esp. Lectures 1930–32, p. 87). Some commentators have argued that the thesis of the autonomy of grammar has a crucial importance for the development of Wittgenstein's mature view. Baker and Hacker emphasize the importance of the first claim contained in this thesis: that "grammar is autonomous, a free-floating structure which is not answerable to reality."[68] Shanker underscores the importance of the second claim: that each "autonomous 'propositional system' [. . .] constitutes a distinct 'logical space,'" that language is "compartmentalised into distinct, autonomous systems, each of which operates on its own specific internal rules."[69] According to these commentators, the thesis of the autonomy of grammar constitutes the final rejection of the Tractarian view of language and the hallmark of Wittgenstein's later philosophy. On this interpretation, propositional systems are "*language games* in embryo."[70] As Shanker puts it: "In a short time (. . .) from these *Satzsysteme* would evolve 'language games'."[71]

In subsequent chapters, I will argue that the thesis of the autonomy of grammar was progressively qualified and finally abandoned in the 1930s, and that the changes from the Satzsystem conception of language to Wittgenstein's mature view have been underestimated. As a first step to assess the role of the autonomy thesis in the evolution of Wittgenstein's thought, in what follows I will examine the arguments that Wittgenstein offered in support of this thesis in 1930–32. I will argue that these arguments were not directed against the *Tractatus*, but against the metaphysical realism that was already shown to be untenable by the logical analysis of the *Tractatus*, as well as against the phenomenalism transitorily adopted in SRLF.[72] So, on my interpretation, the thesis of the autonomy of grammar constitutes a return to the Tractarian view of language, not a departure from it. Indeed the Satzsystem conception of language involves important modifications of the Tractarian view. In particular, it involves a strong conventionalism and pluralism absent in the *Tractatus.* But these changes do not constitute a complete break with the Tractarian system. As Kenny puts it, "the effect of these changes was to make the system of the *Tractatus* more supple and closer to ordinary language."[73]

The thesis of the autonomy of grammar is first introduced as a repudiation of "the idea that language is kept in bounds by reality" (Lectures 1930–32, p. 103). Strictly speaking, this is not a Tractarian idea. In the *Tractatus,* language is "kept in bounds" by its own logical form, not by some reality outside language.[74] Similarly, Wittgenstein now argues that transgressing the bounds of sense is not getting into a special kind of conflict *with reality,* for "you can only get into conflict with reality by saying something which is not true" (Lectures 1930–32, p. 95). Speaking nonsense is going beyond the limits of significance established by the grammar of particular propositional systems. For instance, "a sound is red" is indeed "nonsense—i.e. not language at all" (Lectures 1930–32, p. 47)—not because it conflicts with certain logical structure external to language, but because it conflicts with the rules of grammar we have adopted for the description of sounds and colors. "To call a thing a colour is to say it obeys certain grammatical rules" (p. 47). For instance, the attribution of a color to a thing implies that that thing is a visible object, which sounds are not. Color words and the word "sound" belong to two different Satzsysteme, and there is no overarching Satzsystem in which the grammars of these words can be combined.

In "Some Remarks on Logical Form" Wittgenstein claimed that in order to determine whether the conjunction of any two predicates is admissible in language, we have to investigate first whether the properties they denote are compatible. But Wittgenstein now argues that this is a mistake: we know that a point in the visual field cannot have two colors at the same time independently of any particular investigation or experience (PR §84; cf. also WWK, p. 67). Wittgenstein emphasizes that color incompatibilities derive from the inferential structure of the Satzsystem for the description of color, not from some external reality that can be independently investigated. Given the grammatical rules of color attribution, if I know that a point in the visual field is blue, I automatically know that it is not red, nor green, nor yellow. And "this," Wittgenstein remarks, "is also *the reason why* a point cannot have different colours at the same time" (WWK, p. 64; my emphasis). It is the inferential relations among statements of color attribution that *explains* the phenomenon of color exclusion, not the other way round. What marks the transition from the phenomenalism of 1929 to the conventionalism of 1930 is another reversal in the order of explanation, now concerning the relation between symbolic rules and necessary connections in experience: it is not because certain things appear as necessary or impossible in our experience that we must describe the phenomena in a particular way; it is because we describe the phenomena in a particular way that certain things appear as necessary or impossible in our experience.

In 1930 Wittgenstein contends that logical rules cannot be read off "the logical form of the actual phenomena" (cf. PR §4). He argues that we cannot even make sense of the idea that the phenomena we describe in language have a logical form prior to and independent of the rules that we lay down for their description. According to Wittgenstein, the phenomena we describe have the logical multiplicity that our systems of description ascribe to them. On this view, what counts as a possible description is ultimately up to us; it is fixed by our systems of descriptions. So, in order to determine whether a particular sign or proposition has representational content within a symbolism, all we need to do is to see whether there are grammatical rules that govern the use of that sign or proposition within the symbolism: "The sign plus the rules of grammar applying to it is all we need. We need nothing further to make the connection with reality" (Lectures 1930–32, p. 59). The logical analysis of different kinds of phenomena is thus replaced by the logical analysis of different propositional systems. This crucial move from the realm of phenomena to our systems of description is evoked in an important passage of the *Investigations*: "We feel as if we had to *penetrate* phenomena: our investigation, however, is directed not towards phenomena, but, as one might say, towards the '*possibilities*' of phenomena. We remind ourselves, that is to say, of the *kind of statement* that we make about phenomena" (§90).

In the early 1930s Wittgenstein repeatedly emphasizes that the rules of grammar are *arbitrary* conventions that regulate our symbolic systems (cf. esp. Lectures 1930–32, pp. 57–58 and 85–87). We cannot point to something in the world that necessitates our symbolic conventions: for instance, "I cannot cite a property of colours that make the conventions [for their description] necessary" (PR §4); "Grammar is not determined by facts" (Lectures 1930–32, p. 95). On the Satzsystem view, the rules of grammar are prior to and independent of any investigation of matters of fact. They are not *necessities* that we discover a posteriori through an examination of the phenomena that language describes (as the argument of SRLF suggested). In the first place, what counts as *necessary* is determined by the grammar of our propositional systems: "To a necessity in the world there corresponds an arbitrary rule in language" (Lectures 1930–32, p. 57). According to the Satzsystem view, only the rules of grammar can impart necessity, but these rules themselves cannot be called "necessary," for there is no grammar over and above these rules that can grant them such status. In the second place, we do not come to know grammatical rules a posteriori. In fact, the rules of grammar are not something that we come to *know* in any way, whether a priori or a posteriori; they are conventions that we lay down. We do not have an epistemic relation of any kind with these rules:[75] they call for a decision, not for cognition. As Wittgenstein puts it, "a rule of representation" is not a knowledge claim that "can be justified in propositions: propositions describing what is represented and showing that the representation is adequate" (PR §7). The arbitrariness of grammar derives from the fact that we cannot give *reasons* for or against the grammar of a language being the way it is. It is the arbitrariness of what cannot be justified or refuted, of what is beyond the realm of justification.

In the *Tractatus* Wittgenstein did not regard the rules of logical syntax as arbitrary conventions. He argued that logical rules spring from "the essence of a proposition," from "what *all* propositions, by their very nature, [have] in common" (5.47-5.471).[76] However, it is not a Tractarian thesis that logical rules must (or even can) be justified. On the contrary, according to the Tractarian view of language, the rules of logical syntax are empty tautologies that make no claim and any attempt of justifying these rules would be unintelligible. So the arguments that Wittgenstein developed in 1930–32 against the possibility of justifying or refuting symbolic rules, far from being directed against the *Tractatus*, constitute in fact the revival of a Tractarian idea; namely, that logic does not stand in need of metaphysical grounding. In *Philosophical Remarks* and the lectures we can find three distinct arguments against the attempt of justifying grammar: a *reductio ad absurdum*, a charge of circularity, and a regress argument. Each of these arguments undermines ideas that Wittgenstein played with in the 1929 paper.

Let's consider, first, the *reductio*. Wittgenstein asks: "Can we give a description which will justify the rules of grammar? Can we say why we must use these rules?" (Lectures 1930–32, p. 47). He argues that for something to be susceptible to justification, it must also be susceptible to refutation. So the very attempt to justify grammar "presupposes that I could say 'If reality were otherwise, then the rules of grammar would be otherwise'" (Lectures 1930–32, p. 47). And this is precisely what Wittgenstein suggested in SRLF. But he now argues that grammatical rules are not defeasible: the possibility of their refutation is *unintelligible*, and so is the possibility of their justification. We cannot even make sense of the possibility of refuting grammar through a description of reality because if we were *able to describe* a reality that supposedly contradicted the grammar of our language, then, by definition, that reality would not refute our grammar: the very act of our description would put that reality in harmony with grammar. As

Wittgenstein puts it, "in order to describe a reality in which grammar was otherwise I should have to use the very combinations which grammar forbids" (Lectures 1930–32, p. 47). But "I cannot use language to get outside language" (PR §6).[77]

In the second place, Wittgenstein argues that the attempt to justify the grammar of a symbolism by appealing to something external to it is *viciously circular*: "Grammatical conventions cannot be justified by describing what is represented. Any such description already presupposes the grammatical rules" (PR §7). Symbolic rules cannot be justified by their correspondence with language-independent facts: "A grammatical rule does not stand in a relation to reality such that we can give rule and reality and then see whether they agree or not" (Lectures 1930–32, p. 86). It is the rules of our symbolisms that determine what we can call "facts," and these symbolic rules cannot in turn be grounded in facts, on pain of circularity. The grammar of a symbolism cannot be modeled after the structure of a language-independent reality: "We don't model the grammar of 'red', 'green' and other such words to match reality, because this would mean that we could say 'these qualities have this sort of grammar.' The grammatical rules about 'red', 'green' etc. cannot be justified by anything you can say about colours" (Lectures 1930–32, p. 86). We simply don't have access to the "grammar" of color phenomena independently of the language that we use to describe these phenomena. We cannot carry out a logical investigation of the phenomena we want to describe without relying on a particular grammar. We cannot justify grammar because that would involve using language and therefore grammar.

One might reply that the circularity argument does not undermine the validity of *every* attempt of justification. For we could escape the vicious circle by justifying one grammar or set of rules using another language with a different grammar. But Wittgenstein argues, in the third place, that the justification of one grammar in terms of another opens an infinite *regress* and distorts the nature of the rules of grammar. If you expect "some further set of rules" to justify the rules of grammar, "these rules will then in turn need justification. [But] grammar is not something higher, with another grammar beyond it" (Lectures 1930–32, p. 87). There is no such thing as a hierarchy of grammars. If we move from one grammar to another, we simply move from one language to another, leaving the original intact. The thesis of the autonomy of grammar implies that all symbolisms stand on a par, that they are autonomous systems, independent from one another. This undercuts the impetus to develop a "perfect notation" whose grammar we can use as the paradigm to measure the adequacy of the grammatical rules of other symbolisms.

As pointed out above, the idea that the grammar of one propositional system is independent of the grammar of any other is a second sense in which grammar is said to be "self-contained" or "autonomous" (cf. Lectures 1930–32, p. 87). When the autonomy of grammar is combined with the pluralism of grammatical systems, it results in the *logical independence* of Satzsysteme. The separatism of elementary propositions of the *Tractatus* is thus replaced with the separatism of propositional systems. The idea of the autonomy of each propositional system from every other plays *the same* role in the Satzsysteme view that the thesis of the logical independence of elementary propositions played in the *Tractatus*: it is supposed to allow logical (or grammatical) analysis to get off the ground and to draw sharp boundaries around a domain of significance (though now there is room for a plurality of such domains, which are analyzed in a top-down fashion, proceeding from the whole to its parts). In the next chapter, I will argue that the thesis of the logical independence of Satzsysteme involves problems similar to those concerning the logical independence of elementary propositions. It is important to notice that the thesis of logical independence is parasitic on the idea of "the most basic units of significance": it is only when there are linguistic units that can stand on their own (whether sentences or entire propositional systems) that there is room for this thesis.

To conclude, the arguments that Wittgenstein offers in support of the thesis of the autonomy of grammar strongly suggest that this thesis is the direct outcome of his recantation of the ideas defended in SRLF, not in the *Tractatus*. What this thesis achieves is the reestablishment of the Tractarian claim that our ordinary language is "in perfect logical order" (5.5563). What immediately precedes the discussion of the autonomy of grammar in *Philosophical Remarks* (§§4–7) is a critique of the idea that logical analysis can go beyond ordinary language and lay the foundations for a perfect notation: "How strange if logic were concerned with an 'ideal' language and not with *ours*. [. . .] Logical analysis [. . .] is the analysis of propositions *as they stand*" (PR §3). The source of Wittgenstein's discontent with the argument of the 1929 paper soon after he wrote it was probably the strong revisionism that he was led to adopt in his search for a solution to the color-exclusion problem. With the introduction of the autonomy thesis Wittgenstein restores the antirevisionary spirit of his philosophy. The Satzsystem view of the early 1930s enabled Wittgenstein to recover the idea that the distinction between sense and nonsense is drawn within language.

3

THE CALCULUS VIEW OF LANGUAGE

MEANING AND RULES

A recurrent theme in Wittgenstein's writings and lectures from 1930–34 is the critique of the idea that there is a single calculus of propositions that underlies every possible symbolism. He remarks that "Frege and Russell made up a calculus which looked to be *the* calculus underlying the correct use of language" (Lectures 1932–35, p. 68). He also points out that in the *Tractatus* he shared this "mistaken idea" with Frege and Russell:

> I had the mistaken idea that propositions belong to just one calculus. There seemed to be *one* fundamental calculus, viz., logic, on which any other calculus could be based. This is the idea which Frege and Russell had [. . .]. If one has the idea of a single logic then one must be able to give one general formula of logic, the general formula of a proposition. I thought I had found this formula in the T-F table, an equivalent of the word "proposition" and the word "logic." (Lectures 1932–35, p. 138)

Wittgenstein now argues that the logical calculus is just "one calculus among others" (Lectures 1932–35, p. 13), and its rules do not have any special privilege. Each propositional system determines the form of its propositions *autonomously*, that is, according to its own rules of grammar. So Wittgenstein proposes to adopt "as a leading principle" in philosophy that there is no such thing as "the calculus of all calculi" (PG §72).

However, as some commentators have pointed out,[78] the view of language as a calculus remains at the core of Wittgenstein's philosophy in the early 1930s. In *Philosophical Remarks* Wittgenstein refers to a system of proposition as "a calculus" or "system of rules" (PR §152). In a conversation with Schlick and Waismann from September 1931 he remarks: "I am saying that our way of using signs constitutes a calculus, and I am saying this deliberately. For this is not a mere analogy between our way of using words in a language and a calculus" (WWK p. 168). And in *Philosophical Grammar* he argues that "philosophy is concerned with calculi," although not with "the calculus of all calculi" (PG §72). What Wittgenstein finds objectionable is the idea that there is a privileged, overarching calculus that can fix the logical form of every proposition. But he retains the idea that "a general propositional form determines a proposition as part of a calculus" (PG §80). There is nothing wrong with the idea of a calculus as long as it is diversified so as to account for the specificity of a genuine plurality of propositional forms.

As late as 1933–34 Wittgenstein still holds that "language is a calculus" (PG §140). But although the calculus view of language of this period has its roots in the *Tractatus*, it contrasts with the Tractarian account of language in important respects. In the early 1930s the Tractarian view of language as a calculus is transformed in three ways. In the first place, the notion of calculus is *pluralized*: language cannot be reduced to a single propositional calculus; it is composed of a set of autonomous calculi. In the second place, propositional calculi are thought to be *conventional* systems: their rules are arbitrary stipulations (PG §§81–82); they do not spring of necessity from the essence of the proposition ("what we call a proposition is more or less arbitrary"; Lectures 1932–35, p. 12). In the third place, the propositional calculi in which language consists are *no longer hidden* beneath the statements of ordinary language: these calculi operate on the very surface of language use; they are composed of ordinary-language statements (cf. PG pp. 210–211).

This chapter will cover the development of the calculus view of language from 1930 to 1934. The main point of evolution in this period is the repudiation of the thesis of the logical independence of propositional systems. This repudiation marks the transition from the *local* holism of the Satzsystem view to the *radical* holism[79] of *Philosophical Grammar* and the 1932-35 lectures. In section 1, I will examine the leitmotif that gives unity to Wittgenstein's thought during this period: the attempt to develop a *deflationary* account of meaning as use. In section 2, I will analyze the problems facing the account of meaning sketched in *Philosophical Remarks* and the 1930–32 lectures, which finally led to the rejection of the thesis of logical independence. Finally, in section 3, I will discuss the revised version of the calculus view of language that Wittgenstein defended in *Philosophical Grammar*, where he abandoned the Satzsystem conception of language in favor of a radically holistic view according to which language is composed of *interrelated* calculi or "language games."

3.1. Rules as Constitutive of Meaning

The calculus view of meaning of the 1930s arises as a generalization of the semantic *deflationism* characteristic of the Tractarian view of logic. In the *Tractatus* Wittgenstein argued against semantically inflated views of logic according to which logical laws flow from the meaning of the logical constants (the logical connectives and quantifiers). On these inflated views, the laws of logic describe the realm of logical objects that the logical constants designate. Against these views Wittgenstein argued that logical propositions are empty tautologies (6.12). According to the *Tractatus*, the propositions of logic simply show the necessary formal features of every proposition; and the whole of logic is already contained in the general logical form of the proposition: "One could say that the sole logical constant was [. . .] the general propositional form" (5.47). Wittgenstein's deflationay view of logic in the *Tractatus* tries to establish that there is no realm of logical objects that logic describes: logic is "the theory of forms and of inference" (6.1224); it has "no 'subject-matter'" (6.124). In order to eradicate semantic inflation in logic, Wittgenstein developed an alternative, nonreferentialist account of the logical operators: the so-called *disappearance theory* of logical constants.

In the *Tractatus* Wittgenstein expressed the core idea of his view of logic as follows: "My fundamental idea is that the 'logical constants' are not representatives" (4.0312). That is, logical constants do not denote, they stand for nothing. They are not names of objects,[80] they are propositional links. They make a peculiar contribution to the sense of complex propositions. On Wittgenstein's view, the connectives and quantifiers of the propositional calculus simply abbreviate logical operations performed on propositions. These logical signs reveal *how* propositions are combined in complex statements, but they are not further *representational constituents* of the sense of these statements: they are blueprints for truth-functions. Now, if logical constants are just abbreviations for the truth-functions involved in the construction of complex propositional configurations, it should be possible to devise a notation that lays out the complete construction of these configurations down to their ultimate constituents without the help of these abbreviations. This is what the TF-notation of the *Tractatus* is supposed to achieve. As Wittgenstein explained it in the 1930s, "we could do away with *negation*, *disjunction*, *conjunction*, etc. [. . .] making up a notation containing only the words 'true' and 'false'. I once did that, with the notation for truth-functions" (Lectures 1932–35, p. 106fn; see also pp. 135–39). The TF-notation makes it "manifest that there are no 'logical objects'" (*Tractatus* 5.4; cf. also 4.441). By replacing logical constants with configurations of T's and F's,

Wittgenstein shows that the only representational ingredients of propositional manufacturing are elementary propositions. The truth-functional analysis of complex propositions ultimately results in "the vanishing of the apparent logical constants" (5.441). At the last level of analysis, the logical constants disappear because the truth-functions that they abbreviate are carried out in full. The upshot of this analysis is that all there is to the significance of logical connectives and quantifiers is a set of rules for the truth-functional combination of propositions.

In the 1930s Wittgenstein can no longer hold the disappearance theory of logical constants as formulated in the *Tractatus*. On his new view of language there is no room to perform disappearing tricks, since there is no underlying calculus of elementary propositions into which complex statements can be resolved. However, the fundamental insight of the Tractarian account of logical constants is maintained: these logical signs have a combinatorial (not a representational) essence, and their significance is reducible to the rules of logical syntax curled up in them. Wittgenstein emphasizes that it is a mistake to give primacy to the meaning of logical constants over the rules for their use, as if there were logical entities corresponding to the signs of the propositional calculus, entities whose nature determines the use of these signs: "As if the rules for the negation sign *follow from* the nature of negation. So that in a certain sense there is first of all negation, and then the rules of grammar" (PG §15). Wittgenstein's thesis is that the rules for the use of logical signs do not derive from the meaning of these signs, they *constitute* their meaning (PG §14). As he puts it in the lectures:

> Are the rules, for example, $\sim\sim p = p$ for negation, responsible to the meaning of a word? No. *The rules constitute the meaning*, and are not responsible to it. [. . .] how is the meaning of "negation" defined, if not by the rules? $\sim\sim p = p$ does not follow from the meaning of "not" but constitute it. Similarly, $p.\ p\text{->}q.\ \text{->}.\ q.$ does not depend on the meaning of "and" and "implies"; it constitutes their meaning. (Lectures 1932–35, p. 4; my emphasis)

Notice that the mistake of inflationist philosophy of logic is not to endow logical signs with meanings, but to conceive of their meanings as objects. So in order to avoid semantic inflation in logic, we do not need to deny meaning to the logical signs; we just have to construe their meaning differently. This was already achieved by the Tractarian analysis of the meaning of logical constants in terms of combinatorial rules. However, in the *Tractatus* Wittgenstein did not develop explicitly the implications of this deflationary analysis for *meaning* in general. In the early 1930s Wittgenstein uses this analysis to disarm the denotational view of meaning (and not just to criticize its inflationist implications in the philosophy of logic). The calculus view of meaning of the early 1930s is developed by generalizing the Tractarian deflationary strategy toward logical constants. Wittgenstein now argues that it is not only the peculiar trait of a logical sign, but the general trait of any significant sign whatever, that its meaning is entirely determined by the symbolic rules that regulate its use. As Wittgenstein puts it in the 1930–32 Lectures: "We are apt to think that the meaning of words lies outside language [. . .], but the meaning of a word must be entirely given, or determined, if you describe the language or its rules" (p. 64); "The meaning of a word is not the object corresponding to it, but the grammatical rules which apply to it" (p. 85).

Thus, on Wittgenstein's view in the early 1930s, the sentential connectives become the paradigm for the elucidation of word meaning. According to this paradigm, the meaning of a sign is "its place in the calculus, the way it is used" (Lectures 1932–35, p. 29); and this "is determined by all the grammatical rules that apply to it" (Lectures 1930–32, p. 48).[81] He even uses the paradigm of the sentential connectives to explain the meaning of proper names: "Proper names do not function differently as symbols from such words as 'and'. Their meaning is given by their use, by the rules applying to them" (Lectures 1930–32, p. 112). Wittgenstein argues that the semantic locutions "meaning of a name" and "bearer of a name" have completely different uses: "The latter can be replaced by 'Watson', but not the former. Obviously, 'use of a word', if adopted as the definition of 'meaning of a word', is not replaceable by 'bearer of a word'" (Lectures 1932–35, p. 44; cf. also PG §27). He goes on to argue that the meaning of a sign is its rule-governed use, which is captured by its grammar: "What interests *us* in the sign, the meaning which matters for us is embodied in the grammar of the sign" (PG §44). But precisely because "meaning" is a grammatical notion, we cannot identify the meaning of a term with an object corresponding to it, for that would be treating a language-independent entity as a reified piece of grammar, and therefore "inventing a mythology of symbolism" (PG §15). This is what Wittgenstein calls the mythology of "meaning-bodies" [*Bedeutungskörper*] (PG §16):

> We are tempted to think we can deduce the rules for the use of a word from its meaning. [. . .] To say that the use of a word, e.g., "cube," follows from its meaning is to treat the word as if it were the visible face of *a hidden body*, its meaning. (Lectures 1932–35, pp. 50–51; my emphasis)

Wittgenstein argues that this *Bedeutungskörper* mythology arises from the *static* view of signs characteristic of the denotational approach. According to this static view, what turns an arbitrary mark into a linguistic sign is a rigid connection between that mark and an object. Against this view Wittgenstein argues that what is important is the dynamics of the sign, the way it is used, for nothing is a sign unless it has a use: "What I want to say is that to be a sign a thing must be dynamic, not static" (PG §17). Using the sentential connectives as paradigmatic examples, Wittgenstein emphasizes that an arbitrary mark becomes a sign in virtue of "the way it *works*—I mean, the way it is used" (PG §17). And a sign has a use in a calculus only if there are rules in that calculus that govern the application of the sign. What Wittgenstein urges us to recognize is that there are no meanings prior to and independent of the symbolic rules of use that we lay down. The reification of meaning has to be banished from language just as it was banished from the logical calculus; that is, by recognizing that the rules for the use of signs are constitutive of their meaning. As Wittgenstein puts it: "The system of rules determining a calculus thereby determines the 'meaning' of its signs too" (PR §152); "It is grammatical rules that determine meaning (constitute it)" (PG §133).

The core idea in the calculus view of language of the early 1930s is that rules are constitutive of meaning. This idea is the cornerstone of a unified account of semantic content in which word meaning and propositional content are explained in a similar fashion: the contentfulness of both words and propositions consists in their use or role in a calculus as defined by rules. The fundamental principles of this account of content are formulated as follows: first, at the subsentential level, "The meaning is the role of the word in the calculus" (PG §27; cf. also PG §23); and second, at the sentential level, "A proposition has its content as part of a calculus" (PG §27), "The role of a sentence in the calculus is its sense" (PG §84).

In order to determine the precise sense of Wittgenstein's identification of meaning with use in the early 1930s, we need to examine the notion of *use* that is at work in the calculus view of language. In this period—as in the *Tractatus*—when the meaning of a sign is identified with its use, "use" refers to *all* the *possible* applications of the sign within the language or calculus (cf. Lectures 1930–32, pp. 48-49), to its "applic*ability*" (PG p. 319), rather than to its actual applications. What Wittgenstein means by "use" in the early 1930s is a definite set of possible applications fixed by rules, not an open-ended stock of actual applications. Accordingly, the idea that meaning is use should not be understood as the idea that the meaning of our signs is established in and by our actual practices of language use. Rather, Wittgenstein's thesis is that what constitutes the meaning of a sign is "the grammatically *possible* ways of applying it" (PG §10; my emphasis).

On the calculus view of language, the range of possible applications of a sign has priority over its de facto use in actual practice. For Wittgenstein, the former is a grammatical issue, the latter a matter of empirical detail. In

Philosophical Remarks he uses an interesting analogy to distinguish between actual and possible uses and to emphasize the grammatical significance of the latter. He compares the use of a sign with the use of a lever, emphasizing that a sign has application only within a symbolism just as a lever has application only within a mechanism, for instance, a gearbox (PR §§14–15). The analogy illustrates what Wittgenstein means by "use":

> Imagine a gearbox whose lever can take four positions. Now of course it can only take these positions in succession, and that takes time; and suppose it happened that it only ever occupied one of these positions, since the gearbox was then destroyed. Wasn't it still a gearbox with *four* positions? Weren't the four *possible*? Anyone who saw it would have seen its complexity, and its complexity is only to be explained by the use for which it was intended, to which in fact it was not put. (PR §15)

It is the possible applications of the lever as fixed by the structure of the gearbox, and not any finite set of actual applications, that give us a complete picture of its use. Similarly, it is the possible applications of a sign as fixed by the grammatical conventions of a symbolism, and not its de facto applications, that define its use. When we establish the grammar of a symbolism—as when we set the mechanism of a gearbox—we fix the range of applicability of its signs. But one might reply to Wittgenstein's analogy as follows: if there are parts of a mechanism that do not figure at all in its actual use, in what sense can we say that they are nonetheless part of its use?; if there are possible applications of a sign that do not get actualized, in what sense are they part of the identity of the sign? In a *grammatical* sense: they are *possibilities* that lie in the background of any actual application of the sign. Wittgenstein asks: how can one application of the sign presuppose "another that strictly speaking isn't there at all"? He answers: "It presupposes its possibility; its possibility in sign-space (in grammatical space)" (PR §110). So the realism of *possibilia* of the *Tractatus* discussed above (see 1.4) is still very much alive in Wittgenstein's view in the early 1930s. On this view, a sign signifies against a background of possibilities; and the same goes for the proposition: "A proposition is a sign in a system of signs. It is one combination of signs among a number of *possible* ones, and as opposed to other *possible* ones" (PG §84; my emphasis).

On the calculus view of language of the early 1930s, the grammar of a symbolism fixes all its possible applications; and this totality of possible uses gives significance to any particular application that gets actualized. The actual use of language has, therefore, only an empirical interest. For the *possibility* of any actual use of language is already contained in its grammar. By distinguishing between actual and possible uses of language in this way Wittgenstein draws a sharp boundary between two different kinds of investigations: the examination of the possible uses of a symbolism is what he calls a "logical" or "grammatical" analysis; the investigation of matters of fact concerning language use is what he terms the study of the "natural history" of language. Thus Wittgenstein concludes from the analogy of the gearbox: "the natural history of the use of a word can't be any concern of logic" (PR §15).

The actual application of a sign necessarily has a *temporal* dimension. By contrast, what Wittgenstein calls the *grammatical* use of a sign, its applicability, is not conceived as something *essentially* extended over time. As Wittgenstein puts it, when we are dealing with grammar "time does not enter in" (Lectures 1932–35, p. 87). The rules of grammar determine *sub specie aeternitatis* the whole range of possible applications of a sign within a symbolism. Thus, in the calculus view of language of the early 1930s, the Tractarian idea of a sempiternal range of possible uses of language is maintained, though in a new way: this range of significant possibilities is no longer fixed by the logical form of the proposition, but by the grammatical conventions of each symbolism. Wittgenstein argues that the range of possible applications of a sign are built into the very identity of the sign. By using a sign we become *committed* to a set of rules and hence to a range of possible applications (cf. Lectures 1930–32, p. 37). And the rules governing the applicability of a sign cannot be altered by any actual practice, for using the sign according to different rules would be simply using a different sign (cf. Lectures 1930–32, p. 58).

The priority of grammatical rules over the actual use of language is underscored by the dynamic view of signs that Wittgenstein held in the early 1930s. According to this view, an arbitrary mark becomes a sign only when the rules for its use have been fixed. Therefore, the grammatical rules that regulate the applicability of a sign must already be given before any actual application of the sign takes place; for in the absence of these rules we do not even have the sign yet, all we have is an arbitrary mark, and using an arbitrary mark without rules is not using language at all. As Wittgenstein puts it, "the place of a word in language" is set up by all the grammatical rules "that can be given *previous to its use*"; "The rules prepare for the game which may afterwards be used as a language. *Only when the rules are fixed* can I use the game as a language" (Lectures 1930–32, p. 49 and p. 57; my emphasis). In the calculus view of language there is not a more fundamental explanatory notion than the notion of a rule. As we shall see in later chapters, this view of rules will undergo important changes: the priority of rules over actual applications and their independence from facts of natural history will be questioned in the mid and late 1930s when Wittgenstein abandons the calculus view and starts to regard language as an actual practice of use.

In this section I have examined the features of the calculus view of language that remain constant from 1930 to 1933–34. These features provide the fixed background against which important changes take place. In what follows I will discuss these changes by considering the details of the account of meaning that Wittgenstein developed in the early 1930s. According to this account, in order to determine the possible applications of a sign and hence its meaning, we need to determine first the calculus to which the sign belongs and, second, the rules of grammar that apply to the sign within that calculus. In the next section I will discuss the issue of whether there can be a satisfactory method for the individuation of propositional calculi. This issue is particularly pressing for the Satzsystem view of 1930–32 in which each propositional calculus is conceived as an autonomous system *logically independent* from any other calculus. As we shall see, in trying to keep propositional calculi apart from one another Wittgenstein came to realize that the compartmentalization of language into autonomous Satzsysteme was more problematic than he originally thought.

3.2. Local Holism, Verificationism, and the Proliferation Problem

The idea that propositional systems are logically independent of one another gives a peculiar twist to the semantic holism that Wittgenstein defended in 1930–32. The semantic holism of the Satzsystem view is *local.* On this view, what determines the semantic content of a particular word or a particular proposition is not language as a whole, but the cluster of tightly connected propositions in which that word or that proposition figures. This local holism maintains the Tractarian idea that the analysis of language should arrive at the most basic units of significance, although these units are no longer, as in the *Tractatus*, the building blocks out of which our significant statements are constructed, but rather the frameworks within which our statements signify. But like the separatism of elementary propositions, the separatism of Satzsysteme burdens the analysis of language with a problem of individuation: a heuristic that enables us to determine the most basic units of significance is needed for semantic analysis to get off the ground. On the Tractarian view, every issue concerning the significance of statements hinged on the logical analysis of statements into elementary propositions, but no method to carry out this analysis was provided. Now, on the Satzsystem view, every semantic question turns on the membership of signs (whether words or propositions) in propositional systems, but we do not yet have a method to determine the Satzsystem identity of signs.

In order to determine the sense of a proposition "p" (or whether it makes sense), we must first determine what other propositions "p" associates with. The kind of associations between propositions that we should be looking for are indeed inferential connections. However, there is no guarantee that all the propositions that are inferentially connected with "p" belong to the same system. The inferential connections in which "p" enters can be quite heterogeneous. So we need to know which propositional systems we have to look out for in order to be able to sort out inferential connections in the appropriate way. For instance, the proposition "A (a point in the visual field) is red" is inferentially related to the proposition "My shirt is blue" (together they imply that A and my shirt have different colors). On the other hand, "A is red" is also inferentially related to "Red has such-and-such wave-length." Now, should we conclude that all these propositions are members of one and the same Satzsystem? Or should we say that the propositions for the ascription of colors to points in the visual field form one system with the propositions for the description of ordinary objects, and another with the propositions for the description of colors in terms of wavelength? Unless we establish what gives unity to a propositional system, the inferentialist analysis of propositions and their component parts is doomed to wander aimlessly in the sea of language.

Wittgenstein repeatedly emphasizes that the same propositional sign "p" can figure in different Satzsysteme and hence express different propositions (e.g., PR §153). So in order to determine the sense of "p," we need to go beyond the propositional sign; we need to find a way of linking the sign with the *relevant* set of propositions. But what can guide us to those inferential connections that endow "p" with a particular sense in each case? In the early 1930s Wittgenstein argues that what determines the sense of a proposition are not the conditions under which the proposition is true as he thought in the *Tractatus* (cf. 4.024), but rather the conditions under which *we* regard the proposition as true. The sense of a proposition is to be determined by examining *how* we go about settling its truth value: "To understand the sense of a proposition means to know how the issue of its truth or falsity is to be decided" (PR §43). Wittgenstein is thus moving away from a truth-conditional semantics and toward a *verificationist* account of meaning: "Every proposition is the signpost for a verification" (PR §150). He draws the contrast between truth conditions and verification conditions as follows:

> Every significant proposition must teach us through its sense how we are to convince ourselves whether it is true or false. [. . .] The sense would have to be revealed to us *from without*—since it can't be obtained from the propositional sign alone—*in contrast with its truth*, where *the proposition itself* tells us how to look for its truth and compare the truth with it. (PR §148, my emphasis)

The holism of the Satzsystem view dictates that the sense of a proposition is not contained in the propositional sign (it is "revealed to us from without"). For Wittgenstein, the sense of a proposition is manifested by those other propositions that can have a bearing on our acceptance or rejection of the proposition in question. So the passage just quoted can be read as saying: if you want to know the sense of a proposition "p," do not ask what is required for the proposition to be true because the answer is already contained in the propositional sign (i.e., "p" is true iff p); ask, rather, what is required for the proposition to be verified and you will then find out what other propositions can be mobilized to support it or to refute it. The evidential relations among propositions determine their place within a system of propositions and hence their sense. For Wittgenstein, the cash value of the move from truth conditions to verification conditions is that the latter (but not the former) can be used as a guide to the Satzsystem indentity of propositions. By examining the way in which a proposition is verified, we can recognize the relevant set of inferentially related propositions, namely, those that can make a contribution in settling the truth value of the proposition. The method of verification of a proposition indicates the propositional system against whose background we can compare the proposition with reality "as a yardstick" (PR §43).

In his analysis of *Philosophical Remarks*, Shanker points out that Wittgenstein appeals to verification procedures as a way of determining the membership of propositions in propositional calculi.[82] What Shanker recognizes with this remark is that the verificationism of the Satzsystem view is primarily a *methodological verificationism*, invoked to give guidance to the semantic analysis of propositions. The methodological significance of Wittgenstein's verificationism in 1930–32 is twofold: the method of verification of propositions is used to individuate Satzsysteme *and* to explore their grammar. In the first place, a common method of verification is what holds propositions together in a cohesive system of description, what defines a particular way of talking about reality (cf. WWK p. 53; PR §16). In the second place, by examining the peculiar method of verification of a Satzsystem, we can identify the rules of grammar of that system. For the grammatical rules of a Satzsystem define the way in which propositions are to be compared with reality within that system; they are constitutive aspects of the method of verification. Wittgenstein characterizes grammatical rules as propositions that are taken for granted in every verification but which are not themselves susceptible of verification. For instance, "two colors cannot occupy the same visual point" is not a proposition that can be confirmed or refuted, for it is presupposed in every verification of statements of color attribution (cf. WWK p. 79). If I want to verify the proposition "A is red," what I need to do is to go to A and observe its color. If I observe that A is blue, that suffices to disconfirm the proposition; no further verification is needed: I do not need to observe A again to check whether or not it is also red, for two colors cannot occupy the same visual point.

Wittgenstein's methodological verificationism arises as a natural development of his inferentialist view of language and his conception of meaning as use. As Black has noted, Wittgenstein saw an intimate connection between "verification's path," "use," and "place in a system."[83] He frequently points out that the method of verification of a proposition reveals its sense by disclosing its use within language: it "determines the meaning, i.e. determines its *use*, or grammar" (Lectures 1932–35, p. 29, my emphasis; see also PR §28).[84] Black suggests that it was Wittgenstein's verificationist account of meaning in the 1930s that led him to link meaning with use. By contrast, on my interpretation, Wittgenstein's view of meaning as use (already present in the *Tractatus*) is not the consequence, but the source and motivation of his verificationist considerations. That the verificationism of the Satzsystem view is at the service of an inferentialist semantics becomes explicit in Wittgenstein's remarks about verification in a lecture from 1932. In that lecture he argues that the import of asking of a proposition "What is its verification?" is that "an answer gives the meaning by showing the relation of the proposition to other propositions. That is, it shows *what it follows from and what follows from it*. It gives the grammar of the proposition" (Lectures 1932–35, pp. 19–20; my emphasis). So, for Wittgenstein, verificationism seems to be a heuristic tool that enables us to analyze the content of propositions in terms of their *inferential use*.[85]

But once Wittgenstein adopts verificationism as a strategy to carry out the inferentialist analysis of language he is interested in, isn't he committed to a verificationist theory of meaning? It is beyond dispute that verificationism is a crucial aspect of Wittgenstein's view of meaning in the early 1930s, but what is the status of this verificationism? To answer this question, Black has distinguished between two different kinds of verificationism. According to Black, semantic verificationism in a general sense is any view according to which the content of a proposition can be *determined* by its method of verification. In this general sense, it is undeniable that Wittgenstein held a verificationist semantics in 1930–32. But there is a stronger kind of semantic verificationism. This is what Black calls "classical" or "radical verificationism": the "view that *identifies* a proposition's meaning with its verification-procedure."[86] Black contends that Wittgenstein held a radical verificationism in the 1930s[87] (though not in the *Tractatus* or in his later writings). This seems to be the general consensus among those commentators who have discussed the status of Wittgenstein's verificationism in the intermediate period. Coffa, for one, argues that in the 1930–32 lectures Wittgenstein identified the sense of a proposition with its verification conditions, ultimately to be cast in sense-data language.[88] Coffa emphasizes that with this radical verificationism Wittgenstein curtailed the domain of significant speech dramatically, as some members of the Vienna Circle were trying to do around that time. Gargani also underscores the affinities between Wittgenstein's view in the intermediate period and logical positivism. In particular, he argues that there are strong similarities between Wittgenstein's and Schlick's verificationism.[89] Some members of the Vienna Circle itself concluded from their conversations with Wittgenstein that he was proposing a verificationist semantics very congenial with the one they were developing.[90] A canonical statement of the radical verificationism of the Vienna Circle can be found in section 6 of Waismann's *Thesen* (WWK pp. 243–46). Let's compare the verificationist theses of the Vienna Circle as stated by Waismann with the verificationism held by Wittgenstein in the early 1930s, to see whether we can actually find the strong convergence that both contemporary commentators and some members of the Vienna Circle have indicated.

I will begin by identifying Waismann's main theses about verification and then I will discuss whether these theses can also be found in Wittgenstein's own remarks about verification. Waismann contends that what determines the sense of a statement is not its logical composition, but how the statement is compared with reality: "A statement has sense, not because it is constructed in a legitimate way, but because it can be verified" (WWK p. 245). Waismann's first substantive thesis is that verifiability is the *essence* of significance: "To say that a statement has sense *means* that it can be verified" (WWK p. 244; my emphasis). Being verifiable is a sufficient condition for a statement making sense; but more importantly, it is also a *necessary* condition (WWK p. 244). And what is required is not simply that the statement be in principle verifiable, but rather that a definite method for its verification be available: "if I cannot specify under what conditions the proposition is to count as verified, I have not given the proposition a sense. A statement that cannot be verified definitively is not verifiable at all" (WWK p. 245).

A second thesis about verification that can be drawn from Waisman's discussion is what Black considers the central tenet of radical verificationism: the *identification* of the sense of a proposition with its verification conditions. As Waismann puts it: "The sense of a proposition *is* the way it is verified" (WWK p. 244; emphasis partially dropped). When I lay down the verification conditions of a proposition, "I thereby lay down the *sense* of that proposition" (WWK p. 244). What a proposition says is exactly equivalent to what is expressed in the propositions that describe its verification conditions: "If I say 'My friend is angry' and establish this in virtue of his displaying a certain perceptible behaviour, I only *mean* that he displays that behaviour" (WWK p. 244).

As a corollary of this verificationist account of meaning, Waismann formulates a third thesis: to a plurality of methods of verification there corresponds a plurality of senses. The claim that verification conditions are constitutive of the semantic identity of propositions thus results in the proliferation of semantic contents. A proposition that can be verified in different ways has different senses. And the same goes for the meaning of a word: if the word appears in propositions that are verified according to different methods, it has a different meaning in each case. As Waismann puts it:

> In order to learn what a sign means, you have to ask, 'How is a proposition in which that word occurs to be verified?' The same word can have different meanings in propositions that are verified in different ways. [. . .] Thus *in everyday life the word 'yellow' means something completely different from what it means in physics*. For in the one case a proposition about yellow is *verified by looking*, in the other case *by measuring wave-length*. (WWK p. 245; my emphasis)

Although in the early 1930s Wittgenstein placed a heavy emphasis on verification, it would be surprising if he subscribed to Waismann's first thesis. Verifiability as the *essence* of significance was the Circle's own way of reading the Tractarian notion of the representational essence of the proposition. But what is most characteristic of the view that Wittgenstein was developing around 1930 is its pluralism and anti-essentialism. The central insight of the Satzsystem view is precisely that propositions with sense do *not* constitute *one* distinctive class (i.e., that there is no such thing as the essence of the proposition). On this view, there can be no universal constraints on what counts as a genuine proposition; this is to be established, autonomously, by the grammar of each propositional system. Wittgenstein held that the availability of a distinct method of verification is a *sufficient* condition for a distinct mode of significance. But it is not clear at all from what he says that the availability of such method should also be taken as a *necessary* condition of significance. It is only in very restricted contexts that he claimed that propositions that cannot be verified lack sense (WWK p. 79; PR §§149–50). In these contexts Wittgenstein talks about propositional systems in science that are defined by particular methods of verification. So it may be hasty to conclude that Wittgenstein thought that *every* propositional system (in ethics, aesthetics, religion, etc.), if it is to be an autonomous realm of significance, must contain a method of verification.

As Coffa emphasizes,[91] in the 1930–32 lectures, Wittgenstein did privilege what he called "experiential" and "scientific propositions" as paradigmatic cases of significant propositions (cf. Lectures 1930–32, pp. 4–6 and 80–81). But he may have done so simply because he thought that, having a distinctive method of verification, the grammar of these propositions is particularly easy to survey. At any rate, in Wittgenstein's writings and lectures, there is no clear statement that verifiable propositions exhaust the category of significant propositions. According to Moore's account of the 1930–32 lectures, after saying that verification determines the sense of propositions, Wittgenstein remarked: "This is necessarily a mere rule of thumb, because 'verification' means different things, and because *in some cases the question 'How is it verified?' makes no sense.*"[92] So, for Wittgenstein, the possibility of significance without verification does not seem to be entirely excluded.

But since Wittgenstein held that verification procedures determine the sense of propositions at least in some Satzsysteme, perhaps he held a restricted version of radical verificationism. Did he endorse the identification thesis (the epitome of radical verificationism) at least for "experiential" and "scientific propositions"? There are passages in which Wittgenstein identifies the sense of a proposition with its verification conditions (cf. esp. WWK p. 79 and PR §166). However, Wittgenstein's formulations of the identification thesis are usually qualified in an interesting way, and perhaps with this thesis he meant something different from what is usually called the "verification principle."[93] As reported by Moore in his summary of the lectures, after stating what looks like a formulation of the identification thesis, Wittgenstein qualified it as follows: "He made the famous statement: 'The sense of a proposition is the way in which it is verified'; but he said this *only* meant 'You can *determine* the meaning of a proposition by asking how it is verified."[94] For Wittgenstein, the sense of a proposition is to be determined by, but not to be understood as identical with, its verification conditions.

In a conversation with Schlick, Wittgenstein draws a clear distinction between the content of a statement and the verification grounds on which it is asserted (WWK pp. 158–59). Imagine, he says, that I assert the proposition "My brother is in that room" and I specify the grounds of my assertion as follows: "He told me that he would be there," "I hear the piano being played and I recognize his way of playing," "Just now I heard steps that sounded just like his" (WWK p. 158). Wittgenstein contends that what my original assertion says is not the same as what is expressed by the propositions that describe my evidence. For my brother's being in that room is certainly not the same fact as his telling me he would be there, my hearing the piano being played in a certain way, or my hearing steps that sound just like my brother's. The latter facts are "symptoms" of the former (WWK p. 159). For Wittgenstein there is a *grammatical* relation between a proposition and those other propositions that specify its verification conditions: they are inferentially related in such a way that the latter *determine* the place that the former occupies in a propositional system. But he seems to reject the idea that the content of a proposition *is* what is specified by a list of verification conditions. For Wittgenstein, the relation between sense and verification is more indirect.

In a lecture from 1932 Wittgenstein is yet more explicit about his rejection of the identification thesis. He remarks that the verification conditions of a proposition about the past are typically couched in propositions about the present and future. And, he asks, "how could the meaning of a sentence about the past be given by a sentence about the present?" (Lectures 1932–35, p. 28). He answers: "My reply is to deny that the verification *gives* the meaning. It merely *determines* the meaning, i.e., determines its use, or grammar" (Lectures 1932–35, pp. 28–29).[95] Wittgenstein emphasizes that "a distinction should be made between '*being the meaning of*' and '*determining the meaning of*'" (Lectures 1932–35, p. 28). The verification conditions of a proposition serve as a guide to establish the use or grammar of a proposition; but they are not what the proposition "*means*": "If you want to know the meaning of a sentence, ask for its verification. I stress the point that the meaning of a symbol is its place in the calculus, the way it is used" (Lectures 1932–35, p. 29). Although the semantic view that Wittgenstein held in the early 1930s has a strong verificationist bias, the most distinctive aspect of this view is not its verificationism, but its inferentialism. For Wittgenstein, the significance of a sign consists in the inferential moves that we can make with it in a propositional calculus: "Understanding a word or a proposition is calculating" (WWK p. 168). So the most fundamental notion of Wittgenstein's semantic view in the early 1930s is *calculation*, not verification; the latter plays only a methodological role.

Now, given that Wittgenstein regards verification as a way of determining meaning but not as what meaning consists in, one might expect that he would admit different methods of verification for one and the same proposition as different ways of establishing the same semantic content. There seems to be no room in Wittgenstein's view for the corollary that Waismann drew from the identification thesis: that to a plurality of methods of verifications there corresponds a plurality of semantic contents. However, on the Satzsystem view, meaning also proliferates as verification methods become diversified: "Where there are different verifications there are also different meanings" (WWK p. 53). As Waismann in *Thesen*, Wittgenstein uses the example of colors to illustrate this proliferation:

> The "colour' I can recognize immediately and the one I establish by chemical investigation are two different things. One source only yields *one* thing. (PR §16)
>
> If, then, I say, "This is yellow," I can verify it in entirely different ways. The sentence has completely different sense, according to what method I allow as a verification. If, for example, I admit a chemical reaction as a means of verification, then it makes sense

> to say, "This looks *grey*, but in reality it is *yellow*." But if I regard what I see as a valid verification, then it makes no sense any more to say, "This looks yellow, but it is not yellow." (WWK p. 97)
>
> These ways of testing give different meanings for "having the same color." (Lectures 1932–35, p. 30)

So Wittgenstein's methological verificationism also results in semantic proliferation. But how can this be, given that verification procedures do not seem to be constitutive of the semantic content of propositions? On the Satzsystem view, the proliferation of meaning arises from verificationist considerations in an indirect way. For Wittgenstein, a particular method of verification is constitutive of the identity of the propositional system in which it has application: it is what holds the propositions of that system together. So different methods of verification indicate different Satzsystem affiliations. When a proposition is verified in different ways, its Satzsystem identity and hence its meaning changes; and the same goes for the terms that appear in it. So semantic proliferation does not result from identifying meaning with verification, but from identifying Satzsystem identity with method of verification. Wittgenstein soon became dissatisfied with this result and tried to liberalize his verificationist criterion of demarcation. In 1932 he admitted that a propositional system may contain more than one method of verification (Lectures 1932–35, p. 29). For instance, he remarked, "Cambridge won the boat race" is a proposition that can be verified in various ways: by witnessing the race, reading about it in the papers, and so forth. All these verification procedures taken together jointly define the identity of the propositional system; but any one of them may suffice to determine the meaning of a term or proposition, its place in the system. However, this more liberal verificationist criterion of demarcation does not stop semantic proliferation. For adding a new verification procedure or discarding an old one would change the identity of the Satzsystem and hence the meaning of its signs: "if we ruled out any one of the means of verifying the statement ['Cambridge won the boat race'] we would alter its meaning. It would upset our grammar if we excluded as a verification something that always accompanied winning. And if we did away with all means of verifying it we would destroy the meaning" (Lectures 1932–35, p. 29).

On Wittgenstein's view, the proliferation of meaning is parasitic on the proliferation of propositional systems. And as long as Satzsysteme are conceived as *logically independent* units to be individuated according to a fixed criterion of demarcation, the proliferation of these systems cannot be entirely ruled out, no matter how liberal their criterion of demarcation is thought to be.[96] The solution to the proliferation problem does not lie in finding the right criterion of demarcation of Satzsysteme, but in abandoning the thesis that these systems are logically independent from one another. Proliferation arises from the *local holism* of the Satzsystem view. So it is not surprising that in *Philosophical Remarks* Wittgenstein mentions the possibility of semantic proliferation as a consequence of his holistic view of language, without relying on verificationist considerations: "Understanding p means understanding its system. If p appears to go over from one system to another, then p has, in reality, changed its sense" (PR §153). The possibility of unwanted semantic proliferation seems to be consubstantial to the fragmentation of language into self-contained units of significance with clear-cut boundaries.

Arguably, it was the proliferation problem that led Wittgenstein to abandon the Satzsystem view of language. Around 1932 or 1933 he gave up the idea that we can compartmentalize the use of language into distinct autonomous systems. And when the thesis of the logical independence of Satzsysteme is abandoned, the very idea of a propositional *system* loses its bite. From 1932 on Wittgenstein no longer uses the term "system" to describe the propositional calculi of which language is composed. These calculi are now compared with "*language games*" (cf. PG §§26ff; also Lectures 1932–35, p. 99). In 1932–33 Wittgenstein uses the analogy of "language games" to underscore that language contains a plurality of different but *interrelated* uses: "What we call 'games' are procedures *interrelated* in various ways with many different transitions between one and another" (PG §35; my emphasis). This view of language as composed of interrelated games or overlapping calculi blocks the proliferation of meaning. For, on this view, a sign does not change its meaning when it moves from one propositional calculus to another; its meaning is not identified with its use in a circumscribed region of language, but with its use in language as a whole. The rules of the different propositional calculi or language games in which a word is used settle different aspects of the use of the word and hence of its meaning. For example, "the use of the word 'good'," Wittgenstein says, "is a combination of a very large number of *interrelated* games, each of them as it were a facet of the use. What makes a single concept here is precisely the connection, the relationship, between these facets" (PG §36, my emphasis; see also Lectures 1932–35, pp. 33–36).

In the period of 1932 to 1933 the holism of the calculus view of language is transformed, becoming *radical* instead of local. This transformation modifies Wittgenstein's view of the grammatical rules that determine the meaning of signs. The rules of grammar now have to be derived not from the inferential structure of self-contained propositional systems but from the vast and fluctuating domain of language use. As we shall see, these symbolic rules of use are still thought to be *autonomous*, but their autonomy is now conceived in a new way. In the next section I will examine Wittgenstein's main arguments for this revised calculus view of language and its rules in *Philosophical Grammar* and the lectures from 1932 to 1933.

3.3. Idealizing Language: The Autonomy of Rules

In 1930–32 Wittgenstein emphasized that there is more than "a mere analogy" between using language and operating with a calculus (WWK p. 168); language *really is* a calculus (or set of calculi). In 1932–33 the conception of language as a calculus is modified. In these years Wittgenstein realizes that the calculus view of language involves a great deal of *idealization*. He still thinks that language is best described as a calculus of fixed and precise rules; but he now underscores that by describing language in this way, we depart from its *actual use* which is in constant "fluctuation" (PG §36). In 1930–32 Wittgenstein had argued that what we do in the "logical" or "grammatical" analysis of language is "*to tabulate rules,*" to "clearly articulate the rules we have been applying unawares" (WWK p. 184 and p. 77). Around 1933 Wittgenstein tries to make explicit the unavoidable idealizations that underlie this analysis (cf. esp. Lectures 1932–35, pp. 47ff). He emphasizes that in order to give a perspicuous representation of the grammar of a language, we have to move from its changing actual use to its possible applications according to rules. As Wittgenstein puts it in *Philosophical Grammar*:

> If we look at the *actual use* of a word, what we see is something *constantly fluctuating*. In our investigations we set over against this fluctuation something more fixed, just as one paints a stationary picture of the constantly altering face of the landscape. When we study language we envisage it *as a game with fixed rules*. We compare it with, and measure it against, a game of that kind. If for our purposes we wish to regulate the use of a word by *definite rules*, then alongside its fluctuating use we set up a different use by codifying one of its characteristic aspects. (PG §36; my emphasis)

What logical analysis does, according to Wittgenstein, is to codify the "characteristic aspects" of language use, to tame the "fluctuating use" of words with "definite rules." The actual use of language is "measured" according to a system of rules that is "set over against" it. In this way the rules of grammar that regulate the applications of signs and determine their meaning go beyond our de facto uses of language. However, Wittgenstein goes on to argue that logical analysis cannot depart from the actual use of language so radically that what we end up with is the grammar of an ideal language, not of ours (PG §36). For Wittgenstein, what logical analysis should offer is not a descriptive model of an ideal language but an *ideal* model of *our* language. But in what sense is the grammar of a language an ideal model? The idealization that separates grammar from actual use in Wittgenstein's view is akin to the idealization used in contemporary linguistics to distinguish between linguistic competence and linguistic performance.[97] A competence model of language is a counterfactual characterization of the use of language according to rules. On this model, those factors that enter into the actual use of language, into linguistic performance, are put aside as extraneous empirical elements.[98] Similarly, Wittgenstein remarks that he is "not interested in any empirical facts about language" (PG §30), in "how *language* meshes with our life" (PG §29), but only in "how we calculate with a word" (PG §31). The counterfactual character of Wittgentein's analysis of language is discussed in the lectures. There he points out that if we examine the actual use of a word, we might conclude that "an exact game was not being played" and so: "It might be said of me that I describe language as if it were in a vacuum, but this is not so. What I do is to talk of language as consisting of fixed rules, which is really *contrary to fact*" (Lectures 1932–35, p. 47; my emphasis).

Wittgenstein emphasizes that the grammatical codification of language use is not simply a simplified and abstract description of the linguistic phenomena.[99] The idealization that grammar involves is of a different nature. The rules of grammar are not empirical generalizations that *describe* natural phenomena; the function of these rules is not descriptive, but *normative*. For Wittgenstein, grammatical rules are the explicit formulation of the tacit conventions that regulate language use (Lectures 1932–35, p. 99; see also p. 48). These conventions are "statable" (though usually not stated) norms that give unity to our fluctuating linguistic practices. Wittgenstein remarks that the "strict rules" of grammar are to the fluctuating use of language as "a figure drawn with sharp outline" in geometry is to "a blurred figure" (Lectures 1932–35, p. 48). In *Philosophical Grammar* §§14–15 he also compares the relation between the grammar of a sign and the actual use of the sign with the geometry of a cube and the actual practice of drawing cubes. He remarks that the geometrical rules of cubic figures are not abstracted from the actual cubes that we draw; they are an ideal characterization of cubic figures that fixes the normative criteria for what counts as a cube: "Geometry defines the form of a cube but does not describe it" (PG §15). The recurrent analogy between grammar and geometry[100] underscores that the rules of grammar, like the laws of geometry, are not used to describe but to define; they are meaning-constituting rules. In fact, there is more than an analogy here, for Wittgenstein used the propositions of geometry and arithmetic as paradigmatic examples of grammatical rules. He argued that these propositions do not treat of actual objects but of the grammar of certain words. For Wittgenstein, the laws of geometry and arithmetic give a normative characterization of a certain region of language by prescribing the possible applications of certain terms in ordinary language. And, he contends, this is the role that all grammatical rules play:

> Geometry does not treat of cubes but of the grammar of the word "cube," as arithmetic treats of the grammar of numbers. [. . .] Arithmetical propositions say nothing about numbers, but determine which propositions about numbers make sense and which do not. Similarly, geometrical propositions say nothing about cubes, but determine which propositions about cubes make sense and which do not. This comment suggests the *relation* [. . .] *between a sentence giving the grammar of a word and an ordinary sentence in which the word figures*. (Lectures 1932–35 p. 51; my emphasis)

What is most characteristic of the calculus view of language is the idea that the normative aspects of language use can be captured in a system of rules. As we shall see later (cf. 5.3), in 1934–35 Wittgenstein will start to question the idea that rules can, by themselves, provide a genuine insight into the normativity of language use; and from the mid 1930s on he will argue that the normative force of rules is misunderstood if it is considered in abstraction from our actual practices of use. But as late as 1933–34 Wittgenstein maintained that the rules of grammar could be thought of as constituting an *autonomous* realm. As Backer and Hacker put it, one of the main thesis of Wittgenstein's view in the early 1930s is "that there is behind the use of language a definite body of *autonomous* rules," that "grammar is a *free-floating* array of rules for the use of language."[101] So now there appears a new sense of the idea of the autonomy of grammar: grammatical rules are called "autonomous" not only because they are in no way contingent on an external, nonlinguistic reality (cf. esp. PG §55), but also because they are independent of our actual practices of use (cf. PG §§36–37).

In the next two sections I will examine Wittgenstein's view of rules as developed in his discussion of meaning and understanding in *Philosophical Grammar*. The central arguments in this discussion are the critique of ostensive definition and the so-called Manifestation Argument.[102] Given the similarity of these arguments with the arguments of the *Investigations*, *Philosophical Grammar* has been considered as a first, early draft of the *Investigations*.[103] I will argue, however, that the critique of ostensive definition and the Manifestation Argument play a different role in the calculus view of the early 1930s and in the later view. Interesting discrepancies between the different versions of these arguments will emerge when we read these arguments in the different contexts in which they were used at different times. As a first step to uncover these discrepancies, in what follows I will try to put the arguments of *Philosophical Grammar* in perspective, bringing to the fore their connection with the calculus view of language of the early 1930s.

3.3.1. Ostensive Definition, Holism and Lingualism

In *Philosophical Grammar* Wittgenstein attacks the semantic reification that results from the denotational approach to meaning. He contends that this approach is at the core of a distorted picture of language that has been pervasive in philosophy: "the Augustinian picture of language" (PG §§19ff). This picture construes the signification of all words on the model of name and designation, and assigns a foundational role to baptismal acts of naming: "*Naming* here appears as the foundation, the be all and end all of language" (PG §19). The critique of ostensive definition is Wittgenstein's master argument against the Augustinian picture of language. But this critique is also used to give support to the calculus view of language and the "dynamic" account of meaning as use that Wittgenstein proposes as an alternative to the denotational approach. The negative points of the critique of ostensive definition are accompanied by positive conclusions about how meaning is to be determined and what meaning is. As we shall see, in *Philosophical Grammar* the critique of ostensive definition contains two main negative points and two corresponding positive conclusions about meaning. In the first place, Wittgenstein argues that an ostensive definition is *insufficient* to establish the meaning of a term; and he concludes that the specification of the meaning of a term is *radically holistic*, involving all the rules that fix the use of the term within language. In the second place, Wittgenstein argues that the meaning of a term cannot be identified with the object pointed at in an ostensive definition; and he concludes that meaning is something *intralinguistic*, constituted by rules of use that are in no way dependent on an external, nonlinguistic reality. According to the interpretation defended above (see esp. 1.2), these two points could be found already in the Tractarian view of meaning. But in the early 1930s Wittgenstein develops new arguments in their support.

In the lectures Wittgenstein remarks that "an ostensive definition is not really a definition at all" (Lectures 1932–35, p. 45), if by "definition" we mean a complete specification of the meaning of a term. He argues that an ostensive definition is in fact a rule for the use of a term, but only one rule among many.[104] Similarly, in *Philosophical Grammar* Wittgenstein argues that an ostensive definition makes a contribution to the meaning of a term, but this contribution can only be understood against the background of many other rules for the use of the term (PG §§24–25). This is why an ostensive definition, by itself, is radically indeterminate. In ostensive definitions we use the same formula (i.e., "This is (or is called) 'x'") to introduce terms with very different grammars (PG §25). Even if there were objects corresponding to each and every word, an ostensive definition would still not be a unitary and self-sufficient way of establishing a connection between words and objects, for the sense of the ostension would vary *pari passu* with the grammar of the word defined: "The *same* ostension might define a numeral, or the name of a shape or the name of a colour. But in the grammar of each different part of speech the ostensive definition has a different role; and in each case it is only *one* rule" (PG §25). It is a mistake to think that an ostensive definition can singlehandedly determine the meaning of a word "as if the other grammatical rules for a word had to follow from its ostensive definition" (PG §24). Understanding the ostensive definition of a term requires a prior grasp of the grammar of the term. So an ostensive definition, far from settling the grammar of a word, actually presupposes (a great deal of) it: "One must already understand a great deal of a language in order to understand that definition" (PG §24).

The ostensive definition of a term is typically disambiguated by noting the sort of thing that the term is supposed to refer to, that is, by using "a sortal" (Geach's term,[105] not Wittgenstein's). But of course the information that the ostensive definition then conveys is parasitic on our knowledge of the grammar of the sortal. We should not think that it is the object itself, being of a certain kind, that determines the sense of the ostensive definition and the grammar of its name—as if the sortal simply described the essence of the referent. A sortal can disambiguate an ostensive definition only because it adds to the definiens a set of rules of use that specify the grammatical identity of the definiendum. For Wittgenstein, what the sortal disambiguation of ostensive definition shows is that this definition can be used to specify the meaning of a term only when *all but one* rule for the use of the term have been established. As Wittgenstein puts it in *Philosophical Grammar* and the lectures:

> Suppose that instead of saying "that is called 'red'" I had phrased my definition "that colour is called 'red'." That certainly is unambiguous, but only because the expression "colour" settles the grammar of the word "red" up to this last point. (PG §24)

> For example, from "This is sosh" you would not understand the use of the word "sosh," though from "This color is sosh" you would. That is, if a person is to learn the meaning of a word from such a definition he must already know *what sort of thing* it stands for. The word "color" already fixes the use of "sosh." *The*

> *ostensive definition is of use if you need to fill in only one blank.* [. . .] [It] can only be understood if it makes the last decision about the word's use, that is, if it supplements a knowledge of the grammar of a word which is *lacking one rule.* (Lectures 1932–35, pp. 45–46; my emphasis)

The upshot of Wittgenstein's discussion is that the specification of word meaning is radically holistic: an ostensive definition is an individual rule that settles only one aspect of the meaning of a term; and it can only do so in conjunction with all the other grammatical rules that regulate the use of the term. It is only the complete set of grammatical rules for the use of a word that captures its meaning. Thus, from the indeterminacy of ostensive definition, Wittgenstein also draws a positive conclusion about how the meaning of words is to be determined: "All the rules together give the meaning, and these are not fixed by giving an ostensive definition" (Lectures 1932–35, p. 3). The important point is that the meaning of a term can only be established by the whole network of interrelated rules that govern its use.[106]

Now, even if the holistic aspects of ostensive definition are acknowledged, it might still be thought that the meaning of a name is the object identified (as holistically as you like) in an ostensive act, that is, the bearer of the name. For instance, in his theses about definition Waismann seems to recognize that the definition of the meaning of signs requires a complex grammatical apparatus; and yet he contends that "ostension steps outside language and connects signs with reality" (WWK p. 246). But Wittgenstein argues that we cannot step ouside language by means of an ostensive definition. When we give an ostensive definition, "all we are doing is to add to the symbolism. The ostensive definition does not get us away from the symbolism" (Lectures 1930–32, p. 23). Since ostensive definitions are rules for the *use* of words, they cannot serve to connect language with an *independent* reality. Wittgenstein emphasizes that the objects we point to in ostensive definitions should not be viewed as language-independent entities, but as elements of grammar: they are "part of the symbolism" (PG §56); they are "samples" (PG §§49ff).

Take the following example: "Suppose I gave you a sample, saying 'This is *green*', and asked you to bring me something green" (Lectures 1932–35, p. 84). Whether the object that you bring is correctly or incorrectly called "green" will depend on whether it agrees or disagrees with the object I pointed at *in some respect.* But it would be a mistake to conclude that it is the physical object, independently of how we talk about it, that dictates what counts as agreement or disagreement and thus determines the use of the term "green." Wittgenstein emphasizes that what plays a normative role in fixing the use of the term "green" is the object qua sample, qua part of grammar, that is, the object as it is used in language:

> To say that something yellow disagrees with the green sample is to give a rule about agreement. That yellow disagrees with green does not follow from anything in the nature of green or yellow. [. . .] That a green or yelow agrees with the green sample is part of the geometry [. . .] of "green"; that is, it is *part of the grammar of "green,"* not a natural law. (Lectures 1932–35, p. 84; my emphasis)

The upshot of this part of Wittgenstein's discussion of ostensive definition is that the meaning of words does not lie outside language: "A name has meaning, a proposition has sense in the calculus to which it belongs. The calculus is as it were *autonomous.*—Language must speak for itself" (PG §27; my emphasis). As in the *Tractatus*, *meaning* is conceived as an intralinguistic notion. We can of course talk about a representational relation between language and the world, but it would be a mistake to think that this relation involves a language-independent reality: "The connection between 'language and reality' is made by definitions of words, and these belong to grammar, so that language remains *self-contained* and *autonomous*" (PG §55; my emphasis). On Wittgenstein's view, the meaning of a term is its use within language as established, *autonomously*, by grammatical rules (cf. PG §§27ff).

3.3.2. The Manifestation of Understanding and the Autonomy of Rules

Wittgenstein's view of meaning as use leads to a peculiar conception of understanding. If the meaning of a sign is its rule-governed use within language, understanding a sign must consist in knowing its entire range of applications. Wittgenstein anticipates resistance to this view of understanding, for we tend to think of undertanding as a "conscious state" that takes place in an instant (PG §10). When we understand a sign, it looks as if we grasped its meaning in a flash, and it does not seem possible that the whole use of the sign can appear before our minds in an instant: "After all, I can't have the whole mode of application of a word in my head all at once" (PG §10). So we are led to believe that understanding a sign must be something different from knowing its use, that it must be an *intuitive* grasp of meaning from which every application of the sign derives: "It can seem as if the rules of grammar are in a certain sense an unpacking of something we experience all at once when we use a word" (PG §12); "As if understanding were an instantaneous grasping of something from which later we only draw consequences which already exist in an ideal sense before they are drawn. As if the cube already contained the geometry of the cube, and I had only to unpack it" (PG §18). Wittgenstein argues that this intuitive conception of understanding is grounded in the mythological idea that there is a "meaning-body" behind each sign that determines its grammar: "As if the grammar were contained in the sign like a string of pearls in a box and [we] had only to pull it out" (PG §10). As discussed above, against the reification of meaning Wittgenstein argues that the rules of grammar are constitutive of the meaning of signs, thus moving from a static to a dynamic view of signs. Correspondingly, Wittgenstein also urges us to move from an intuitive to a *discursive* conception of understanding. What this conception emphasizes is that understanding has an essential *temporal* dimension:

> We can regard understanding a symbol, when we take its meaning in at a glance, as intuitive. Or understanding it may be *discursive*: knowing its meaning by knowing its use. (Lectures 1932–35, p. 29; my emphasis)
>
> We mustn't think that when we understand or mean a word what happens is an act of instantaneous, as it were non-discursive, grasp of grammar. As if it could all be swallowed down in a single gulp. (PG §11)

According to Wittgenstein's discursive conception of understanding, "'to understand the meaning of a word' means to know the grammatically possible ways of applying it" (PG §10). Wittgenstein explains that this knowledge is "knowledge of rules" (cf. PG §11ff). So we can understand now in what sense someone can have the entire use of a sign 'in her head': "I can have the possible ways of applying a word in my head in the same sense as the chess player has all the rules of chess in his head, and the alphabet and the multiplication table" (PG §10). Wittgenstein emphasizes that this knowledge of rules in which linguistic understanding consists is not "a conscious state that accompanies the sentences of the language" (PG §11). He draws a twofold contrast between conscious, intuitive knowledge and the knowledge involved in linguistic understanding. In the first place, the speaker's knowledge of grammatical rules is *tacit* knowledge that remains in the background without being explicitly articulated. For Wittgenstein, whether someone utters a sentence with or without understanding depends on whether she has "in the back of her head" the grammatical rules that endow the sentence with meaning. He remarks that the knowledge of rules provides the "*background* against which a particular sentence acquires meaning" (PG §11; my emphasis). In the second place, linguistic understanding is *practical* knowledge, an ability: understanding the meaning of a word is "*knowing* how it is used; *being able to* apply it" (PG §10); it is "like the understanding or mastery of a calculus, something like the *ability* to multiply" (PG §11).

But what is the criterion for ascribing this ability?—"What is the criterion for this knowledge?" (PG §26). Wittgenstein argues that the criterion for ascribing linguistic understanding cannot be simply "the ability to state rules," for "I might also say of a little child 'he can use the word, he knows how it is applied'," even if the child is not able to recite the rules for the use of the word (PG §26). Wittgenstein compares the mastery of a word with the mastery of a game, suggesting that we use similar criteria for the attribution of these practical capacities. The criterion for someone's understanding a game is "that he can play the game, i.e. that he does in fact play, even if he's baffled when asked for the rules" (PG §26). Similarly, the criterion for undertanding a word is consistently being able to use the word correctly. The only warrant for the attribution of understanding is correct use over time. So understanding requires *explicit manifestation.* Wittgenstein emphasizes that linguistic understanding should not be conceived as "a precondition" for using language, as a condition to be fulfilled prior to and independently of the actual use of language (cf. PG §8). He warns us that if we separate the knowledge involved in understanding from actual applications, then the question arises "But how does this knowledge help me [in what I do]?" and there appears an inexplicable "jump from knowing to doing" (PG §8). We save this jump when we think of understanding as a practical capacity that has to be displayed in actions.

This conception of undertanding as a tacit, practical skill is indeed very similar to the one Wittgenstein will defend in his later work. However, there is an important difference: Wittgenstein's account of understanding in *Philosophical Grammar* is still tied to the view of language as a calculus of rules that he will later reject. Thus in *Philosophical Grammar* Wittgenstein contends: "When someone interprets, or understands, a sign in one sense or another, what he is doing is taking a step in a calculus (like a calculation)" (PG §13). By contrast, in the *Investigations* he considers it a mistake "to think that if anyone utters a sentence and *means* or *understands* it he is operating a calculus according to definite rules" (§81). This difference notwithstanding, Wittgenstein's discussion of undertanding in *Philosophical Grammar* anticipates an important part (though not the whole) of the Manifestation Argument of the *Investigations* (see 6.4.3). But it is important to notice that the Manifestation Argument of *Philosophical Grammar* has a limited scope. This argument provides an insight into the nature of our understanding or knowledge of rules, but this insight is not extended further to shed light on the nature of the rules themselves that are the object of our understanding. For Wittgenstein, understanding language, knowing how to calculate with words, is crucially dependent on the actual use of language; but the rules according to which we calculate in language are not so dependent. Accordingly, the essential temporal dimension that Wittgenstein recognizes in our understanding is not transferred to what is understood. The rules of grammar are not thought to require explicit manifestation over time in our actual practices; they are atemporal (cf. Lectures 1932–35, p. 87). For Wittgenstein, actual regularities in language use are an indicator of the understanding of language users, but they do not determine the *content* of their understanding. Thus, after arguing that understanding a sentence is "related to countless things that happen before and after the reading of *this* sentence" (PG §34), Wittgenstein goes on to argue that the *content* of our understanding does not depend on anything we do: "*what*'s understood is as it were *autonomous*" (PG §37; my emphasis). As late as 1933–34, Wittgenstein thought of language as being regulated by as an *autonomous* system of rules.

In the *Investigations* Wittgenstein will reject the idea of an autonomous system of rules that transcends our de facto activities of language use. The chapters that follow tell the story of how Wittgenstein came to reject this idea. The focus of my discussion will be Wittgenstein's developing view of the relation between rules and their applications. In the early 1930s Wittgenstein thought of this relation as an *internal* one. He insisted that a rule must have a range of possible applications that intrinsically belongs to it, for otherwise there would be a "gulf between rule and application" that no actual practice of use can "bridge."[107]

4

The "Unbridgeable Gulf" between Rule and Application

> The style of my sentences is extraordinarily strongly influenced by Frege. And if I wanted to, I could establish this influence where at first sight no one would see it. (*Zettel* §712)

As discussed in the previous chapter, the core idea in Wittgenstein's view of meaning in the early 1930s is that the rules for the use of a sign are constitutive of its meaning.[108] Wittgenstein's conception of symbolic rules as constitutive of meaning seems to have been influenced by formalist accounts of geometry and arithmetic. Wittgenstein's claim that the meaning of a sign is given by an entire system of rules (e.g., Lectures 1932–35, p. 3) echoes Hilbert's thesis that the meaning of a geometrical sign is defined by a "whole axiom-structure," in which "each axiom contributes something to the definition."[109] More explicitly, Wittgenstein's semantic view in the early 1930s draws on the formalist analogy between arithmetic and the game of chess: "The truth in formalism is that every syntax can be conceived of as a system of rules of a game. I have been thinking about what Weyl may mean when he says that a formalist conceives of the axioms of mathematics as like chess-rules" (WWK p. 103). The semantic import of this analogy was explained by Thomae[110] as follows: "For the formalist, arithmetic is a game with signs, which [. . .] have no other content (in the calculating game) than they are assigned by their behaviour with respect to rules of combination (rules of the game)" (quoted by Frege in BLA II §88). It is against the background of formalist views such as Hilbert's and Thomae's that Wittgenstein uses the laws of geometry and arithmetic as paradigmatic examples of grammatical rules. Following the formalists, Wittgenstein conceives of the rules of grammar as arbitrary symbolic conventions that tell us what we can and cannot do with signs, just as the rules of chess tell us what we can and cannot do with chess pieces (cf. e.g. PG §§11–13).

In the early 1930s Wittgenstein gives special attention to Thomae's formulation of the analogy between arithmetic and chess and to Frege's criticisms of it (cf. WWK pp. 105, 138, and 150ff; and PG II pp. 289–95). Insofar as Wittgenstein's view of the relation between symbolic rules and their applications is based on Thomae's analogy, Frege's criticisms of Thomae's view of arithmetical laws have also critical force against Wittgenstein's view of grammatical rules. In this chapter I will take a detour to examine how the debate between Frege and the formalists shaped Wittgenstein's view of the relationship between rules and their application. I will try to show that Frege's critique of formalism sets the agenda of Wittgenstein's rule-following discussion in the early 1930s.

Thomae's analogy between the laws of arithmetic and the rules of chess is one of the central targets of Frege's critique of formalism in *Grundgesetze* (BLA II §§88–96). Frege's main argument against Thomae is that his formalist approach cannot account for the *applicability* of the laws of arithmetic (cf. esp. BLA II §91). Frege argues that when arithmetic is conceived as a game with signs that have no other content than "their behaviour with respect to rules of combination," the propositions of arithmetic become detached from their applications and lose the importance they have in science and everyday life: "How could we possibly apply an equation which expressed nothing and was nothing more than a group of figures, to be transformed into another group of figures in accordance with certain rules?" (BLA II §91). According to Frege, the laws of arithmetic must indeed fix the applicability of arithmetical terms in ordinary language and in the language of the different sciences. But when arithmetical laws are conceived as arbitrary rules for the manipulation of signs, they cannot explain the use of arithmetical terms in science and ordinary language. For arithmetical terms are used in inferences, and the correct application of a term in an inference cannot be justified simply by appealing to "arbitrarily stipulated" rules (cf. BLA II §91).

To see the kind of applications that, according to Frege, are left out of account by the formalist, let's take as an example the application of the equation "5 + 2 = 7" in the following inference: "If we pour 2 unit volumes of liquid into 5 unit volumes of liquid we shall have 7 unit volumes of liquid" (FA §9). According to Frege, if the equation "5 + 2 = 7" is understood as an arbitrary rule that licenses transformations from one configuration of signs into another, it cannot possibly warrant the inference that by mixing liquids of volume 5 and 2 we must obtain a liquid of volume 7. For the rules that we stipulate to play with signs allow us to utter certain strings of signs after certain others, but they do not allow us to derive true conclusions from true premises. Frege emphasizes that drawing an inference involves more than moving from one group of figures to another according to rules (cf. BLA II §90–91); it involves a lawful transition from one *thought* to another, a "train of thought" (§90). For Frege, arithmetical propositions can warrant the validity of our inferences, not because they are well-formed strings of signs according to our stipulations, but because they express *true thoughts*. So, for instance, the equation "5 + 2 = 7" warrants the validity of our inference about the volume of liquids only because it is a true equivalence.

For Frege, if the propositions of arithmetic are to have application in inferences, they have to be regarded as "sentences expressing thoughts," not as groups of mere figures: "An arithmetic with no thought as its content will also be *without the possibility of application*. Why can no application be made of a configuration of chess pieces? Obviously, because it expresses no thought. [. . .] Why can arithmetical equations be applied? Only because they express thoughts" (BLA II §91; my emphasis). The rules of arithmetic can only regulate the applicability of arithmetical propositions if they establish lawful relations between the thoughts expressed by these propositions. So arithmetical rules should not be understood as rules for the manipulation of signs, but as laws that regulate how true propositions are to be derived from true propositions: "If [the equations of arithmetic] were viewed as having sense, the rules could not be arbitrarily stipulated; they would have to be so chosen that from formulas expressing true propositions could be derived only formulas likewise expressing true propositions" (§91). Since the rules of formal arithmetic are not "so chosen," they do not guarantee the applicability of arithmetical formulas in inferences. The formalist disregards the content that the arithmetical signs have prior to his stipulations. And, according to Frege, it is precisely this *content prior to rule stipulations* that must be taken as the starting point of arithmetic. The science of arithmetic has to be built on the meaning of the arithmetical signs. An arithmetic built on arbitrary conventions with no regard to content would be unrelated to the use that arithmetical signs have in scientific and everyday contexts. On Frege's view, we should start giving a precise meaning to the arithmetical signs and then derive the rules of arithmetic from the meaning of these signs. In formal arithmetic, however, "we do not derive these rules from the meaning of the signs, but lay them down on our own authority, retaining full freedom and acknowledging no necessity to justify the rules" (BLA II §94).

Frege emphasizes that, given the formalist's disregard for content, the application of rules in formal arithmetic becomes a matter of *interpretation*. Whether an arithmetical formula is correctly applied in any given case depends on whether we can find an appropriate interpretation for the formula that fits that application (i.e., "whether the signs can be given a sense compatible with the rules previously laid down"; BLA II §91). In formal arithmetic, Frege remarks, "such matters [. . .] only arise when applications are to be made" (§91). The mistake of the formalist is to think that the use of arithmetical formulas in scientific and everyday inferences is something *extraneous* to arithmetic itself, which is conceived as an autonomous calculus, "a game with signs" that stands on its own. The formalist thinks he can leave the applications of this calculus out of account, as if this could be settled piecemeal by the different scientific disciplines: "The formal arithmetician shifts it [the problem of applicability] to the shoulders of his colleagues, the geometers, the physicists, and the astronomers; but they decline the occupation with thanks; and so it falls into a void between these sciences" (§92). For Frege, the formalist's refusal to take up the issue of applicability is not just a harmless division of labor, but an unfortunate move that ultimately makes arithmetic inapplicable. For since no sense is attached to the arithmetical formulas prior to their application, the issue of how they are to be used in inferences becomes an utterly *indeterminate* matter. Thus, in the hands of the formalists, arithmetic becomes a formal apparatus without application. By detaching the propositions of arithmetic from the thoughts they express, the formalist introduces "a *gulf* between arithmetical formulas and their applications" that cannot "be *bridged*" (§92; my emphasis). "In order to bridge it," Frege contends, "it is necessary that formulas express a sense and *that the rules be grounded in the meaning of the signs*" (§92; my emphasis).

For Frege, a range of possible applications is *intrinsic* to the rules of arithmetic, not something to be added to them at a later point. There is not merely an accidental connection between the propositions of arithmetic and their use in inferences: these propositions have the binding force of *rules* in our inferential practices only because their possible inferential uses necessarily belong to them. And this point can be generalized to any rule that we can appeal to in our inferential practices: what gives normative force to a rule is its connection with a range of possible applications. This is what I will call the *Applicability Principle*, which defines the binding force of rules as follows: if rules are to have any normative power at all, there must be a range of possible applications corresponding to them. Frege's claim is that the rules of arithmetic have an intrinsic range of applicability *in virtue of their meaning*. His argument against formalism is that the rules of arithmetic do not acquire a range of possible applications in virtue of arbitrary stipulations that do not fix their content: as long as rules can be interpreted in various ways, their applicability is up for grabs. In Frege's eyes, what this shows is the priority of the meaning of the arithmetical signs over the rules for their use: the rules have to be "grounded in the meaning of the signs" (§92). So Frege concludes that only an "arithmetic with content," an arithmetic that fixes the meaning of its signs, can guarantee the applicability of arithmetical propositions. And this is what is required for arithmetic to become a science: "It is applicability alone which elevates arithmetic from a game to the rank of a science. So *applicability necessarily belongs to it*" (BLA II §91; my emphasis).

Now, Wittgenstein's rules of grammar are not the rules of a science. However, they are supposed to regulate the inferential relations that hold among the propositions of our language. Among these grammatical rules Wittgenstein counts the laws of logic, geometry, and arithmetic, as well as any rule that can be brought to bear upon the inferential relations among propositions (e.g., "A point in the visual cannot have more than one color"; cf. esp. WWK pp. 148–49; and Lectures 1932–35, p. 51). If these grammatical rules are to have binding force for the use of signs in inferences, they must honor the Applicability Principle, that is, they must have a range of possible applications corresponding to them. Since Wittgenstein's view of rules as arbitrary symbolic conventions draws heavily on formalist accounts, it may also seem to face the danger of creating an *unbridgeable gulf* between symbolic rules and their applications in inference. From a Fregean standpoint, Wittgenstein's conventionalist view of rules may appear to turn the rule-governed use of signs into an arbitrary game utterly unrelated to our inferential practices, just as formalist accounts do. Following the formalists, Wittgenstein denied that the rules for the use of signs can be grounded in the meaning that these signs have prior to the stipulation of rules. But he was very careful to avoid the pitfalls of formalism pointed out by Frege. Frege's critique of formalism in *Grundgesetze* is the most often discussed philosophical text in Wittgenstein's writings, lectures, and conversations in the early 1930s.[111] In these years Wittgenstein desperately tried to meet the challenge that Frege had posed in his critique of formalism: the relation between rule and application must be grounded somewhere, and if not in the meaning of signs, then where?

Despite the influence of formalist ideas on Wittgenstein's view, the primary concern of his discussions of rules is the issue of applicability emphasized by Frege. In this respect Wittgenstein's view of rules is more indebted to Frege's critique of formalism than to formalism itself. It was this critique that motivated Wittgenstein's rule-following considerations in the early 1930s; and, in part, it was also this critique that led Wittgenstein to reject the conventionalist framework of the calculus view of language when he couldn't find a satisfactory answer to Frege'c challenge within it.

In the next three sections I compare Frege's and Wittgenstein's views of the relation between rules and their applications.[112] In the next section I discuss Frege's view of the applicability of the laws of arithmetic. In sections 4.2 and 4.3 I examine how Wittgenstein tried to accommodate Frege's requirements on applicability in his view of rules in the early 1930s.

4.1. Frege on Applicability

Frege was engaged in an ambitious foundationalist project. Whether semantic or epistemological in spirit,[113] Frege's logicist project was to uncover the logical foundations of arithmetic. From *Grundlagen* to *Grundgesetze* his aim was to show that the laws of arithmetic are analytic truths ultimately reducible to the more primitive truths of logic. Against Mill, Frege argued that the truths of arithmetic are not synthetic a posteriori; against Kant, he argued that they are not synthetic a priori. At first sight, it is difficult to see how the issue of the applicability of arithmetical laws fits into Frege's discussions of the status of arithmetical truths. But the difficulty disappears when we examine Frege's construal of the analytic/synthetic distinction. For Frege, the range of applicability that true propositions have—"the domain that they govern" (FA §14)—indicates the kinds of truths they express: analytic, synthetic a priori, or synthetic a posteriori. As Weiner puts it, Frege regarded this threefold classification "as a division of truths according to the domain over which they are applicable."[114] Synthetic a posteriori truths are the product of experience and, accordingly, their domain of applicability comprises what we can experience, that is, "what is physically and psychologically actual" (FA §14). On the other hand, synthetic a priori truths are the product of intuition and, accordingly, their domain of applicability is the intuitable. The applicability of a synthetic a priori truth is only limited by the specific kind of intuition from which it derives. So, for instance, "the truths of geometry govern all that is spatially intuitable, whether actual or the product of our fancy" (FA §14). Therefore, to regard the truths of arithmetic as synthetic a posteriori or a priori would be to restrict their range of applicability to what we can experience or intuit, turning arithmetic into an empirical science or into a special science that relies on a special kind of intuition (like geometry). However, Frege argues, the applicability of arithmetical truths is not so restricted: they apply to everything whatsoever, not only to the possible objects of our experience or intuition. As Frege puts it:

> The truths of arithmetic govern all that is numerable. This is *the widest domain of all*; for to it belongs not only the actual, not only the intuitable, but *everything thinkable*. Should not the laws of number, then, be connected very intimately with the laws of thought? (FA §14)

For Frege, the domain of applicability characteristic of analytic truths is neither what is actual nor what is intuitable, but what is *logically possible*, "everything thinkable." On Frege's view, analytic truths are constitutive of what is thinkable and their denial leads to the dissolution of thought.

So, in order to test the analyticity of the truths of arithmetic, "we have only to try denying any one of them" (FA §14) and see what happens. What happens, according to Frege, is that "complete confusion ensues" and "even to think at all seems no longer possible" (FA §14). So Frege concludes that the truths of arithmetic are constitutive of what is thinkable and hence analytic: they are truths that range over everything that is logically possible.[115]

According to Frege, the intrinsic range of applicability of arithmetical truths cannot be determined piecemeal by examining the different applications that we make of arithmetical formulas in different domains. For instance, against Mill, Frege argues that the applications we make of arithmetical formulas in our calculations of the volume of liquids is extrinsic to the sense of these formulas, for these applications "presuppose observed facts" about liquids and their volume which are in no way contained in what these formulas say (FA §9). The particular applications we make of arithmetical propositions typically contain an empirical element foreign to their content. So, Frege contends, it is "a mistake to see in such applications the real sense of the propositions; in any application a large part of their generality is always lost, and a particular element enters in" (FA §16). This gives us a hint as to the kind of applications which, according to Frege, are intrinsic to arithmetic and determine the status of its truths. What Frege considers to be integral to the sense of an arithmetical formula is not the sum of all its particular applications, but the *general* principle or criterion that determines its applicability. As he puts it in *Grundgesetzse*, the sense that the arithmetician needs to "attach" to his formulas must be "*so general* that, with the aid of geometrical axioms and physical and astronomical observations and hypotheses, manifold applications can be made to these sciences" (§92; my emphasis). Thus Dummett summarizes Frege's view of the applicability of arithmetic as follows: "what is *extrinsic* to arithmetic are all *particular* applications of it: these relate to restricted domains of knowledge [. . .]. What is *intrinsic* to arithmetic [. . .] is the *general principle that explains its applicability* and hence determines the common pattern of all particular applications."[116]

However, the *general* applicability of the truths of arithmetic by itself is not sufficient to distinguish these truths from empirical truths. After all, a more refined empiricist could argue that the sense of an arithmetical formula is not the mere collection of particular applications, but the *general* principle of applicability that can be *abstracted* from those applications. On this proposal, the sense of an arithmetical formula would contain an element of generality, but it would be dependent on the *actual* applications that we make of it, which involve empirical factors. Thus, despite their generality, the truths of arithmetic would remain tied to what is physically and psychologically actual. So the contrast between particular versus general applications is not all that Frege needs in order to distinguish the applicability of arithmetical propositions from the applicability of empirical propositions. This contrast has to be supplemented with another one: the contrast between *actual versus possible* applications. For Frege, our actual applications of arithmetical propositions are not "the business of arithmetic" (FA §20) but the *possibility* of these applications must be contained in the sense of the propositions. What is intrinsic to the propositions of arithmetic and determines the kind of truths they express is not their applicability in practice but their applicability in principle.

The general range of possible applications that the truths of arithmetic must have is not something that we can simply add to them; it is something that must belong to them essentially: their applicability must spring from what these truths are about, from the *meaning* of the arithmetical signs. Arithmetical truths are about numbers. But this does not seem to grant them the maximal generality that they are supposed to have if they are to be considered analytic truths. Prima facie "what is numerable" does not seem to be "the widest domain of all," encompassing "everything thinkable," as Frege claims (FA §14). One might think that there are things to which numbers can be applied and things to which they cannot—we cannot ask "How many?" of anything whatsoever. So Frege needs to show that, contrary to appearances, the truths about numbers are in principle applicable to every possible object of thought and not just to objects with special properties. He tries to show that arithmetical truths have maximal generality by providing definitions that show the *logical nature* of numbers.[117] If arithmetic were a special science with restricted applicability, it would contain primitive terms that cannot be defined. Frege tries to show that even the most basic terms of arithmetic, the numerals, are definable, and that the truths about numbers can be proved drawing "only on general logical laws and on definitions" (FA §3). If he could show this, he would thereby show that the truths of arithmetic are analytic truths of maximal generality. This is, quite explicitly, what motivates Frege to search for definitions of the number one (cf. FA Preface) and of the concept of number (cf. FA §4) from which the truths of arithmetic can be derived by means of logical laws alone.[118]

Definitions play a crucial role in Frege's project: "Their role is to bestow a meaning on a sign or word that hitherto had none"; "A sign has a meaning once one has been bestowed upon it by definition."[119] The derivation of arithmetical truths from definitions is what Frege has in mind in his critique of formalism when he demands that the rules of arithmetic "be grounded in the meaning of the signs" (BLA II §92). Frege repeatedly criticizes the formalists' refusal to define the meaning of the arithmetical signs before laying down the rules that govern their use (cf. BLA Preface xiii; BLA

II §93). As a result, the rules that the formalists stipulate do not have an *intrinsic* range of applicability. Consider, for instance, the commutative law of addition Frege discusses in his critique of formalism (esp. BLA II §107). In formal arithmetic the commutative law "a + b = b + a" is simply a rule for the manipulation of signs: a rule that allows us to use the patterns of signs in the right- and left-hand sides of the equation interchangeably. So considered, the commutative law is simply an arbitrary stipulation that does not have any *intrinsic* binding force: it is simply a convention that we choose to enforce, a convention that, without our enforcement, does not have any normative force of its own. The relation between this rule and its applications remains arbitrary as long as the meanings of the signs that appear in it are not taken into account. But when the letters in the equation "a + b = b + a" are taken to stand for numerical variables and the plus sign is taken to designate the binary function of addition, we can recognize that there is nothing arbitrary about this rule and its applications: the equation expressess a *truth* from which all its possible applications can be derived. In order to ground this rule in the meaning of the arithmetical signs involved, we need a definition of the function of addition and a definition of the concept of number that determines all the possible arguments of this function (cf. BLA II §65). From these definitions we can prove that the sum of any two numbers must always yield the same result, whatever the order in which these numbers are taken. Thus, in arithmetic with content, the commutative law expresses a truth about addition; and since the definition of the concept of number delimits what can and cannot enter as an argument of this function, this law has a fixed range of applicability.

So, according to Frege, in order to derive rules that govern the applicability of the arithmetical signs, we need to define these signs. Frege argues that expecting someone to learn how to use the plus sign from certain patterns in which this sign appears, such as "a + b = b + a," would be like expecting someone to infer the rules of chess from certain configurations of chess pieces on the chessboard. But if someone wanted to learn the permissible moves in chess and he were shown "groups of chessmen on the chessboard," "he would probably say he could find no rules there" (§106). "The case only seems different here," Frege remarks, "because we already know from arithmetic that has content the plus sign, the equality sign, and the use of letters" (§106).

But what kind of definitions do we need in order to provide the laws of arithmetic with an intrinsic range of applicability? According to Frege, most definitions in mathematics do not actually succeed in assigning meaning to the terms defined. This is because the method of definition that pervades mathematical practice is "the procedure of piecemeal definition," which Frege finds "inadmissible" (BLA II §57). It is customary mathematical practice, Frege says, to define a symbol "for a limited domain" and then, when the need arises, "to define the same symbol once more for a wider domain" (§58). What's wrong with this procedure of piecemeal definition? The piecemeal definition of a term does not draw "sharp boundaries" around the use of the term and, therefore, the term so defined does not acquire a precise meaning: the concept expressions and object names defined according to this procedure do not pick out definite concepts and objects; they "only create an illusion of so doing" (§64). Frege argues that "any procedure of piecemeal definition must be rejected" because it makes it indeterminate whether and when the definition of a term is complete (§65). He concludes: "Every symbol must be completely defined at a stroke, so that, as we say, it acquires a meaning" (§65). This requirement is what Frege calls "the principle of completeness in definitions" (discussed in BLA II §§56–65). What the principle of completeness underscores is that a definition must fix the complete range of possible applications of a term, that it must draw *sharp boundaries* around the use of the term.

The "Sharp Boundary" Requirement is the most substantive requirement for the admissibility of scientific definitions that Frege proposes in *Grundlagen*.[120] This requirement determines whether a definition succeeds in assigning meaning (*Bedeutung*) to a term: for a term to have *Bedeutung*, to pick out a concept or object, "the limits of its application should be sharp" (e.g., FA §74). In the case of object words, the Sharp Boundary Requirement amounts to the demand that the definition of a name pick out exactly one object and provide a criterion for the identification of this object in all the possible applications of the term: "If we are to use the symbol *a* to signify an object, we must have a criterion for deciding *in all cases* whether *b* is the same as *a*, even if it is not always in our power to apply this criterion" (FA §62; emphasis added). On the other hand, the demand that the definition of a concept word fix "sharp boundaries" amounts to the demand that the definition "unambiguously determine, as regards any object, whether or not it falls under the concept (whether or not the predicate is truly ascribable to it). Thus there must not be any object as regards which the definition leaves in doubt whether it falls under the concept; though for us men, with our defective knowledge, the question may not always be decidable."[121] (BLA II §56; cf. also FA §74).

In constructing the science of arithmetic from the foundations up, as Frege takes himself to be doing, we must only admit signs that have been sharply defined. For only when the complete range of applicability of our signs has been fixed can we "lay down precise laws for them" (BLA II §56). The Sharp Boundary Requirement on definitions guarantees the possibility of formulating precise laws, laws with a well-defined set of applications. The fulfilment of this requirement is what is needed to honor the

Applicability Principle discussed above: by formulating definitions that draw sharp boundaries around the use of the arithmetical signs, we guarantee that the rules derived from these definitions have also a definite range of applications. As we saw, Frege thinks that we cannot settle the applicability of the rules of arithmetic piecemeal as the issue of their application arises in different domains (cf. BLA II §92). If we do not draw sharp boundaries around the applicability of a rule prior to its actual application, the issue of whether the rule has application in each particular case becomes wholly indeterminate. On Frege's view, for there to be more than an arbitrary relation between a rule and its applications, the rule must have a sharply bounded range of applicability.

But are sharp boundaries all we need to establish a nonarbitrary relation between a rule and its applications? We could draw sharp boundaries around the use of the arithmetical signs in different ways; and hence we would have arithmetical rules with different ranges of applicability depending on our choice of boundaries. So it appears that, even on Frege's view, whether or not a given range of applications belongs to an arithmetical rule ultimately depends on our decisions. So what is gained by shifting the ground of the applicability of arithmetic from the stipulation of rules to the definition of signs? Are Frege's definitions any less arbitrary than the stipulations of the formalists? If we can draw whatever boundaries we want around the applicability of signs and their rules as long as they are sharp, Frege's critique of formalism cannot amount to anything more than a demand for precision. However, this is only one aspect of Frege's critique. He also criticizes the formalists for making the rules of arithmetic "appear as *arbitrary* as those of chess" (BLA II §89; my emphasis). For Frege, what distinguishes arithmetic from a game like chess is that its "applicability cannot be an accident" (BLA II §89): it is an accident that we move chess pieces as we do when we play chess, but it is not an accident that we use the signs of arithmetic as we do in our calculations.

The applicability of the rules of chess is unconstrained by anything objective; it is entirely dependent on the arbitrary conventions laid down and enforced by chess players. By contrast, for Frege, the applicability of the laws of arithmetic involves an *objective* element, namely, "that numbers having certain properties *exist*" (BLA II §89; my emphasis). The range of possible applications that belongs to an arithmetical law is not up to us; it is something objective. The applicability of arithmetical laws must have not only precise limits, but also an objective dimension. So, on Frege's view, there is a further requirement for the applicability of the laws of arithmetic, which I call the Objectivity Requirement: the correct application of an arithmetical rule is not contingent on the subjective judgment of its users; there must be *a fact of the matter* that determines each and all the applications of a rule.

On Frege's view, it is the "complete definitions" of the arithmetical signs that are supposed to provide an *objective* ground for the applicability of rules. So there must be more to the establishment of sharp boundaries through definitions than meets the eye.

According to Frege, his definitions can establish a fact of the matter that determines objectively the correct applications of the laws of arithmetic because, unlike the rule stipulations of the formalists, they concern something objective: what the signs designate, the concepts or objects they pick out (cf. esp. BLA II §93). In the Preface to *Grundgesetze* Frege describes scientific definitions as baptismal acts that name sharply defined bits of reality and their properties, which are the objects of scientific investigation. Against a constructivist view of the role of definitions in mathematics, he contends that it is "a scientific superstition" to credit definitions "with a creative power," to think that we can "by a mere definition magically give to a thing a property which it has not got" (Preface xiii). For Frege, "all there is to definition is that something is brought out, precisely limited and given a name" (xiii). But this "something" that is "brought out" is not something of our own making. Arriving at correct definitions in science is not a matter of invention, but of discovery. This is what his analogy between mathematics and geography underscores: "The geographer does not create a sea when he draws border lines and says: The part of the surface of the ocean, delimited by these lines, I am going to call the Yellow Sea; and no more can the mathematician really create anything by his act of definition" (xiii). Of course the mathematician could have drawn different boundaries around mathematical objects and concepts, just as the geographer could have drawn different boundaries delimiting the world's seas. On Frege's view, there seems to be room (at least in principle) for different systems of definitions. But his discussion of definitions suggests that these different systems of definitions would simply result in different theoretical descriptions of the *same* objective domain, in different (but necessarily compatible) arithmetics or geographies. We must be able to evaluate these alternative theoretical descriptions against each other, that is, by commensurable standards, since there is a common reality that they describe. These are not the autonomous and independent theoretical systems that the formalists fancy (e.g., Euclidean geometry peacefully coexisting with non-Euclidean geometries, not as competing theories of space, but as different languages).

The important point is that, for Frege, the freedom of choice that we have in the initial definitions of a scientific discipline in no way undermines the objectivity of that discipline. There is an arbitrary element in the definitions of arithmetical signs, just as there is an arbitrary element in the naming of a sea. But with these definitions we fix the reality against which the correctness of arithmetical propositions must be judged. As long as the boundaries we draw in the definition of a sign are "sharp," there is a fact of the matter concerning the applicability of the sign. Once the choice of boundaries has been made, what lies within the boundaries is fixed and objective. As Frege put it in *Grundlagen*, using the same analogy, there is a fact of the matter about the truth of our assertions about the North Sea (FA §26): the truth of the assertion "The North Sea is 10,000 square miles in extent" is "something quite objective," although of course we would not have been able to grasp the thought expressed in it and to evaluate its truth, had we not drawn the boundaries we drew to delimit that body of water. But if we had not drawn those boundaries, there would still be an object in the world (although unrecognized) which we could call "the North Sea" and it would still be 10,000 square miles in extent. As Frege puts it: "The objectivity of the North Sea is not affected by the fact that it is a matter of our arbitrary choice which part of all the water on the earth's surface we mark off and elect to call the 'North Sea'. [. . .] In the same way number, too, is something objective" (FA §26).

The Objectivity Requirement can be satisfied by grounding the laws of arithmetic in the meaning of the arithmetical signs *only if* what these signs designate is something more than the product of our fancy. So, for Frege, the concepts and objects that the arithmetical signs pick out must be *in some sense* independent of us: not created but discovered. This *seems* to commit Frege to a robust scientific realism that involves strong ontological commitments. If, as Frege thinks, there are entities that exist independently of our recognition corresponding to the well-defined expressions of science, it seems to follow that the world must come structured into self-identifying objects and properties that can be discovered by science. Worse yet, since Frege's view of objectivity applies first and foremost to the science of arithmetic, he seems to be forced to postulate not only language- and mind-independent entities in the natural world, but also mathematical objects and concepts that exist independently of us. This realist and Platonist interpretation has been the standard reading of Frege's view of objectivity. This interpretation has been recently questioned by a more austere reading that finds in Frege a *deontologized* notion of objectivity. This deflated Fregean notion of objectivity is particularly interesting for our purposes, for, as we shall see, it brings Frege's view closer to Wittgenstein's. In what follows I will try to show that, even on this deflationary interpretation, Frege's view of objectivity presupposes a certain kind of realism, a logical realism without ontological commitments, that is, the realism about *possibilia* that we already encountered in chapter 1.

What motivates the standard Platonist interpretation of Frege's view of objectivity? The main source of textual support for this interpretation can be found in Frege's remarks about a "third realm" of thought distinct and apart from the physical and psychological world. Here is Frege's argument for the existence of this realm:

> If every thought requires an owner and belongs to the content of his consciousness, then the thought has this owner alone; and there is *no science common to many on which many could work*. [. . .] So the result seems to be: thoughts are neither things in the external world nor ideas. *A third realm must be recognized.* Anything belonging to this realm has it in common with ideas that it cannot be perceived by the senses, but has it in common with things that it does not need an owner so as to belong to the contents of his consciousness. Thus for example the thought that we have expressed in the Pythagorean theorem is *timelessly true, true independently of whether anyone takes it to be true. It needs no owner.*[122]

According to Frege, the existence of a "third realm" is required by the very possibility of a shared science. In order to have a shared science, thoughts cannot be the private property of particular individuals; they must be intersubjectively sharable. And if thoughts are to be shareable, they cannot belong to the psychological world of ideas; and they certainly do not belong to the world of physical objects that we can experience. So Frege concludes that there is an intersubjective domain of thought which is independent of what is physically and psychologically actual. For Frege, this is what makes science possible: a "third realm" that contains "timeless" thoughts and the concepts and objects of which they are composed. Is this "third realm" an ontological realm? Does Frege conceive of thoughts as the abstract denizens of a Platonic world?

Thomas Ricketts (1986), for one, has argued that it is a mistake to think that Frege's view of the objectivity of science is based on ontological categories, rather than on logical ones. According to Ricketts, Frege's distinction between the world of ideas and the world of thought does not rest on a metaphysical contrast between two distinct ontological realms, but rather on a logical contrast between the subjective and the objective contents of our utterances: it "lodges in the contrast between asserting something and giving vent to a feeling."[123] And for Frege, Ricketts remarks, the crucial difference between an assertion and the expression of a feeling is that the former (but not the latter) requires intersubjectivity. On Ricketts' interpretation, Frege's claim that thoughts are independent of us thinkers does not express the thesis that thoughts are mind-independent, abstract entities (and so are the concepts and objects of which they are composed); Frege's claim is simply that thoughts (unlike "ideas") are independent of individual thinkers, that they admit no owner. As Frege puts it, thoughts are "independent of me; other men can grasp them just as much as I; I can acknowledge a science in which many can be engaged in research. We are not owners of thought as we are owners of our ideas."[124] Frege's "third realm" is certainly not the product of the workings of anybody's mind. But thoughts, for Frege, are not independent of the *possibility* of being "grasped" by different thinkers: what defines a thought is that it is judgeable and expressible in assertions.

Joan Weiner has also defended an austere reading of Frege that tries to do away with any unnecessary metaphysical baggage.[125] On her interpretation too, Frege's "third realm" is the realm of what is thinkable and expressible in language, not a separate ontological realm populated by language- and mind-independent entities. Arguing against Burge's defense of the traditional Platonist reading of Frege,[126] Weiner draws attention to a passage from "Negation" in which Frege denies the thesis of the language- and mind-independence of thoughts: "The being of a thought may also be taken to lie in the possibility of different thinkers' grasping the thought as one and the same thought."[127] As Weiner puts it, this passage makes it clear that for Frege the existence of a thought is "dependent on something linguistic or communal," namely, "on the *possibility* of the thought's being expressed in language or communicated."[128] Indeed, for Frege, thoughts constitute an *objective* realm, but this is not an ontological domain separable from what *can* be grasped by our minds and expressed in language. Weiner reminds us that Frege identifies "what is objective" with "what is subject to laws, what can be conceived and judged, what is expressible in words" (FA §26). So Frege's view of objectivity does not seem to force us to go beyond the bounds of language and the mind to a separate realm. As Weiner puts it: "An interpretation that ignores the connection Frege draws between objectivity and expressibility in language or conceivability leaves too much of his view in penumbra."[129]

But how about Frege's view of scientific definitions as naming sharply defined bits of reality? As we saw, Frege emphasizes that the concepts and objects of a science such as arithmetic are *discovered*, not invented, that they are *there* before (and whether or not) they are in any way recognized by us and expressed in our language (FA §26; BLA Preface xiii). Doesn't this suggest a strong metaphysical realism? Doesn't it suggest that science must carve reality at the joints? Consider, for instance, the following passage:

> A law of nature is not invented by us, but discovered, and just as a desolate island in the Arctic Ocean was there long before anyone had set eyes on it, so the laws of nature, and likewise those of mathematics, have held good at all times and not just since they were discovered. This shows us that these thoughts, if true, are not only true independently of our recognizing them to be so, but that

> they are *independent of our thinking as such*. (Frege 1979, p. 133; my emphasis)

It seems almost natural to read passages like this as a defense of a metaphysical realist picture of science in general and of mathematics in particular. Frege seems to be attributing some kind of independent existence to the concepts and objects of mathematics and the laws governing them: these are said to be utterly unaffected by our recognition of them and by "our thinking as such." So isn't Frege after all the uncompromising Platonist he was always thought to be?

Weiner argues that when we interpret the apparent expressions of realist and Platonist theses in Frege's writings in the light of his logical doctrines, a very different picture emerges. To begin with, for Frege, the discovery of a concept does not require some abstract entity being there, corresponding to our concept expression: "The only requirement to be made of a concept is that it should have sharp boundaries."[130] On Frege's view, Weiner contends, the discovery of concepts consists simply in "the formulation of precise distinctions."[131] The discovery of an object, however, requires more than precise distinctions; "it requires existence and uniqueness proofs."[132] But this does not mean that, for Frege, the objects that we can discover in science are independent of what is thinkable and expressible in language. As Weiner emphasizes, the concept expressions we use (and therefore the distinctions we have drawn) play a crucial role in determining which objects we can discover.[133]

But Frege insists that mathematical objects and concepts and the laws governing them are *there* independently of our grasp and of the sharp boundaries that we draw in language which enable us to grasp them (cf. BLA II Preface xiii; FA §26).[134] How is this claim to be interpreted on a non-Platonist interpretation such as Weiner's? What was *there* before we "discovered" a concept or an object, before we marked off their boundaries in language? What was there, according to Weiner, was "the *possibility* of marking off [their] boundaries in language."[135] On Weiner's interpretation, this is what the objectivity of the North Sea (and, by analogy, what the objectivity of numbers and mathematical concepts) consists in: "To say that unrecognized objects exist, then, is simply to say that it is possible to mark off, in language, boundaries that have never actually been marked off by anyone."[136] What was *there* before we "discovered" a mathematical law, that is, before we grasped the thought expressed by it, was the *possibility* of that thought's being grasped and expressed in language. So, for Frege, the objects, concepts, and thoughts that can be discovered in mathematics are crucially dependent on what is thinkable and expressible in language: these objects, concepts, and thoughts preexist their discovery, not as abstract entities subsisting in a language- and mind-independent world, but as *possible* objects of scientific inquiry. On Frege's view, it is logic alone that constrains the objects, concepts, and thoughts that *can* be discovered in science. As Weiner emphasizes, it is not Frege's view that there is a prelinguistically structured reality which determines a unique set of correct definitions: "Nothing in Frege's writings suggests that we can go wrong by failing to carve the world (or, reality) at the joints."[137]

So Frege's view of the objectivity of science does not require ontological inflation.[138] For Frege, what is objective is what is expressible in his Begriffsschrift, that is, what can play a role in inference, what can be a "content of possible judgment" (see esp. *Begriffsschrift*[139] Preface and §2). But notice that this is still a *realist* view. Even on the deflationary interpretation I have considered, Frege's view of objectivity involves a strong (though peculiar) realism about the objects, concepts, and thoughts we *can* discover in the course of our inquiries: these must be *already there*, prior to any scientific investigation, in the realm of *logical possibilities*. For Frege, logic delimits what is thinkable and expressible in language *sub specie aeternitatis*; and therefore it predetermines *all* the possible objects of scientific inquiry: they are already there, that is, their possibility is already given.[140] Frege's realism about logical possibilities does not depend on an inflated ontology. Frege does not assume that there are such things as "*the* joints" of reality which science must uncover. On his view, reality can have as many joints as precise definitions we can come up with. However, this view does assume that, in any domain of scientific inquiry,[141] there are *absolute standards of precision* that determine the possible "sharp boundaries" we can draw and hence the possible objects and concepts we can discover. For Frege, these immutable standards of precision are fixed by the laws of logic. So Frege's realism rests mainly on logical considerations, not on ontological ones.[142] But this realism is not as *minimal* as it may seem: it relies on substantive assumptions concerning the logical *essence* of thought and language.

Does Frege conceive of the objective existence of thoughts as "dependent on something linguistic and communal," as Weiner claims? Indeed, on Frege's view, thoughts are judgeable contents that *can* be shared and expressed in language. But, for Frege, what is sharable and expressible is fixed by logic independently of our *actual* linguistic practices (see, e.g., BLA Preface xv–xvi). For Frege, thoughts do not depend for their existence on any *actual* language or any *actual* community of language users; they depend, rather, on a logically perfect language (such as his Begriffsschrift) and the notional community of its users. The "linguistic and communal" component of Frege's view of objectivity resides in the *possible* languages and the *possible* communities of language users that logic permits.

Remember that what defines Frege's "third realm" is its independence from what is physically and psychologically *actual.* This is the realm of what is *possible.* As Frege puts it, "what is objective," "what is independent of our mental processes," is that which "does not *have* to be [. . .] actual."[143]

As we have seen in previous chapters, from the *Tractatus* to the early 1930s, Wittgenstein was committed to a realism about *possibilia* very similar to Frege's. Frege's view of logic as that which establishes the bounds of conceivability and expressibility bears striking similarities with the Tractarian view. In the *Tractatus* Wittgenstein argued that logical form determines what is thinkable and expressible in any possible system of representation. In the early 1930s, however, he rejected the idea that there is a single logical structure underlying all symbolisms, an overarching logic that captures the essence of language and thought. But despite its anti-essentialism, Wittgenstein's view of language in the early 1930s retains the idea that there are fixed limits to what is thinkable and expressible in any given system of representation: the grammatical conventions of each system draw a sharp distinction between what makes sense and what does not within the system. On this conventionalist view, the limits of significance and conceivability are established piecemeal by the symbolic conventions of different languages or calculi. The grammatical rules of a symbolism determine the whole range of possible applications of its signs; and they do so *autonomously*, independently of our actual practices of language use. Thus, with the so-called thesis of the autonomy of grammar, Wittgenstein maintains the Tractarian realism about *possibilia* in the conventionalist framework of the early 1930s. Until the mid 1930s he thought of the priority of logical possibilities over actual uses as a fundamental tenet that no account of language can renounce, for its denial would amount to dissolving the normativity of language use.

The realism about *possibilia* that Frege and Wittgenstein shared provides an interesting link between their views of the applicability of rules. I will try to show that remnants of this realism are still present in Wittgenstein's discussions of rule following as late as 1933–34. In what follows I examine how Wittgenstein's view of rules in the early 1930s accommodates the requirements that derive from Frege's account of the applicability of arithmetical laws. Section 2 focuses on the Applicability Principle and the Sharp Boundary Requirement, section 3 on the Objectivity Requirement.

4.2. The "Internal Relation" between Rule and Application

Echoing Frege, Wittgenstein contends that the applicability of arithmetic cannot be something accidental and extrinsic to it: "It must be essential to mathematics that it can be applied. [. . .] Its applic*ability* isn't the kind of thing I mean of a piece of wood when I say 'I will be able to find many applications for it" (PG II p. 319). Like Frege, Wittgenstein criticizes the formalist's refusal to take up the issue of the applicability of arithmetic, arguing that a language or calculus "is not something that is first given a structure and then fitted on to reality" (PG §46). According to Wittgenstein, a calculus cannot have applications whose correctness has not already been established by its rules (PG II pp. 311ff). But for Wittgenstein, as for Frege, the applications that are intrinsic to the rules of arithmetic are not our de facto uses, but their *possible* applications. The "applic*ability*" of arithmetic must be fixed by its rules, but it is not the business of arithmetic to describe the ways in which we actually use its formulas (PG II p. 319). Frege and Wittgenstein are also of one mind in their rejection of the empiricist view of arithmetic: the rules of arithmetic cannot be empirical generalizations; the content of a rule cannot be the contingent sum of the particular applications that we happen to make of it. What agrees with a rule and what does not is not a matter of experience: "The agreement we want is not experiential at all" (Lectures 1932–35, p. 85). If it were, Wittgenstein continues, what counts as correct would be a "natural phenomenon" and it would call for a "psychological investigation." Wittgenstein emphasizes that nothing outside the arithmetical calculus can have any bearing on the applicability of its rules. He argues that "you can develop arithmetic completely autonomously and its application takes care of itself, since wherever it's applicable we may also apply it" (PR §109); "arithmetical constructions are *autonomous* . . . [they] themselves *guarantee their applicability*" (PR §111; my emphasis).

Wittgenstein generalizes the Applicability Principle beyond the rules of arithmetic. On Wittgenstein's view, every rule of grammar is required to have a range of applications that intrinsically belongs to it. For Wittgenstein, a grammatical rule is an arbitrary symbolic convention; but once established, there is nothing arbitrary about what the rule commands, about what accords with it and what does not: "Grammatical rules are arbitrary, but their application is *not*" (Lectures 1930–32, p. 58). As long as the relation between rule and application remains arbitrary, we have not succeeded in laying down a rule and there is not yet the possibility of rule following (cf. Lectures 1930–32, pp. 37–39). According to Wittgenstein, there are no idle rules, rules without application. On his view, a rule and its applications are not separable elements that can be independently established: the range of possible applications licensed by a rule is *constitutive* of the content of the rule. This is what Wittgenstein repeatedly emphasizes by saying that there is "an *internal* relation" between a rule and its application (e.g., Lectures 1930–32, p. 31).

In the early 1930s Wittgenstein's writings and lectures are full of references to "internal relations": there is an internal relation between a true proposition and the fact that verifies it, between an expectation and its fulfilment, between an order and its execution, and so on (see esp. PR §§16–34). Calling the relation between rule and application "internal" underlines two (related) aspects of this relation. First, it underscores that the relation between rule and application is *constitutive* of its terms, that they would not be what they are without it: *this* rule would not be the rule it is if it did not have the applications it has, nor would *this* act be the act it is if it did not accord with *this* rule. Second, it stresses that the relation between rule and application is *unmediated*, that no intermediary can be interpolated between its terms to glue them together: there is nothing "that interposes itself between the expression 'x/x^2' and its application to numbers, like the mortar between bricks" (WWK p. 155). For Wittgenstein, it is a fatal mistake to think that what determines the applications of a rule is something other than the rule itself. To introduce a third thing mediating between a rule and its applications (e.g., an interpretation) would be to break up an internal relation and, once an internal relation is broken up, the identity of its terms can never be recovered. Once a rule is detached from its applications, a truly "*unbridgeable* gulf between rule and application" is introduced (PR §164).

For Wittgenstein, the normative content of a rule resides in the internal relation between a general instruction or rule formulation and a pattern of application and, as he puts it, "an internal relation cannot be there unless both its terms are" (Lectures 1930–32, p. 31). Neither explicit principles or laws nor patterns of application can, by themselves, encapsulate the normativity of rules. The normative content of a rule cannot be reified in either of the two poles of this relation. For these poles cannot be isolated: the relata of an internal relation belong necessarily to each other; the very identity of each is bound up with the other, and they cannot, therefore, be grasped independently. One cannot, for instance, understand the rule of squaring and yet deny that "16" follows "1, 4, 9, . . ." in the application of that rule to the natural number sequence. So Wittgenstein argues that in going from a formula to its instantiation, or from a particular instance to the general law, nothing can help me, I must grasp the internal relation: "I must see it. [. . .] This is the unbridgeable gulf between rule and application, or law and special case" (PR §164). The "unbridgeable gulf" that Frege talked about goes both ways: from rule to application, and from application to rule. We cannot start with patterned actions and then figure out what rule they accord with; likewise, we cannot start with a rule formulation detached from its applications and then bridge our way to them. Wittgenstein emphasizes that we can only grasp a rule when we "see" the internal relation between a formula and its applications, that is, when we read into a rule formulation the pattern of applications that intrinsically belongs to it, or when we read a certain configuration of signs as the necessary instantiation of a general formula (cf. PR §§164ff; in particular, the discussion of "2 + (3 + 4) = (2 + 3) + 4" and "a + (b + c) + (a + b) + c" in §164).

By arguing against the one-sided identifications of the norms that govern language use with rule formulations or patterns of applications, Wittgenstein rejects two opposed conceptions of normativity. These are the conceptions that Robert Brandom has aptly described as "regulism"[144] (the view that norms must take the form of explicit rules or principles) and "regularism"[145] (the view that identifies norms with behavioral regularities). Wittgenstein's developing view of rules is an attempt to articulate an account of normativity that avoids a double danger, warily steering its course between the Scylla of regulism and the Charybdis of regularism, to use McDowell's metaphor.[146] It is Scylla that Wittgenstein's conventionalism in the early 1930s (a "rule"-based account of normativity) is at pains to avoid, while the danger of avoiding Charybdis will grow larger as we move toward Wittgenstein's later view (a practice-based account of normativity). In what follows I will discuss the indeterminacy arguments that Wittgenstein offers in the early 1930s against regulism and regularism (which resemble in some respects Frege's criticisms of formalism and psychologism). As we shall see, these arguments are at the service of the conventionalism of the calculus view of language. They support the view that there is an internal relation between rule and application. After discussing these arguments, I will examine what this internal relation consists in and how it can be forged by convention according to Wittgenstein.

Wittgenstein argues that the regularity view of normativity rests on a category mistake: it confuses "what ought to be done" with "what is done." For Wittgenstein, this view is a nonstarter because it remains in the empirical realm of conjectures and predictions, the realm of "what is and will be," and cannot reach "the realm of the 'must'" (Lectures 1932–35, p. 85). This view treats the agreement with a rule "as though it were a question of time. But time does not enter in" (Lectures 1932–35, p. 87). For Wittgenstein, regularities have a purely empirical interest, they are "mere history" (cf. PR §15). Mere regularities of use cannot provide standards of correctness: take any pattern of actions and for anything you might go on to do, there is some regularity with respect to which your action counts as "going on in the same way."[147] So rule following cannot be reduced to behavioral regularities; the distinction between correct and incorrect applications of a rule cannot be reduced to the distinction between regular and irregular performance. Something more than a behavioral pattern is needed for rule following: what is needed, according to Wittgenstein, is a rule of grammar that governs that pattern nonaccidentally, an underlying convention. Reacting to traffic lights in certain regular ways, for instance, would not be rule-following behavior if there were no conventions that regulated those reactions, certain implicit or explicit norms in virtue of which those reactions can be deemed correct or incorrect (cf. Lectures 1930–32, pp. 40–41).

According to Wittgenstein, regularism makes the relation between rule and application wholly indeterminate: a pattern of applications is not sufficient to uniquely identify a rule that governs the pattern, for there are infinitely many rules that can be brought to agree with any finite collection of applications. Similarly, Wittgenstein argues that regulism makes rule following equally indeterminate: the formulation of a rule is not sufficient to uniquely identify its correct applications, for there are infinitely many patterns of application that can be brought to agree with it. Here the "gulf" between rule and application is opened before us when we consider that a rule formulation is just a sign and that "no sign leads us beyond itself" (PG §71).

Wittgenstein urges us to distinguish between rules and rule formulations (WWK pp. 154–56; Lectures 1930–32, p. 113). As long as we fail to make this distinction, we find ourselves at a loss to answer the question How *can* a rule be applied? (WWK p. 155). How do we go from the rule "x/x^2" to the series "1, 4, 9, 16 . . ."? The algebraic rule "x/x^2" *in isolation* does not suffice to single out the series "1, 4, 9, 16 . . ." as the correct application of the rule of squaring to the series of natural numbers. One may think that the correct application of the rule "x/x^2" has to be fixed "by means of another rule" (WWK p. 155)—for instance, a substitution rule that enables us to raise every number to its second power (e.g., "$x = y/x^2 = y \cdot y$"). But Wittgenstein replies that "in this way you would never get off the ground" (WWK p. 155). We can only fix the applicability of a rule "by means of another rule" if the applicability of the latter has already been fixed, but how is this done? One may think that we can always do that by appealing to a new rule of a higher order, but this of course opens an infinite regress: "I should again not have got any further—I should have needed a further rule that told me how to apply it, etc." (WWK p. 154).

The Regress Argument is Wittgenstein's master argument against regulism. A possible rejoinder to this argument is to appeal to the explicit interpretation of rule formulations. The regulist can reply that a rule formulation seems to lack normative force only when it is considered as an uninterpreted string of signs; but if we supplement the rule formulation with an explicit interpretation, we thereby provide a bridge to its applications. Wittgenstein remarks that "in all languages there is a bridge between the sign and its application" (Lectures 1930–32, p. 67). But he emphasizes that this bridge cannot be built with verbal explanations or interpretations: "Any explanation of a symbol can do nothing but add to the symbol"

(Lectures 1930–32, p. 32). If we need to make a jump from a sign to its application, we need a similar jump to put the explanation of the sign to use, for, after all, the explanation is just a further sign (or a collection of signs): "No explanation ever saves the jump, because any further explanation will itself need a jump" (Lectures 1930–32, p. 67). As discussed above (3.3.1), not only verbal explanations, but even ostensive definitions (the most likely candidates to give a jumpstart to the application of a symbolism), fail to bridge the gulf between signs and their application (cf. PG §45). If a formula needs to be supplemented with an interpretation, so does the interpretation of the formula, which is a further formula. So the appeal to interpretations cannot save regulism from "an infinite regress" (Lectures 1930–32, p. 32). And this shows that interpretations cannot fix the applicability of rules. Against regulism, the Regress Argument underscores that rule following cannot be a matter of rule formulation or interpretation *all the way down*.

As is well known, this Regress Argument against the intrinsic normative force of rule formulations and interpretations also appears in Wittgenstein's later writings. According to Brandom, the Regress Argument of the *Investigations* is "Wittgenstein's master argument for the appropriateness of the pragmatist, rather than the regulist-intellectualist, order of explanation."[148] If this were the case, one should expect that the first appearance of this argument in Wittgenstein's writings would be a decisive turning point in the development of his thought. However, the Regress Argument of the 1930s does not seem to be *yet* at the service of a practice-based account of normativity. Nothing in the writings and lectures of these years suggests that Wittgenstein already held a pragmatist view of normativity or that he arrived at it through this argument. What seems to be the most distinctive idea of a pragmatist approach to normativity—namely, that "rule-based proprieties of performance depend on practice-based ones"[149]—is lacking in the calculus view of language Wittgenstein defended in the early 1930s.

Both in the early 1930s and in the *Investigations* Wittgenstein uses the Regress Argument to show that rule formulations lack prescriptive power when considered in isolation, that explicit rules can have normative significance only against a *background*. But in the early 1930s the background that gives normative force to rule formulations is not an actual practice of application, but a system of conventions. According to Wittgenstein, rule formulations codify "grammatical conventions," which he usually describes as "stipulations" (e.g., PR §167; PG §81; Lectures 1932–35, p. 86). And the idea that rule formulations codify conventions is not supplemented with the insight that conventions are maintained alive through actual practices. So the critique of regulism that results from the Regress Argument in the early 1930s is not as radical as in the *Investigations*. Wittgenstein's view seems to be that regulism is right in pointing out that the normative constitutes an autonomous realm, but its mistake is to identify this autonomous realm with disembodied rule formulations, rather than with the "internal relations" that they codify.

Wittgenstein's critique of regulism in the 1930s is very similar to Frege's critique of formalism. Like Frege, Wittgenstein argues that we cannot see a rule in a mere configuration of signs. For instance, the arithmetical equation "1 + 1 = 2" can be taken to express a rule, a "general instruction" (WWK p. 155). But from the configuration of signs "1 + 1 = 2" alone, we cannot gather what we are supposed to do. The normative content of the equation, the rule expressed in it, can only be appreciated when we associate the equation with "a certian kind of application," in this case, a substitution pattern: "Wherever there is an expression in which 2 occurs, you may substitute 1 + 1 for 2" (WWK p. 155). The equation would be an idle rule formulation if it did not relate to this pattern of application. It is not until we "see" the relation of the equation with this substitution pattern that we can grasp its normative content: "We now *see* what the rule really is. It relates to this whole pattern; it is not a part, an isolated element of it. I have already to read this whole pattern into the equation '1 + 1 = 2' —only then shall I have the rule in front of me. The isolated equation is not yet the rule." (WWK pp. 155–56; my emphasis). The equation in isolation does not express the rule, just as a configuration of chess pieces by itself does not express a rule of chess: "*Basically the rule is the internal relation* [. . .]. As an internal relation it cannot be expressed by means of a configuration of the game" (WWK p. 157).

But what does the *internal relation* between a formula or general instruction and its applications consist in? It consists in a definite *method of application* that determines what counts as the correct application of the rule in each case (cf. PR §§149–50). According to Wittgenstein, it is a particular method of application that correlates a rule formulation with a pattern of application, enabling us to go from the general formula to its specific applications and from any given application to the general formula. Wittgenstein argues that the rules of grammar of a symbolism always presuppose a particular "method of application" or "method of projection," and that it is in virtue of this method that a certain range of possible applications intrinsically belongs to the symbolism (cf. PR §45, §54, §58; PG II p. 319; Lectures 1930–32, p. 115; Lectures 1832–35, p. 72).

The method of application or projection that Wittgenstein appeals to in his rule-following discussions may appear as a *deus ex machina* invoked to bridge the gulf between rule and application. But Wittgenstein emphasizes that this method is not a mysterious third thing that glues together a rule and its applications but rather the very relation in which rule and application stand to one another. As Wittgenstein puts it in *Philosophical Grammar*, "if the method of projection is a bridge, it is a bridge which is not built until the application is made" (p. 213). According to Wittgenstein, the method of application or projection is precisely what the regulist leaves out of account, for this method is not something that can be captured in a list of rules. As Baker and Hacker put it in their discussion of these passages, "a description of a bridge is not a bridge."[150] The method of application of a calculus of rules is the part of the grammar of the calculus that remains unavoidably *implicit*: "You can only explain the method of projection by projecting; and the projection is only made when it is made" (Lectures 1930–32, p. 68). For Wittgenstein, the grammar of a symbolism does not consist simply in the rules that we can enunciate, but also in the particular way in which these rules are applied. Laying down a convention for the use of a term or proposition in a symbolism requires more than stating a rule; it requires settling the use of the term or proposition with a definite method of application, which can only be *shown*.[151]

Against regulism, Wittgenstein contends that laying down a rule is more than the mere enunciation of a rule formulation: it requires a demonstrative use of the rule in which its method of application is exhibited. This is how, according to Wittgenstein, the internal relation between rule and application is forged by convention. But he also emphasizes, against regularism, that we should not identify the rule with its manifestation in actual practice. Although the method of application of a rule can only be exhibited through actual applications of the rule, the actual applications have only an "empirical interest," they are "mere history" (cf. PR §15, Lectures 1930–32, p. 54, PG §29). For Wittgenstein, the method of application is not only what determines the actual use of a rule, but also what fixes its *possible* applications. And therefore it goes beyond any series of actual applications: it belongs to the realm of grammatical possibilities. He argues that only when we regard the method of application in this way can we understand how a rule can *contain* all its applications before they are carried out: a grammatical rule does not contain all its applications in actuality, but it contains their possibility (cf. esp. PR §141). Wittgenstein remarks that the confusions surrounding the issue of whether or not an arithmetical rule such as "m = 2n" somewhat "contains" the infinite totality of its applications can only be cleared away by distinguishing between grammatical possibilities and actual cases: "It all hangs on the syntax of reality and possibility. *m = 2n* contains the *possibility of correlating any number* with another, *but doesn't correlate all numbers with others*" (PR §141). On Wittgenstein's view, the totality of possible applications of a rule is fixed by the method of carrying them out, just as all *possible* measurements are determined by "the method of taking measurements": "The use, the application, of a yardstick doesn't presuppose any particular length for the object to be measured," but it presupposes a "method of taking measurements" which is equally applicable to objects of all sizes (PR §44).

According to Wittgenstein, when the use of a rule formulation is demonstrated in actual applications, "something does as it were *adhere* to" it (Lectures 1930–32, p. 116). What "adheres" to the rule formulation (e.g., "an algebraic schema") is "the way in which it is applied," which "must always be behind it" (PR §167). As Wittgenstein puts it in the lectures, the method of application endows the rule formulation with a "grammatical body" (cf. Lectures 1930–32, p. 59 and p. 116). It may seem paradoxical that Wittgenstein allows himself to talk about "grammatical bodies" while he makes such a fuss about "meaning bodies." However, despite the ontological overtones of the metaphor, Wittgenstein's appeal to "grammatical bodies" does not involve any kind of reification: the "grammatical body" of a rule is not an abstract *thing* or hidden object, but its range of possible applications. (These "grammatical bodies" are akin to the *hidden bodies* that the Tractarian view of language postulated as lurking beneath the statements of ordinary language.) The metaphor of "grammatical bodies" underscores that there is something immutable (though not a thing) that accompanies all the applications of a rule. This constant accompaniment is the applicability of the rule as fixed by a particular method of application. It is in this sense that, as we saw, Wittgenstein thinks of the entire range of possible uses of a rule as the indispensable background that accompanies any particular application of the rule that gets actualized in practice.

Wittgenstein describes the range of possible applications of a rule, its "grammatical body," as having *sharp boundaries*, as "a figure drawn with sharp outline" (Lectures 1932–35, p. 48). It is the particular method of application of a rule that draws a sharp boundary around its possible uses. So, on Wittgenstein's view, the method of application is what guarantees not only that grammatical rules have intrinsic applicability (i.e., that they honor the Applicability Principle), but also that their applicability have definite limits (i.e., that they meet the Sharp Boundary Requirement). Wittgenstein demands that the extension of a rule be "*complete*" (cf. PR §154); and his explanation of this demand for completeness closely resembles Frege's rationale for the Sharp Boundary Requirement on definitions.[152] He argues that grammatical rules must have a *fixed* range of applicability if the signs whose use they govern are to have a definite sense. Given that the sense of a sign is "defined" by rules of use, if a sign has a definite sense, we must be able to determine when and how the rules that govern its use can be applied. These rules must be fixed and complete, for "any alteration (e.g., supplementation) of the rules" would result in "an alteration of the sense" (PR §154). Grammatical rules must remain immutable: we cannot alter their applicability without thereby changing the rules themselves, "just as we can't alter the marks of a concept without altering the concept itself (Frege)" (PR §154).

As late as 1933–34 (cf. PG §10), Wittgenstein's view of rules retains the idea that there must be a unitary core underlying all the possible applications of a rule. This is a result of accepting the challenge that Frege posed to the formalists; namely, to formulate and elucidate rules in such a way that their applicability becomes intrinsic to them (the Applicability Principle) and it acquires definite limits (the Sharp Boundary Requirement). The acceptance of this challenge forces us to view the applicability of a rule *sub specie aeternitatis*, for it forces us to single out something immutable that determines the entire range of possible applications of the rule. Trying to meet Frege's challenge, in the early 1930s Wittgenstein contends that what fixes the applicability of a rule is something that we can isolate from particular contexts of use and particular practices: what he calls "the method of application." According to Wittgenstein, a particular method of application establishes an internal relation between a rule and its possible uses; and an internal relation, once established, is not contingent on anything we do or fail to do; it is always binding. These internal relations between rules and their applications do not belong to the realm of actual practices but to the sempiternal realm of grammatical possibilities. The autonomous realm of grammar, like Frege's "third realm" or the "logical space" of the *Tractatus*, is not a realm of abstract entities but the realm of what is thinkable and expressible in language. Thus, as discussed above, the realism about *possibilia* shared by Frege and the author of the *Tractatus* is still maintained in Wittgenstein's conventionalist view of language in the early 1930s.

4.3. Is Grammar Up to Me?

Wittgenstein emphasizes that "grammar consists of conventions" (PG §138), which he describes as "stipulations" or "decisions" (cf. e.g., PR §149). But if the accord with a rule ultimately depends on our decisions, doesn't this mean that what counts as correct in the application of a rule is a purely arbitrary and subjective matter? On Wittgenstein's view, grammatical rules are stipulations, but *once established*, what count as their correct applications is not up to any individual or particular community to decide. Grammatical conventions have a *contractual* nature: by accepting a grammatical convention "I am committed to a future usage" (Lectures 1930–32, p. 37); and the same goes for the comunity of rule followers: by laying down a rule "we thereby commit ourselves" to a range of possible applications (p.

39). Wittgenstein emphasizes that when we use a symbolism we are bound by its rules: the correct application of its signs is determined by its conventions, not left to the discretion of its users. This is the inexorable bindingness of symbolic conventions that Wittgenstein talks about: they themselves are arbitrary, "but their application is *not*" (Lectures 1930–32, p. 58).

According to this *contractualist* view of rules, there is no fact of the matter *prior* to the stipulation of a rule that can determine its correct applications. For Wittgenstein, what accords with a rule and what does not can only be determined by the rule itself, that is, by the convention that we lay down and the commitments that go with it. But he agrees with Frege that the agreement between rule and application cannot be a purely subjective matter; that is, he endorses what I have called the Objectivity Requirement. He emphasizes, for instance, that there is nothing subjective about the application of the rules of arithmetic, even though they are mere stipulations. Wittgenstein tries to elucidate the objectivity of arithmetical rules through an analogy with traffic lights (Lectures 1930–32, pp. 40–41). He argues that the relation between the rule of squaring "x/x^2" and the series "1, 4, 9, 16 . . ." is like the relation between "the red, amber, green of traffic lights" and "traffic movements": "The choice of colours is arbitrary, but once we adopt it we are committed" (Lectures 1930–32, p. 41); what counts as correct responses to the colors has been fixed and we are bound to react to them in certain ways. This analogy contrasts sharply with the analogy with geography that, as we saw, Frege repeatedly used to underscore the objectivity of arithmetic.

For Frege, the objectivity of arithmetic springs from something prior to the rules that we lay down; namely, from what is thinkable and expressible in language. As we saw, Frege emphasizes that the laws of arithmetic cannot be mere arbitrary stipulations; they require *justification* (cf. esp. BLA II §94): it needs to be shown that they are truths about numbers that govern "everything thinkable" (cf. FA §14). According to Wittgenstein's contractualism, by contrast, the objectivity of an arithmetical rule (or of any grammatical rule, for that matter) springs from the contract put forth (whether tacitly or explicitly) when the rule is laid down. Wittgenstein emphasizes that rules are arbitrary conventions that are not susceptible to justification. As we saw in chapter 2 (cf. 2.2), the arguments he provides in the early 1930s for the autonomy of grammar are intended to show the impossibility of grounding symbolic rules in a language-independent reality: the rules of grammar cannot be justified by appealing to extralinguistic facts because they determine what we call "facts." But this does not seem to be the kind of justification that Frege asks for in his discussion of formal arithmetic. He does not claim that the objectivity of rules requires *metaphysical* grounding; his demand is that "rules be grounded in the meaning of the signs"

(BLA II §92). As suggested by a deflationary reading of Frege's view of objectivity, this demand can be construed as a request for logical (rather than metaphysical) justification of the correctness of rules; that is, as the requirement that rules be grounded in complete and precise definitions. Would Wittgenstein accept this kind of justification?

For Wittgenstein, the attempt to justify grammar by appealing to the logical essence of language and thought is just as objectionable as the attempt to justify grammar by appealing to a language-independent reality. He insists that the rules of grammar do not admit justification of any kind, for there are no standards (logical, metaphysical, or of any kind) that swing free from particular symbolisms and can be used to assess their conventions (see, e.g., PR §7). In *Philosophical Grammar* Wittgenstein explicitly rejects the possibility of grounding symbolic rules in the *meaning* of signs. He argues that we cannot intelligibly ask whether the rules for the use of a sign "accord with its meaning," for these rules *define* the meaning of the sign. This is how he puts it:

> It is grammatical rules that determine meaning (constitute it) and so they themselves are *not answerable to any meaning* and to that extent are *arbitrary*. There cannot be a question whether these or other rules are the correct ones for the use of "not" (that is, whether they *accord with its meaning*). For without these rules the word has as yet no meaning. (PG §133; my emphasis)

What Wittgenstein rejects in this passage is the very idea that signs can have meanings prior to the establishment of rules governing their use. And it is quite immaterial for his rejection of this idea how these meanings are conceived, whether they are reified entities or possible objects of thought and communication. Wittgenstein's claim is that the meaning of a sign (however conceived) cannot be given prior to (and independently of) the rules that determine the use of the sign. According to Wittgenstein, grammatical rules *define* the meaning of our signs and they are, therefore, the ultimate foundations of our symbolisms.[153] Interestingly enough, in Wittgenstein's view grammatical rules play the same role that definitions play in Frege's: they are supposed to endow signs with meaning by drawing a sharp boundary around their possible applications. However, there is a fundamental difference between Frege's definitions and Wittgenstein's rules. For Frege, successful definitions constitute the *discovery* of something preexisting (i.e., the possible objects and concepts that we can think and talk about). For Wittgenstein, by contrast, the rules of grammar create *ex nihilo* an autonomous domain of significance; they do not describe a preexisting domain.

Wittgenstein emphasizes that it is a mistake to think of symbolic rules as objects of investigation and discovery: "*We cannot make discoveries in syntax*" (PR §154). Grammatical rules cannot be the product of an investigation, for any investigation (whether empirical or a priori) presupposes a grammatical framework that remains fixed. Only within a grammatical framework can we pose meaningful questions and acquire knowledge, but the framework itself is not a further object of investigation:[154] "We can only ask from a standpoint from which a question is possible. From which a doubt is possible. [. . .] We cannot ask about that which alone makes questions possible at all. Not about what first gives the system a foundation" (PR §168).

On Wittgenstein's view, there is a crucial distinction between symbolic rules and propositions with a descriptive content: the latter can be deemed true or false; the former are norms of representation which cannot be subject to semantic evaluation (cf. e.g., Lectures 1932–35, p. 90). The failure to recognize this crucial distinction gives rise to a *descriptivist view of rules*. According to this view, the rules of a symbolism express a special kind of *truth*: a truth that can be asserted but not denied. Against this view, Wittgenstein argues that if a proposition cannot be denied it cannot be asserted either: it is a convention that we lay down. He emphasizes that the grammatical statements that constitute the foundations of a propositional system or calculus are not fact-stating propositions, but symbolic conventions: "A basic rule of a system [. . .] can only be laid down, but not *asserted*, or denied" (PR §163). In the early 1930s grammatical rules play the same role that logical propositions played in the *Tractatus*. They are characterized by their emptiness, by their lack of representational content.[155] They are not assertions but rules for description: they structure the "grammatical space" (PR §110) where we make assertions and draw inferences.

According to Wittgenstein, it is a descriptivist view of rules that has led philosophers to "confuse two different things, a law of nature and a rule which we ourselves lay down" (Lectures 1932–35, p. 83); and hence "to confuse mathematics with a natural science" (p. 101). But statements that express symbolic rules and statements that express laws of nature should be distinguished because they play radically different roles: the latter describe facts of nature, whereas the former do not concern how the world *is* but how it *ought* to be described (cf. Lectures 1932–35 p. 84). The descriptivist view of rules leads to the conflation of symbolic rules and natural laws and, consequently, to the assimilation of all science to natural science, imposing the logic of empirical research on all scientific endeavors and thus distorting the purely "grammatical" nature of logic, mathematics, and geometry (cf. Lectures 1932–35, pp. 51ff).

Does Frege's view of rules discussed above fit the descriptivist paradigm of rules that Wittgenstein criticizes? As we saw, Frege used the language of description to talk about the laws of logic and mathematics; and he even compared mathematics with the natural sciences.[156] So it appears that Frege could be read as an advocate of the descriptivist paradigm. However, according to Wittgenstein, this paradigm of rules betrays the normative nature of the laws of logic and mathematics and makes it impossible to appreciate their special status. But Frege can hardly be accused of neglecting the normativity of logic and mathematics and the special status of their laws!

Recently Putnam[157] has argued that there is a tension between a descriptivist and a prescriptivist conception of rules in Frege's view of the laws of logic and mathematics. According to Putnam's interpretation (elaborated in more detail by Conant),[158] Frege's view of the laws of logic (and mathematics) is pulled in two different and irreconcilable directions: toward a Kantian view in which the laws of logic are *constitutive* of thought and toward a positivistic view, in which the laws of logic have a subject matter (the most general domain of all) and constitute a branch of positive science (the most general science of all).[159] On the one hand, Frege maintains that the laws of logic are "laws which *prescribe* universally the way in which one ought to think if one is to think at all."[160] On the other hand, Frege contends that there is something that the laws of logic *describe*; namely, *everything* thinkable.[161] This latter strand in Frege's view of logic is responsible for the thesis that the laws of logic (and hence the laws of arithmetic too) are, as Putnam puts it, "the most general laws of nature."[163] According to Putnam, the tension in Frege's view of logic can be summarized as follows: as *statements*, the laws of logic are not different from the laws of the natural sciences: they are "simply quantifications," although "quantifications over 'all objects'—and all concepts as well—in *Begriffsschrift*";[163] as laws of thought, however, "their *status* [. . .] is very different from the status of empirical laws":[164] they have a transcendental status. But how can the laws of logic (and mathematics) *describe* and at the same time *define* objects and concepts? How can they be the product of *generalizations* and yet be *constitutive* of that from which they are generalized?

In "Thoughts" Frege contends that the laws of logic are laws about "what is" and that from them "there follow prescriptions about asserting, thinking, judging, inferring."[165] But how can we derive prescriptions from descriptions, an 'ought' from an 'is'? Burge argues that it is the postulation of a Platonic realm of abstract entities that enables Frege to make this move: "This is a paradigmatic Platonic direction of explanation: from what *is* in an abstract realm to what is reasonable."[166] According to Burge's Platonist interpretation, Frege's thought is that logic prescribes the form that our judgments and inferences must take by describing the ideal entities of the abstract realm of thought. Weiner argues that this interpretation is not faithful to what Frege says: for he does not say that the laws of logic are laws about a special domain, but rather, that they are "laws about *every-*

thing," about all concepts and all objects, "including everyday spatio-temporal objects."[167] And since nothing escapes the laws of logic, since there is no concept or object which is not subject to them, we can derive from them prescriptions about what can be judged and expressed in language. According to Weiner, "there is no need for any reference to an abstract realm"; in virtue of their universal applicability, the laws about 'what is' license "prescriptive laws about judgment."[168]

Frege's descriptivist view of the laws of logic and mathematics does not rest on Platonism, but it does rest on a realist view of what is thinkable and expressible in language. In order to derive prescriptions about what is thinkable and expressible from these laws, what must they describe? They must describe the logical features of everything thinkable and expressible in language. All the possible contents of judgment must be given or prefigured by the laws of logic and mathematics. Only then can these laws be descriptions and prescriptions at the same time: by describing the essence of conceivability and expressibility, they prescribe how we ought to think and talk.

An integral part of Wittgenstein's critique of essentialist views of thought and language in the early 1930s is his attack on the descriptivist approach to the symbolic rules according to which we think and talk. According to Wittgenstein, the descriptivist approach misunderstands the special status of symbolic rules, which derives from the *normative role* they play in language, not from the special nature (or the generality) of what they describe. For Wittgenstein, what is special about logical and mathematical laws (and symbolic rules more generally) is not what they describe, but the fact that they describe nothing at all, that they only prescribe (cf. Lectures 1932–35, p. 51). The 'ought' of grammar cannot be derived from an 'is', and it does not make any difference whether the 'is' pertains to the natural world, to a Platonic heaven, or to the logical realm of what is thinkable and expressible in language.

The impossibility of deriving an 'ought' from an 'is' is a fundamental Kantian tenet that runs through Wittgenstein's arguments against Frege from the *Tractatus* to the *Investigations*. Already in the *Tractatus* Wittgenstein departed from Frege's view of logic arguing that the laws of logic "have no 'subject-matter'" (6.124), that they have no content, that they describe nothing. However, like Frege, Wittgenstein also thought that there was such thing as the logical structure of what is conceivable and expressible in language. Now, in the early 1930s, Wittgenstein criticizes the realist assumptions about the structure and limits of significance underlying the views of logic of Frege and his earlier self. He argues that "we mean all sorts of things by 'proposition', and it is wrong to start with a definition of a proposition and build up logic from that" (Lectures 1932–35, pp. 12–13). The rules of grammar of each propositional system or calculus determine, autonomously, what is and what is not significant within that system or calculus. There are no "super-rules" or privileged calculus that can determine the grammar of every calculus (cf. PG §72 and Lectures 1932–35, p. 13 and p. 68).

But is this move from the logical structure of language to the rules of grammar of particular symbolisms a radical departure from the Tractarian view and its realist assumptions? By grounding the bounds of significance in the conventions of particular symbolic systems, rather than in the essence of language, Wittgenstein introduces a pluralism and a conventionalism that were absent from the *Tractatus.* But the notion of "grammar" of the early 1930s is essentially the Tractarian notion of logical syntax relativized to different symbolisms (cf. 2.2). Like the rules of logical syntax, the rules of grammar are the conditions of possibility of representation in a symbolism, and therefore not part of what can be represented in that symbolism. Like the rules of logical syntax, the rules of grammar say nothing, but they determine what *can* be said. The grammar of each symbolism fixes, *sub specie aeternitatis*, the *possible* uses of its signs (cf. esp. Lectures 1932–35, p. 51). So the realism about *possibilia* that the *Tractatus* shared with Frege is not entirely abandoned, but simply qualified: the realist assumptions about the range of what is thinkable and expressible in language are relativized to particular symbolisms.

Indeed Wittgenstein's contractualist view of rules rests, crucially, on substantive realist assumptions about the possible applications of rules. Only if a certain realism about *possibilia* is maintained can Wittgenstein's contractualism meet the Objectivity Requirement. For only on the assumption that rules bring with them a fixed range of possible applications can there be objective commitments that attach *themselves* to the use of a rule. On Wittgenstein's view, the commitments that the use of a rule brings with it go beyond the subjective judgment of its actual users because when the rule is laid down a contract is made that is binding for everyone at all times. It is in this sense that what accords with a rule and what does not is still viewed *sub specie aeternitatis* on Wittgenstein's conventionalist view of the early 1930s. In the next chapter I will examine how Wittgenstein starts to call into question these realist assumptions about the applicability of rules in the mid 1930s (cf. esp. 4.3). As we shall see, in *The Brown Book* (1934–35) the notion of rule loses the absolute protagonism it previously had, being no longer the most fundamental notion in Wittgenstein's view of normativity.

5

Internal Relations in Action

Following a Rule versus Conforming with It

In this chapter I will examine the account of rule-following actions that goes with the conventionalist view of normativity Wittgenstein held in the early 1930s. According to Wittgenstein's contractualist view of rules, following a rule requires, so to speak, signing a contract that fixes the applicability of the rule, a contract by virtue of which one becomes committed to do certain things and not others. But how does an individual enter into such contract when she uses a rule? What determines that she is in fact endorsing this contract, rather than merely acting randomly and uncommittedly? As Wittgenstein puts it, we need to find a criterion that enables us to determine when one is "acting *in obedience to*, not just in accordance with, particular rules" (PG §61).

Any action that falls under a rule can be subject to normative assessment and deemed correct or incorrect. When I write down "2 + 2 = 4," what I write is correct according to the rules of addition, whether I am in fact doing addition or simply playing about with figures. But it is only in the former case that I am following a rule. Rule-following and rule-conforming actions belong to the same *genus*; namely, actions that can be regarded as being in accord with rules. But it appears that rule-following actions must exhibit a *surplus* of some sort when compared with rule-conforming actions. In the early 1930s Wittgenstein thought that there must be a distinctive feature or *differentia specifica* that makes rule-following actions a special class of normative actions. He contended that when we follow a rule, the rule must be involved in the production of our actions in a way in which it is not when we merely act in accordance with it (cf. e.g., PR §149 and PG §61). But notice that although it is a trivial fact that one can act in accord with a rule without following it, it is contentious to conclude from this fact that there must be something *intrinsic* to the act of following a rule that distinguishes it from the mere conformity with the rule: a fact about the action or about the agent that makes that action special.

As Baker and Hacker point out, in the early 1930s Wittgenstein was misled by "the natural thought that following a rule is doing something *more* than merely acting in accord with it," and consequently he tried to answer the question What more?[169] As we shall see, from 1930 to 1934 Wittgenstein gave various tentative answers to this question, but none of these answers succeeded in drawing a distinction between rule-following and rule-conforming actions to his satisfaction. However, the important point of evolution concerning Wittgenstein's view of this distinction does not lie in his recantation of any particular answer that he tried out, but rather, in the rejection of the question itself; that is, in the rejection of the idea that there is something intrinsic to the act of rule-following that distinguishes it from rule conforming, a special (super strong) connection between the act and the rule in question. This is not to say, of course, that Wittgenstein will come to reject the distinction between rule following and rule conforming. The point is, rather, that the basis and nature of this distinction will be seen in a new light. In the mid 1930s Wittgenstein starts to argue that we can only draw this distinction against the complex background of our *actual* practices of rule application.

In the next section I discuss the different proposals that Wittgenstein offers in *Philosophical Remarks*, *Philosophical Grammar*, and *The Blue Book* to account for the distinction between rule-following and rule-conforming actions. This discussion will bring to the fore what made these different proposals appealing to Wittgenstein as well as the problems that make them unsuccessful.

5.1. Searching for a *Differentia Specifica*

Wittgenstein's discussion of rule following in *Philosophical Remarks* focuses mainly on the solution of mathematical problems and the construction of proofs. He emphasizes that the solution of mathematical problems requires the use of rules and of their methods of application, and not simply writing down the right figures. He gives the following example: "Suppose I wanted to construct a regular pentagon but didn't know how" and, trying out different things "at random," I finally stumbled "upon the right construction by accident" (PR §157). Did I solve the problem in that way? According to Wittgenstein, I did not solve the problem because I followed no method and hence no rules for the construction of a regular pentagon, even though the product of my actions was a regular pentagon. But why does it matter that I arrived at the correct solution by accident? It matters because "the accident can only refer to something *purely external*, as when I say 'I found that out after drinking strong coffee.' The coffee has no place in what I discovered" (PR §157; emphasis added). In rule following, by contrast, the rules are not adventitious elements externally related to my actions, they are not simply part of the *history* of my actions. They are, rather, what *defines* my actions. Conforming to a rule is something that can be done by accident, but following a rule is not. The latter involves something *more* than a purely accidental or external connection between my action and the rule; it involves an *internal* relation.

But how do we know when an action is internally related to a rule? Wittgenstein remarks that an action is carried out in virtue of a rule, and not merely in conformity with it, when the action stems from an understanding of the rule: "Of course I can write down the solution of a quadratic equation by accident, but I can't understand it by accident" (PR §157). Understanding is precisely what I lacked when I constructed a regular pentagon by accident, and that is why my actions were not properly described as the rule-governed activity of constructing a regular pentagon: "If I don't understand this construction, as far as I'm concerned it doesn't even begin to be the construction of a pentagon" (PR §157). But what does the understanding of a rule consist in? Wittgenstein emphasizes that to understand a rule is to *grasp the internal relation* between the rule and its range of possible applications (cf. Lectures 1930–32, p. 56). So in order to be able to follow a rule, we must be able to see the rule and its applications as bound up with each other. But must every act of rule following be accompanied by the grasp of a conceptual connection of this kind? Or does this grasp, once achieved, guarantee that I follow the rule every time I act in accordance with it? In 1930 Wittgenstein argues: "I must recognize each time afresh that this rule may be applied *here*. No act of foresight can absolve me from this act of *insight*" (PR §149). So it appears that in order to follow a rule on a particular occasion, I have to recognize, through an act of insight or intuition, that the action in question belongs to the range of applicability of the rule. The grasp of the internal relation between a rule and its permissible applications is not, therefore, a general prerequisite that one has to meet to qualify as a rule follower; it is, rather, a necessary condition for following the rule on any given occasion.

But an insight or intuition is just the wrong kind of thing to establish *objectively* whether or not our actions qualify as rule following! For one may perceive an internal relation between a rule and her action where there is none, where the rule does not even have application. The fact that the application of a rule is accompanied by an "act of insight" whereby we "recognize [. . .] that this rule may be applied *here*" (PR §149) certainly shows that we take ourselves to be following a rule. But taking oneself to be following a rule should be distinguished from actually doing so. As Wittgenstein put it in a lecture from 1932–1933, "we get into difficulties when we believe ourselves to be following a rule. We must examine to see whether we are" (Lectures 1932–35, p. 32). And this cannot be settled by examining the insights that agents have while applying rules, because the veridicality of these acts of insight is precisely what is in question.

It did not take Wittgenstein long to reject the idea that an "act of insight" is what is distinctive of rule-following actions. In a marginal note to the passage from *Philosophical Remarks* quoted above (a later addition to the original manuscript),[170] he wrote: "Act of *decision*, not *insight*" (PR §149, fn 1). This shift from insights to decisions puts the emphasis on rule-following actions as voluntary actions, as actions that engage the will of the agent. What is required for the application of a rule to a particular case, it is now emphasized, is not an intellectual recognition that the rule applies to that case, but a decision to apply the rule to that case. As Baker and Hacker point out, a natural conclusion that seems to follow from the recognition that there is nothing that can glue together a rule and its applications, is that "pure acts of the will are required. One is tempted to say that a new *decision* is necessary at each application of a rule."[171] But the appeal to an act of decision of the agent as indicative of an internal connection between her action and the rule is no less problematic than the appeal to an act of insight. Here again we find the same problem as before: we still don't have the requisite conceptual space to draw a distinction between taking oneself to be following a rule and actually doing so. Worse yet, the dependence of rule following on acts of decision strongly suggests that such distinction *cannot* be drawn. For if the application of a rule ultimately depends on a sheer decision on the part of the agent, it seems to follow that rule following is something purely subjective and arbitrary. So Wittgenstein's appeal to the agent's decision as criterial for rule following seems to commit him to something akin to a *normative existentialism*.

But how can this be? A radical decisionism of this kind is at odds with Wittgenstein's contractualist view of rules and its emphasis on the commitments that we unavoidably acquire when we use a rule (cf. 4.3). In the early 1930s Wittgenstein often appeals to decisions to describe how rules are laid down (e.g., PR §167 and PG II p. 303), but not to describe how they are applied. And this is just as should be, since "grammatical rules are arbitrary, but their application is *not*" (Lectures 1930–32, p. 58). There is no room for decisions once a rule has been established, for the rule brings with it certain obligations for its users (a contract, so to speak). So the passage added to the *Remarks* (circa 1930–31) is indeed very peculiar. For there

Wittgenstein claims that the application of a rule, and not just its establishment, requires an act of decision (PR §149). How are we to understand this claim?

If a rule brings with it a fixed range of applications, we are not free to decide whether or not a rule has application on a particular occasion; our decisions cannot have the power to make the rule fit our actions. But, of course, we are free to decide on any given occasion whether or not we want to apply *this* rule. This suggests a more charitable interpretation of Wittgenstein's appeal to decisions at §149 of the *Remarks*. The kind of decision that is required for rule following cannot be a decision as to whether or not the rule has application in this particular case. Rather, it must be a decision to subdue one's will to the normative standards of application of the rule. In other words, Wittgenstein's claim that rule-following actions spring from acts of decision should be interpreted as the claim that following a rule requires having the appropriate *intention.*

According to Baker and Hacker's interpretation, the agent's intention to follow a rule is a crucial component of Wittgenstein's mature view of rule following. As they put it: in order to follow a rule one "must understand what the rule requires (permits, etc.) and *intend* to act in conformity with it"; the rule follower "knows that there is a rule, understand it, and *intentionally* moulds his actions to it."[172] Around 1930–31 Wittgenstein did consider the agent's intention to act in accordance with the rule as the *surplus* that rule-following actions exhibit over rule-conforming actions. But, *pace* Baker and Hacker, this account of the distinction between rule-following and rule-conforming actions does not survive in Wittgenstein's later view.[173] In a lecture from 1933–34 he already attacked the idea that what characterizes rule following is having a certain intention. "How do you know that you are playing chess and not draughts?" (Lectures 1932–35, p. 49). A natural answer is to say "that whether one is playing chess [. . .] is assured by knowing one's intentions" (Lectures 1932–35, p. 49). But Wittgenstein rejects this answer, arguing that whether or not one is following a rule cannot be decided by any "state of mind" of the individual. Again, it is the veridicality of such a state that is in question. Since the agent can be quite confused about what the rules of chess are, her intention to play chess cannot be what guarantees that she is in fact following the rules of chess, rather than the rules of some other game, or none at all.[174]

In the period of 1932–34 Wittgenstein contends that the *differentia specifica* that distinguishes rule-following from rule-conforming actions cannot be an insight, an intention, or any state of mind of the agent. He argues that for there to be an objective distinction between these two different kinds of actions, there must be something *publicly checkable* that enables us to determine when an action springs from an understanding of a rule and when it does not. As we saw in chapter 3 (cf. 3.3), in *Philosophical Grammar* Wittgenstein argues that the understanding of a rule does not consist in an insight or intuition, but in a practical ability or skill that requires explicit manifestation in actual use. This "discursive" conception of understanding is also defended in the *Blue Book* (from 1933–34; p. 40). So one should expect that during this period Wittgenstein would hold that what determines whether or not someone is following a rule on a particular occasion is what she does before and after that act; for the agent's correct application of the rule over time is the only warrant we have for attributing a mastery of the rule to her. However, Wittgenstein argues that the distinction between rule-following and rule-conforming behavior cannot be drawn by appealing to the behavioral regularities of the agent (cf. PG §3, §39, §43; and BLB p. 14). Wittgenstein's thought seems to be that although the correct use of a rule over time is our only criterion for the ascription of understanding of the rule to an agent, it is not a *sufficient* criterion to determine whether the agent is actually following the rule on any particular occasion. Remember that for an action to qualify as rule following, there must be an *internal* relation between what the agent does and the rule. And to say that when I follow a rule the relation between my action and the rule is mediated by an actual history of use would be to interpose an intermediary between my action and the rule, thus externalizing an internal relation. On Wittgenstein's view, to think of a regularity of use as that which forges the link between an action and a rule would be to let something empirical and contingent be the glue of an internal relation. This is the rationale behind his arguments against the normative significance of learning histories, which I will discuss in the next section.

So how do we know when an internal relation between a rule and our actions obtains? In *Philosophical Grammar* and the *Blue Book* Wittgenstein argues that an action qualifies as rule following only when a rule is *explicitly* "involved" in its production, that is, when the action involves the *explicit* use of "a rule (a table, a chart, or some such thing)" (BLB p. 11). Consider the following example that Wittgenstein examines in the *Blue Book*: the use of the rule of squaring x/x^2. When can my manipulation of numerical figures be properly considered as squaring? If I wrote down the series "1, 2, 3, 4" and then "1, 4, 9, 16" underneath, "what I wrote is in accordance with the general rule of squaring; but it obviously is also in accordance with any number of other rules" (BLB p. 13). So what else does my action need to exhibit, beyond this accord, in order to be considered an application of the rule of squaring? Wittgenstein answers: "Supposing, on the other hand, in order to get to my results I had written down what you may call 'the rule of squaring', say algebraically. In this case this rule was involved in a sense in which no other rule was" (BLB p. 13). So the criterion for rule following that Wittgenstein arrives at is the following: a rule is "involved" in the production of an action only when the rule is *formulated* in the course of the action. As he puts it: "We shall say that the rule is *involved* in the understanding, obeying, etc., if, as I should like to express it, the symbol of the rule forms part of the calculation" (BLB p. 13). In *Philosophical Grammar* Wittgenstein also appeals to rule-formulations to distinguish between rule-following and rule-conforming behavior. He argues that there is rule following only when the rules "enter into the conduct of the game itself," when the players "use the rules by looking up in each particular case what is to be done" (PG §43).

Given Wittgenstein's critique of regulism (cf. 4.2), it seems paradoxical that he would arrive at this view of rule following. For, indeed, the view that we follow rules only when our actions are accompanied by rule formulations is a radical version of the regulist paradigm of normativity. But when we consider how Wittgenstein arrived at this view, it is not so surprising (though still paradoxical) that he felt forced to make this regulist move. Wittgenstein was engaged in a misguided search for the characteristic mark of our rule-following actions. He was searching for something *within* the act of following a rule that could guarantee the internal relation between this act and the rule. And since "an internal relation cannot be there unless both its terms are" (Lectures 1930–32 p. 31), the presence of a rule formulation seems to be the only fact that can guarantee that an internal relation obtains. But this regulist move is highly problematic and it introduces important tensions in Wittgenstein's view of rules.

In the first place, the regulist criterion that Wittgenstein defends in *Philosophical Grammar* and the *Blue Book* results in a very restrictive view of rule following. As Wittgenstein himself recognizes, "primitive games are played without their rules being codified, and even without a single rule being formulated" (PG §26; cf. also BLB p. 25). But, according to Wittgenstein's regulist criterion, these primitive, unsophisticated normative activities would not count as genuine instances of rule following. On the other hand, according to this criterion, the behavior of the masters of a rule-governed activity who no longer need to make explicit use of rule formulations (algebraic formulas, tables, charts, diagrams, etc.) would appear as rule-conforming behavior.[175] So the upshot of the regulist criterion that Wittgenstein is forced to adopt is that rule following becomes a very rare phenomenon and loses most of its interest. This may have appeared to Wittgenstein as a welcome result in the *Blue Book*, where he starts to criticize the idea that the use of language should be conceived as operating a calculus of rules (cf. esp. p. 25). However, as we shall see later, although in 1933–34 Wittgenstein tries to place some strictures on intellectualist views of normativity that make rule following ubiquitous, he does not yet articulate an alternative, nonregulist account of the norms that govern the use of language.

In the second place, and more importantly, the thesis that rule-following actions require the explicit formulation of a rule is untenable in the light of Wittgenstein's own criticisms of regulism. If the problem is that an act that accords with a rule "is also in accordance with any number of other rules" (BLB p. 13), and we need an internal relation between the act and the rule, the presence of a rule formulation will not help to establish this relation *unless* the rule formulation uniquely picks out a particular rule. But, as we saw, Wittgenstein's arguments against regulism show that rule formulations do not have the power to do that. A rule formulation does not single out a unique rule until it is given a definite range of possible applications. So we haven't got any closer to an internal relation between a rule and its application when an action is supplemented with a rule formulation. The question "What rule is this action an instance of?" is not answered, but simply supplemented with the question "What range of applicability corresponds to this rule-formulation?" And we cannot answer these questions as long as the rule formulation and the action in question are considered in isolation. One may reply that the presence of a rule formulation at least indicates that a rule is being followed, even if it leaves underdetermined what rule exactly is being followed. But this too is a regulist mistake. For, taken by itself, independently of any practice of rule application, what is usually called the formulation of a rule is just an inscription. And writing down an inscription cannot guarantee that one is following a rule, any more than having an intuition or making a decision can. There is rule following only when there are standards of correctness for the application of a rule. And, indeed, an isolated rule formulation and a single application that (supposedly) accords with it are not enough to draw a distinction between the correct and incorrect applications of a rule.

The very restrictive, regulist view of rule following that Wittgenstein espouses in *Philosophical Grammar* and the *Blue Book* is the product of a misguided attempt to find what is constitutive of rule following in isolated actions. Wittgenstein emphasizes that a rule cannot "act at a distance" (PG §39; BLB p. 14), but he seems to assume that it can act in contact ("It acts only by being applied"; PG §39). Accordingly, he set out to investigate how this *contact* is produced: through insights, decisions, or rule formulations. The failure of this investigation led him to a radical rethinking of what is involved in rule following. In the late 1930s he came to realize that rules do not "act" at all, neither at a distance nor in contact; that the normative efficacy of a rule derives from its use in "a certain practice" (LFM p. 237). Once this is recognized, it is clear that in order to determine whether or not a given action is an instance of rule following, we cannot consider that action in isolation, we need to place that action in a wider *context*. It is not a special feature of the action or the agent who performs it that makes the difference, but the *context* in which the action is carried out. Whether in a particular case acting in accord with a rule qualifies as rule following depends on whether the action takes place in the appropriate surroundings, that is, on whether the action is part of a *practice*. As Wittgenstein put it (circa 1943–1944): "What, in a complicated surrounding, we call 'following a rule' we should certainly not call that if it stood in isolation" (RFM VI §33).

Of course, when actions are considered in the context of rule-governed practices, the use of a rule formulation can be a reliable indicator that the agent is following a rule. But there is nothing special about the use of a rule formulation. There can be other contextual hints that can tell us whether an action can be considered the application of a rule, hints not necessarily confined to the immediate context in which the action takes place. These contextual hints encompass also the agent's past and future actions, including the instruction she received and the reasons she can cite for her action when challenged, for these too can help us to locate a particular action within a rule-following practice. However, in the early 1930s Wittgenstein argues that the normative significance of an action cannot derive from what the agent does before or after the action is carried out. Of particular interest are Wittgenstein's arguments for the thesis that training processes are devoid of normative significance. To the examination of these arguments I now turn.

5.2. The Irrelevance of Learning: Reasons and Causes

According to Wittgenstein's view in the early 1930s, being trained into a rule stimulates the grasp of the internal relation between rule and application, but once the training is completed it becomes "mere history."[176] Wittgenstein repeatedly emphasizes that the training we have received in following a rule cannot be what determines our subsequent rule following. Indeed, having received the appropriate training in the use of a rule is not a *sufficient* condition for attributing rule following to an agent every time that her actions can be deemed correct (or incorrect) according to the rule. But Wittgenstein's claim is not just that the learning processes that agents undergo give us only insufficient criteria for their rule following, criteria that leave some room for indeterminacy. His claim is, rather, that the training we receive in rule-governed practices is *irrelevant* to our subsequent rule following: when we learn something, "the way in which we learn it is irrelevant to our future use and understanding of it. [. . .] It is a matter of purely historical interest" (Lectures 1930-1932, p. 116). Wittgenstein emphasizes that in rule following the only rules that "interest us" are those that are explicitly "involved" in our actions. And when a rule is "involved" in an action, we do not need to look beyond the action itself to see its internal connection with the rule. In particular, we do not need to look back at the training the agent received to establish a connection between her action and the rule: "The rule which has been taught and is subsequently applied interests us only so far as it is involved in the application" (BLB p. 14). On the other hand, when no rule is explicitly "involved" in an action, we can only establish a *hypothetical* relation between the action and a rule that the agent was taught, for the training that the agent received is something purely external to her present action.[177] According to Wittgenstein, the external and hypothetical relation between the training we received and our subsequent actions cannot explain the normativity of rule following: "Teaching as the hypothetical history of our subsequent actions (understanding, obeying, estimating a length, etc.) drops out of our considerations" (BLB p. 14).

In the early 1930s Wittgenstein argues that to make rule following depend on the learning histories of rule followers involves a *category mistake*: a conceptual "confusion between 'reason' and 'cause'" (PG §61; cf. also BLB p. 15, and Lectures 1932–35, p. 28). He remarks that when we explain someone's actions by citing a rule, saying that she did so and so *because* of such and such rule, the statement that the "because" introduces is ambiguous: it can be either "a statement of the cause" or "of the reason" (PG §61 and BLB p. 15). But it is only when a rule is cited as a *reason* for one's action that there is a *normative* relation between the rule and the action. When rules function as reasons for one's actions, they *define* what one does (e.g., playing chess, adding, etc.). By contrast, the rules that function as causes have only an empirical and contingent relation with what one does. Wittgenstein argues that the rules that belong to our learning history bear an external relation to our present actions, for they function as the *causes* of our behavior and a cause is not contained in its effect: "The way in which language was learnt is not *contained* in its use. (Any more than the cause is contained in the effect.)" (PG §39). And this is why "the *process* of learning does not matter" (Lectures 1930–32, p. 54); only the *product* (the rule we learn) does (cf. BLB p. 11). "The rule we learnt which makes us now behave in such and such a way is of no interest to us considered as the cause or history behind our present behaviour" (PG §43).

The core of Wittgenstein's critique of learning-based accounts of rule following is that normativity can find no place in the realm of causes. According to Wittgenstein, an account of rule following in terms of learning histories can only produce behavioral hypotheses based on causal considerations, such as "the hypothesis that the two people who sit at the chess board will behave (move) in such and such a manner" (PG §43). He contends that a learning-based account of rule following leads to a causal-mechanistic view of language that is unable to accommodate the normative aspects of language use. On this view, the connection between symbolic rules and our verbal behavior is supposed to be established through the teaching of language by means of certain mechanisms, such as "the mechanism of association" (PG §33). Against this view Wittgenstein argues that there is a normative relation between grammatical rules and our use of language, not a "mechanical, electrical, [or] psychological" one (PG §56). So, he concludes, "hypotheses about learning and using language and causal connections don't interest us" (PG §74); "causal connections in the mechanism of language are things that I don't scruple to *invent*" (PG §139).

Wittgenstein's master argument against learning-based accounts of normativity is first given in *Philosophical Remarks* (esp. at §23) and later expounded in *Philosophical Grammar* (esp. at §33). In the *Remarks* he offers an *argument by dilemma* to show that the rule-governed use of language cannot be explained in terms of causal mechanisms set up by the teaching of language. The dilemma for causal accounts arises from the following question: "If when a language is first learnt, speech, as it were, is connected up to action—i.e. the levers to the machine—then the question arises, can these connections possibly break down?" (PR §23). On the one hand, if these causal connections *cannot break down*, "then I have to accept any action as the right one" (PR §23). There would be no room for mistakes in my verbal behavior if everything I say or write were causally determined by the mechanisms set up by the teaching of language. And of course when we cannot draw a distinction between correct and incorrect, our behavior lacks a normative dimension. On the other hand, if the defender of a causal account answers that the mechanisms that cause our verbal behavior *can break down*, we obtain the other horn of the dilemma: "What criterion have I for their having broken down?" (PR §23). Wittgenstein's point seems to be that we cannot reduce the normative distinction between correct and incorrect to the distinction between the proper functioning and the malfunctioning of causal mechanisms, for the latter distinction in turn requires normative criteria that cannot be obtained from the examination of the workings of causal mechanisms. He elaborates on this point in the lectures when he considers the analogy between our verbal behavior and the mechanical behavior of a pianola (Lectures 1930–32 pp. 39–40). He argues that "the pianola may go wrong," but whether or not the pianola is functioning properly cannot be determined simply by examining how its mechanism is (and has been) working: "There is nothing in the machine itself that can be right or wrong. The machine goes as it goes [and] never commits itself" (Lectures 1930–32, p. 40). This is the crucial point that

Wittgenstein derives from his discussion of the mechanical behavior of a pianola (cf. also PG §33 and BRB pp. 118–19): the brute force of causal mechanisms can only produce conformity with rules, but not rule following.[178] There is genuine rule following only when an agent is guided by rules, and being guided by rules contrasts sharply with being "mechanically led," as the movements of the hammers of a pianola are led by the pattern of holes on the pianola roll (Lectures 1930–32, p. 39).

So Wittgenstein concludes that the process of learning lacks normative significance. The causal relations between our actions and the training we have received can only explain how, as a matter of empirical fact, we come to do things in a certain way, but not how, in the light of standards of correctness, we *ought* to do things that way. We cannot deduce how a mechanism ought to function from how it functions (or has been functioning). We cannot derive an 'ought' from an 'is'. This is also Wittgenstein's main objection against *dispositionalist* accounts of rule following. For Wittgenstein, dispositionalism is just one version of the misguided attempt to explain rule following in terms of causal mechanisms fixed by training processes. He emphasizes that dispositions are "static" mechanisms that we postulate to explain the etiology of our behavior (Lectures 1932–35, p. 83): "A disposition is thought of as something always there from which behavior follows. It is analogous to the structure of a machine and its behavior." (Lectures 1932–35, p. 91). Wittgenstein's objection is that our dispositions may determine what we do, but they cannot instruct us in what we *ought* to do. This is the point that Kripke elaborates in his critique of dispositionalist accounts of meaning and rule following.[179]

Kripke argues that "almost all objections to the dispositional account boils down to this one": that a disposition does not qualify as "a candidate for a 'fact' that determines" the meaning of my words and the rules that I follow, for "it fails to satisfy the basic condition on such a candidate"; namely, "that it should *tell* me what I ought to do in each new instance."[180] That is, the problem is that behavioral dispositions cannot provide normative guidance. If the meaning of a rule for a given subject consists in her dispositions to use that rule, then *whatever* she does with the rule will be an actualization of those dispositions, and therefore it would have to be regarded as in perfect accordance with the rule that she is following. Therefore, Kripke concludes, in a dispositionalist account there is no room for mistakes.[181] The upshot of Kripke's discussion is that a subject's possession of a disposition to act in a certain way is not sufficient for our attribution of normative (rule following) behavior to her: for example, to produce certain sounds because one is inclined to do so is not the same as speaking; to write certain squiggles after the equals sign because one is so disposed is not to carry out a mathematical operation. The import of saying that someone is following the rules of addition is not that she *will* or *would* answer "125" to the problem "68 + 57 = ?" but rather that she *ought* to give that answer.

Wittgenstein's arguments against causal-mechanistic accounts of rule following and Kripke's arguments against dispositionalism converge on a point of quite general significance: they cast doubts on the very possibility of *naturalizing normativity*. In causal accounts of language and rule following, Wittgenstein remarks, the accord between rules and actions is treated as "a natural phenomenon" (Lectures 1932–35, p. 85). But, for Wittgenstein, this involves a mistake, for what accords with a rule is the product of convention, not of nature (cf. esp. PG §138). The assimilation of symbolic conventions to facts of nature leads to the vain attempt to reduce the normative and necessary to the factual. Wittgenstein emphasizes that the correctness of the use of a word cannot be settled by means of an empirical investigation, for in such investigation "we are in the realm of hypotheses, about effects and causes, and not in the realm of the 'must'" (Lectures 1932–35, p. 85). Thus he contends that the idea that psychology can explain the normative aspects of language use involves a deep misunderstanding: "We are mixing up two different things, a process which happens in our minds or brains, whose causes and effects can be studied by psychological methods as in other sciences, and certain rules which we lay down" (Lectures 1932–35, p. 85).

On Wittgenstein's view, our rule-following actions should not be regarded as the product of causal determinations, for we can only appreciate the normative aspects of our actions when we place them in the *autonomous space of reasons*. The normative power of a rule resides in the fact that it can be used as a reason for acting in a certain way, whether or not one is causally predisposed to act in that way. It is this essential connection between rules and reasons for action that, according to Wittgenstein, makes rule-following behavior a kind of intentional behavior that cannot be naturalized in causal terms. In order to capture this essential connection that Wittgenstein emphasizes, Baker and Hacker propose the following "principle":

> X's Øing counts as his following the rule R only if R is his *reason* or part of his reason for Øing. Part of his *justification* for Øing must involve reference to the fact that Øing accords with R. It is not enough to support the statement that X is following R in Øing to observe that X has previously received instruction including formulations of R or that prior exposure to R plays a role in the causal explanation of his Øing.[182]

But this principle doesn't do justice to Wittgenstein's view. For, according to Wittgenstein, it is not the case that an agent is following a rule every time she invokes the rule as the *reason* for what she does. He distinguishes two ways in which rules can be cited as reasons for our actions: "Giving a reason for something one did or said means showing a *way* which leads to this action. In some cases it means telling the way which one has gone oneself; in others it means describing a way which leads there and is in accordance with certain accepted rules" (BLB p. 14). In the latter cases we appeal to rules to give "a justification *post hoc*" of our actions; that is, we justify our actions by their *conformity* with certain rules, whether or not we carried out those actions in the light of those rules. But Wittgenstein argues that an action does not qualify as an instance of rule following simply because the agent can cite rules for its justification after the fact: "That just shows that in certain circumstances he can enunciate the rules, not that he makes explicit use of them while playing" (PG §43). One's capacity to cite (or "recite") rules in support of one's actions is just another kind of "disposition," another "static mechanism," which bears only a hypothetical relation to one's actions: "It is a hypothesis that he will if asked recite a list of rules; if a disposition or capacity for this is postulated in him, it is a psychological disposition analogous to a physiological one" (PG §43). Neither rules that precede my action (in training), nor those that can be called for after it (in justifications 'post hoc'), are rules contained in my action, rules that guide and structure my behavior (remember: rules cannot "act at a distance"; BLB p. 14).

Wittgenstein emphasizes that there is rule following only when rules function as *guiding reasons or motives* of our actions: that is, when the rule cited as the reason for one's action refers, not just to one possible path that leads to one's action, but to the path "which one has gone oneself" (BLB p. 14). Only when rules function as reasons in this sense can they enter into *direct contact* with our actions: "The reason may be nothing more than just the one he gives when asked. Again, a reason may be the way one arrives at a conclusion, e.g., when one multiplies 13 x 25. [. . .] The reason here might be said to be *included in the act* he performs. A cause could not be included in this sense" (Lectures 1932–35, p. 5; my emphasis). While causes and justificatory reasons post hoc are external to our behavior, guiding reasons or motives are internally related to our actions: they *define* the kinds of actions they are. And this internal relation between an action and its motive, Wittgenstein emphasizes, is utterly independent of the causal processes that determine our behavior. Motives should not be confused with causes;[183] they belong to the autonomous space of reasons.

Wittgenstein's arguments against the significance of learning for rule following relies heavily on this radical divide between reasons and causes. Given that reasons and causes belong to two different realms, since rule-following actions belong to the realm of reasons and learning processes to the realm of causes, it follows that learning cannot be but irrelevant for rule following. This is the gist of the arguments that Wittgenstein uses in the early 1930s to establish that learning processes are devoid of normative significance. It is important to notice that these arguments rest on two *substantive assumptions*: first, they assume that there is a radical dichotomy between actions done for reasons and behavior determined by causes; and, second, they assume a particular (and, in fact, very restrictive) view of learning: learning as a purely causal process that proceeds by "building up psychical mechanisms" (BLB p. 12). The validity of Wittgenstein's arguments against the normative significance of learning is tantamount to the validity of these assumptions. But these assumptions are highly questionable. As we shall see in the next chapter, Wittgenstein himself will reject them in his later writings. To cast doubts on these assumptions now, I will draw on the developmental approach to normative behavior articulated by Stephen Toulmin, which is very congenial with Wittgenstein's later view.

In the first place, the distinction between deliberate acts carried out in the light of reasons and automatic behavior blindly determined by causes does not constitute an exhaustive typification of human action. So it is not fair play to establish a radical dichotomy between these two different kinds of actions, presenting them as mutually exclusive alternatives and thus inviting the identification of rule-following behavior with the former. As Toulmin points out, there seems to be "a scale" running from deliberate actions clearly done for reasons to uncontrolled, blind, and instinctual behavior: a gradual progression "passing from carefully thought-out actions, through instrumental and ritual acts, to inattentive or compulsive ones, and finally to pure reflexes."[184] When this progression is appreciated, new questions arise: How do we advance in this continuum? How do we move from pure causal determinations to reasons and standards of correctness? How does our behavior become normatively structured?

Notice that the important conceptual difference between causally determined, mechanical behavior and normatively structured, intentional behavior is not undermined by placing these two different kinds of behavior in a continuum: we have a genuine distinction here, but not an absolute one—just as there is a genuine difference between a jungle and a garden, although "the contrast between a jungle and a garden is not an *absolute* one."[185] Insofar as there is a genuine distinction between actions done for reasons and behavior triggered by causes, it is a mistake to reduce one to the other; for example, to explain normative behavior in terms of causal mechanisms alone, as a crude naturalism may try to do. But insofar as this distinction is not absolute but gradual, it is also a mistake to introduce a radical divide between what is done in the light of standards of correctness and what is done automatically or mechanically,[186] keeping reasons and causes in two completely independent realms, as if they constituted autonomous spheres that cannot overlap. It is this latter mistake that Wittgenstein made. In the early 1930s he fell victim of a radical construal of the distinction between reasons and causes, which distorts their relation and their involvement in actions.[187]

In the second place, it may be a mistake to assume that the only possible relation between the training processes through which we acquire rules and our subsequent use of those rules is a causal one. That the process of learning can *only* serve to fix causal mechanisms is an unwarranted assumption. If anything, we should assume the opposite. For when we consider how the contrast between causally determined behavior and normatively structured actions comes progressively to be established in the course of the individual's lifetime, learning processes seem to play a crucial role. As Toulmin emphasizes, while those acts that can be performed correctly or incorrectly are typically actions that involve the skillful application of "some learned procedure, ritual or technique,"[188] those acts which lack a normative dimension are typically "unlearned responses which operate autonomically, regardless of all learned procedures and techniques."[189] Toulmin offers convincing examples of how our most automatic and primitive behavior can be radically transformed through simple learning processes so that it becomes structured by norms and subject to standards of correctness.[190] And there is indeed ample empirical evidence suggesting that the dividing line between normative behavior and causally determined behavior runs roughly between the learned and the unlearned.[191]

However, appreciating the normative significance of learning requires going beyond a purely behavioristic conception of the process of learning: it requires viewing learning as a process of *enculturation*, of training into normative practices. As we shall see in the next section, in the mid 1930s Wittgenstein already started to appreciate the normative significance of learning—viewing it not merely as a causal process but as a process that structures the learner's behavior according to norms.

5.3. From Possible Applications to Actual Uses

Since an action qualifies as the application of a rule only when there is an *internal* relation between rule and application, we must be able to locate rule-following actions within the fixed range of grammatical possibilities licensed by rules without appealing to external, empirical factors. In order to situate an act of rule following in the *autonomous* space of reasons, we have to consider the act in question, not against the background of how things are done in practice but against the background of how things *can* be done within a grammatical framework or calculus of rules. This was

Wittgenstein's view in the early 1930s. But he soon learned that the internal relation between a particular action and a range of free-floating grammatical possibilities was harder to pin down than he had originally thought. As we saw (cf. 5.1), the only criteria for the presence of an internal relation that he could come up with were self-undermining subjective criteria (the insights or decisions of the agent), and a public criteron (the presence of a rule formulation), which was too thin to do the job. Consequently, Wittgenstein started to look for a broader context in which rule-following actions could be elucidated. In the mid 1930s he emphasized that the normative background required for rule following cannot consist in disembodied *possibilia*, that it must include typical circumstances of applications and the shared reactions of a community of rule followers. Arguing that the permissible applications of a rule cannot be determined independently of what we actually do with it, Wittgenstein connected the applicability of a rule with its actual use. This link will grow so strong that the priority that he initially attributed to possible applications over actual uses will be reversed, and what *can* be done according to rules will come to be seen as the product of our *actual* and *changing* practices of application.

In a lecture from 1935 Wittgenstein contends that "a distinction is to be made between *use* and *application*" (Lectures 1932–35, p. 142). He suggests that we should use the term "application" to refer to the possible ways in which a rule can be employed, and reserve the term "use" for the actual employment of the rule in practice. While in the early 1930s it was the notion of "application" that dominated Wittgenstein's discussions of rule following, in the mid 1930s he starts to turn his attention toward actual uses. The way in which a symbolic rule "meshes with our life," which was previously considered as a matter of mere empirical interest (PG §29), now acquires a new significance: "Whether an application has a use in practice depends on the kind of life we lead" (Lectures 1932–35, p. 142). With these considerations Wittgenstein starts to depart from the view of language as an *autonomous* calculus of rules that he had defended in the early 1930s. In what follows I will examine the shift from a conventionalist view of language and its rules to a practice-based view of normativity that starts to take place in Wittgenstein's writings and lectures in the mid 1930s. First, I will discuss the strictures that he places on the calculus view of language in the *Blue Book*. These strictures, however, do not yet give a new direction to Wittgenstein's rule-following considerations. The *Blue Book* (perhaps the most transitional of Wittgenstein's works) contains a battery of negative arguments against different views of language and its rules, but scarce glimpses of a possible alternative. A different picture of language and rule following starts to emerge in the collection of examples and thought experiments that Wittgenstein analyzes in the *Brown Book* and the lectures from 1934–35.

In the *Blue Book* Wittgenstein rejects the idea that the rules that govern the use of language must have a *unitary core*. He emphasizes that the idea that there must be something underlying the entire use of a rule, a "common element in all its applications," "has shackled philosophical investigation" (BLB p. 19). He argues that when we look at the repertoire of actual uses of a word we find many different cases with "many common features overlapping," and these cases "form a family; they have family likenesses which are not clearly defined" (BLB p. 20).[192] According to Wittgenstein, the idea that the use of a word must have definite limits derives from "our craving for generality" (BLB p. 17), which leads us to seek after a synoptic overview of language. But the actual use of language cannot be encapsulated in clear-cut definitions and exact rules. Wittgenstein now argues that the applicability of symbolic rules in actual practice has an open-ended texture: there are clear cases in which the rule does or does not have application and cases in which the application of the rule is quite undetermined. Thus he rejects the Sharp Boundary Requirement (cf. 4.1–4.2). He emphasizes that what underlies the rule-governed use of a word cannot be a definition or anything akin to a definition: "If [. . .] you wish to give a definition [. . .], *to draw a sharp boundary*, then you are free to draw it as you like; and this boundary will never entirely coincide with the *actual* usage, as this usage has *no sharp boundary*" (BLB p. 19; my emphasis).

As we saw in chapter 3 (cf. 3.3), in *Philosophical Grammar* Wittgenstein had already noticed that there is a sharp contrast between the "constantly fluctuating" use of language and the "fixed" system of rules that "we set over against" it (PG §36). However, he did not use this contrast to cast doubts on the calculus view of language. He argued that viewing language as a calculus of rules involves *idealizations*, but idealizations that are necessary in order to account for the normative aspects of language use: we have to go beyond the actual use of language because this fluctuating use cannot provide standards of correctness; the use of language has to be "measured" according to "definite rules" (PG §36). In the *Blue Book*, however, the usefulness of these idealizations is called into question. Wittgenstein emphasizes that they play no role in the actual use of language (they are *idle wheels*); and that far from providing a genuine insight into the normativity of language use, they actually distort it. Thus he remarks that viewing language as "a calculus proceeding according to exact rules [. . .] is a very one-sided way of looking at language," for "in practice we very rarely use language as such a calculus," "in general we don't use language according to strict rules" (BLB p. 25). And to suppose that these rules *must*, nonetheless, be there underlying our use of language would be to attribute to rules a privileged status that they do not have in our practices, clinging to an unwarranted philosophical picture of language: it "would be like supposing that whenever children play with a ball they play a game according to strict rules" (BLB p. 25).

In the *Blue Book* Wittgenstein emphasizes that there are "primitive" uses of language that are not properly described as calculating according to precise rules; namely, those "with which a child begins to make use of words" (BLB p. 17; cf. also Lectures 1932–35, pp. 77ff, esp. p. 81). He refers to these "primitive forms of language or primitive languages" as "language games" (BLB p. 17). This marks an important evolution in Wittgenstein's use of the expression "language game," which was initially introduced (around 1932) as a synonym of "calculus" (cf. PG §26). A language game is no longer conceived as a circumscribed region of language that can be described by means of a system of rules. Wittgenstein now thinks that our linguistic activities are not as highly regimented as he had previously supposed. He emphasizes that what characterizes a language game is not an underlying system of rules but a certain array of actions and reactions: "When we look at such simple forms of language [. . .] we see activities, reactions, which are clear-cut and transparent" (BLB p. 17). A system of rules can be found only in very sophisticated uses of language governed by explicit regulations (e.g., in the construction of proofs in mathematics). It is only in sophisticated activities of this kind that the use of a sentence can be construed as taking a step in a calculus (cf. BLB p. 42). And even here, Wittgenstein remarks, this model can be dangerous and it must be used with caution, for it can easily lead to mystifications: "We are *tempted* to imagine this calculus, as it were, as a *permanent background* to every sentence which we say" (BLB p. 42; my emphasis). Wittgenstein now argues that we cannot make sense of the idea that when we use a sign a "whole calculus must be present at the same time" (BLB p. 42).

Wittgenstein's arguments in the *Blue Book* constitute indeed an important step in the evolution of his thought, but one that is mainly *negative*. These arguments are warnings that are supposed to put us on our guard against philosophical mistakes that we are "tempted" to make. In order to eradicate these mistakes Wittgenstein emphasizes that we should pay attention to how language is used in our *actual* practices (cf. esp. BLB p. 56). He reminds us of the strong *diversity* that we find in the actual uses of language and, in particular, of the contrast between primitive language games and more sophisticated ones. But he gives us no hint as to why we should think of all these different linguistic activities as anything more than mere behavioral regularities. In fact, the only criterion he offers to distinguish a linguistic practice regulated by norms from mere noise making is the explicit use of rule formulations (cf. BLB p. 13), which can be found only in sophisticated language games. So in the *Blue Book* Wittgenstein leaves us in the lurch as to where the normativity of our most primitive uses of language resides. In the *Brown Book*, however, he elucidates the normativity of linguistic activities of all kinds: from very simple games such as calling out names and fetching objects (BRB p. 83), to sophisticated ones such as calculating according to the formula "$a_n = n^2 + n-1$" (BRB p. 112).

In all the different language games that Wittgenstein examines in the *Brown Book* he underscores that a normative activity presupposes certain characteristic surroundings, a taken-for-granted *background* (cf. e.g., pp. 113–15). And this background is no longer thought to consist in an autonomous calculus of rules and their *possible* applications, but in our *actual* practices of use. Wittgenstein includes two distinct elements as essential ingredients of the background against which language games are played: the characteristic *circumstances* in which these games are carried out and the *natural reactions* that the players share. On the one had, Wittgenstein emphasizes that our linguistic activities do not take place in a vacuum, that they are crucially dependent on certain environmental conditions. It is only under particular circumstances, in an environment with certain stable features, that we can identify objects and name them, count them, measure them, and so forth. Wittgenstein remarks that, if need be, we could enumerate some of the typical circumstances in which a language game is played (particularly if alternative surroundings became available). But he argues that it would be a mistake to think that the characteristic surroundings of a language game can be codified in an exhaustive list of conditions that "describes all these circumstances, i.e., the whole situation which is the background of our game" (BRB p. 114).

On the other hand, Wittgenstein also emphasizes that our linguistic activities take place agaisnt the background of natural reactions that we all share. In a language game the players coordinate their behavior in a particular way, and this coordination requires that they share certain responses, that they regard certain courses of action as *natural*. According to Wittgenstein, the natural reactions that one needs to exhibit in order to participate in a language game are of two kinds: *learned* and *unlearned*. By being trained into a linguistic activity we acquire certain spontaneous reactions, that is, we become compelled to do things in a particular way, acting and responding to the actions of others almost automatically. Wittgenstein describes the process of learning that supplies us with these spontaneous reactions as consisting "a) of a training in a limited range of actions, b) of giving the pupil a lead to extend this range, and c) of random exercises and tests" (BRB p. 98). But in order to acquire automatic responses through training, one must be responsive to these drills and tests and be able to imitate the teacher's behavior and follow her lead. Thus Wittgenstein emphasizes that there are certain unlearned reactions that make the process of training possible in the first place:

> [The teacher's] acts of encouragement [. . .] will only be possible if the pupil responds, and responds in a particular way. (BRB pp. 89–90)
>
> When in counting the pupil arrives at the numeral 20, one makes a gesture suggestive of "Go on." [. . .] If a child does not respond to the suggestive gesture, it is separated from the others and treated as a lunatic. (BRB p. 93)
>
> All then depends on whether the child will react to this "inducement." (BRB p. 105)

Wittgenstein argues that without a background of typical circumstances and shared reactions we could draw no distinction between correct and incorrect uses of language in our practices. The normativity of even the most basic linguistic activity cannot be captured in a decontextualized list of symbolic rules, no matter how specific these rules are. Take, for instance, the following language game often discussed by Wittgenstein:[193] a game in which the letters "a," "b," "c," and "d" are used to command people to move in different directions—right, left, up and down, respectively. One may describe this game using a table of rules correlating letters with arrows pointing in different directions: "a = —>"; "b = <—"; etc. In fact, the players themselves might very well codify the norms of their game in this way and use the table as a tool to teach the game to others, or as a way of settling disputes among themselves. But it would be a mistake to think that the table of rules *by itself* can determine what one is supposed to do in this game. In fact, the table *alone* makes utterly indeterminate what counts as a correct move in the game, for the correlations between letters and arrows can be interpreted in many ways; for example, as commanding us to move in "the direction which we should call the opposite of that of the arrow" (BRB, p. 97). However, there is no indeterminacy whatsoever about what one is supposed to do in this simple game. The indeterminacy arises when we disregard the characteristic circumstances in which the game is played and the natural reactions of the players.

Wittgenstein draws two important conclusions from his discussion of this language game. In the first place, he concludes that rules have an essentially situated character. We cannot detach the rules of a game from the background against which the game is actually played, for it is only against this background that rules can have any normative significance at all. In the second place, Wittgenstein concludes that a normative activity does not require the presence of explicit regulations, for there is *nothing* particularly special about rule formulations. We engage in a normative activity whenever our actions can be deemed correct or incorrect against the background of what practitioners actually do, as a matter of course, in those circumstances; and it makes no difference whether or not there are explicit regulations sanctioning those actions. Thus Wittgenstein concludes that we can rightly say that "'A game is played according to a rule' [. . .] even in cases where the rule is neither an instrument of the training nor of the practice of the game" (BRB p. 97).

The notion of "background" that Wittgenstein articulates through his examination of language games in the *Brown Book* brings with it an important change in his view of the *holistic* aspects of language use. From the *Tractatus* to the early 1930s Wittgenstein thought of the background against which a proposition signifies as a "logical space" or "grammatical space" composed of those other propositions to which the proposition in question is inferentially related. Wittgenstein tried out different versions of this inferential holism in the *Tractatus*, *Philosophical Remarks*, and *Philosophical Grammar*, but all these different versions elaborated the same holistic insight; namely, that a proposition acquires sense only when it is embedded in an inferential network of propositions.[194] This kind of inferential holism is what Williams has termed "*homogeneous* holism";[195] that is, the kind of holism in which there is no qualitative difference between the whole and the parts. On this holistic view, what is required in order to make sense of a proposition is "more of the same." Williams has argued that Wittgenstein's later philosophy involves a holism of a different kind, a *heterogeneous* holism. This is the holism that starts to emerge in the mid 1930s when Wittgenstein abandons the calculus view of language. On this holistic view, the context or background required for the rule-governed use of language cannot be assimilated to an inferential network or propositional calculus. In the first place, the context in which an utterance is to be embedded is not an *autonomous* system of signs defined by rules but a practice composed of *actual actions and their surroundings*. In the second place, the context in which the rule-governed use of language takes place is not an *immutable* logical or grammatical space, the sempiternal realm of *possibilia*; it is a context that has an essential *temporal or historical* dimension: the context of our actual and changing practices.

This new holistic view that Wittgenstein starts to develop in the mid 1930s led to a radical transformation of the conventionalist view of normativity that he had defended in the early 1930s. In the first place, Wittgenstein now argues that symbolic conventions *by themselves* cannot determine our rule-governed uses of language: these conventions do not operate autonomously; they need the support of the environment and of the natural reactions of their users. In the second place, Wittgenstein now holds that a convention is not established by stipulation but by an actual practice of use extended over time. In a lecture given at the time of the dictation of the *Brown Book* (Lectures 1932–35, pp. 87–90), he remarks that "a convention [. . .] is one of two things, a rule or a training" (p. 89). Wittgenstein notes that there are indeed conventions that we establish "by saying something in words." But he argues that those symbolic conventions given in a propositional form cannot be primary, for when a convention is "something laid down by a sign," it presupposes the normative use of signs. If the normativity of language use is to be grounded in conventions, there must be conventions of a more primitive kind, conventions not reducible to signs. So Wittgenstein concludes: "By a convention I mean that the use of a sign is in accordance with *language habits or training*. There can be a chain of conventions at the bottom of which is language habit or training to react in certain ways. These latter we do not call conventions, but rather only those which are given by signs. One can say these signs play the role they do because of certain *habitual ways of acting*" (Lectures 1932–35, pp. 89–90; my emphasis).

This view of conventions contrasts sharply with the one offered in *Philosophical Grammar*. There conventions were treated as rule stipulations (cf. e.g. §§81–82); and Wittgenstein explicitly rejected the idea that the conventions that underlie the normative use of language can be established through training processes without formulating rules explicitly. He asked: Can we "speak of a grammar in the case where a language is taught to a person by a mere drill?" (PG §138). And he answered: "It is clear that if I want to use the word 'grammar' here I can do so only in a 'degenerate' sense, because it is only in a degenerate sense that I can speak [. . .] of 'convention'" (PG §138). However, the training processes regarded here as establishing grammatical conventions "only in a degenerate sense" are considered shortly thereafter—around 1934–35—as what always lies "at the bottom" of the rule-governed use of language (Lectures 1932–35, p. 89). In the *Brown Book* Wittgenstein emphasizes that it is through training processes that we are initiated in language games. The process of learning that, even in the *Blue Book* (cf. p. 14), was considered as something of mere empirical interest and devoid of normative significance thus comes to be seen as a prerequisite for rule following.

The emphasis that Wittgenstein starts to place on learning and actual practices of use around 1934–35 marks the abandonment of the so-called thesis of the autonomy of grammar. *Pace* Baker and Hacker, the view of language as "an *autonomous* calculus of rules"[196] informed Wittgestein's thought *only* up to 1933–34. In the mid 1930s Wittgenstein's view starts to move away from a rule-based conventionalism and toward a practice-based view of normativity. In the next chapter I will examine how this move is completed in the late 1930s with the introduction of the notion of "technique" (in RFM I, from 1937–38; and in LFM, from 1939).

6

Normativity in Practice

LEARNING AND TECHNIQUES

With the introduction of the notion of "technique" in the late 1930s the focus of Wittgenstein's rule-following discussions shifts from stipulations and their range of possible applications to actual practices of application and situated contexts of use. This shift brings with it a reversal of the *order of explanation* in Wittgenstein's view of rule following. In the view of the early 1930s the "internal relations" between rules and their applications were regarded as logically prior to any actual practice of application. By contrast, in the late 1930s Wittgenstein emphasizes that the normative relation between rule and application presupposes a regular activity of use. Priority is thus given to actual practices: there can be rule following only when a *technique* of usage has been fixed (cf. LFM p. 95). And "internal relations" become derivative, something forged in and by practices: what we call "internal" is what is taken "as a matter of course" in our practices (cf. RFM I.85).[197]

Wittgenstein's rule-following discussions in the late 1930s underscore that what is thinkable and expressible in language is not fixed once and for all by an overarching *logic* or by the *grammar* of particular propositional systems. According to Wittgenstein's mature view, what is thinkable and expressible in language can only be *contextually* determined: it depends, in each case, on the techniques available in our practices (cf. RFM I.116; LFM p. 69). Thus, with the thesis of the priority of actual practices, Wittgenstein finally does away with the realism about *possibilia* that haunted his view since the *Tractatus* and until the mid 1930s. But at this point another Fregean worry sets in. If, from a Fregean standpoint, the view of the early 1930s was suspicious because of its similarity with formalism, the practice-based account of normativity of the mature view is also suspicious, for it appears to be just another version of *psychologism*. If the pressing challenge for the conventionalism of the intermediate period was to avoid regulism (i.e., the attribution of intrinsic normative force to rule formulations), the central challenge for the pragmatism of the mature view will be to avoid regularism (i.e., the attribution of intrinsic normative force to regularities of use).

Indeed, the attempt to ground the normativity of rules in actual practices of application seems to entail a crude psychologism and regularism; namely, the view that the norms according to which we *ought* to act and talk in rule-governed practices simply *describe* psychological regularities—that is, the regular ways in which, as a matter of *empirical* fact, we do act and talk in those practices. According to this psychologistic view, the necessity involved in rule following (i.e., in how we *must* see things and how we *must* act according to rules) is ultimately reducible to a psychological compulsion enforced by repeated practice.[198] But doesn't this view of normativity rest on a fundamental confusion between what is correct and what we count as such? This is the worry articulated by Frege's critique of psychologism, which plays an important role in Wittgenstein's rule-following discussions from the late 1930s on.

In the next section I try to show how Frege's critique of psychologism sets Wittgenstein's philosophical agenda in the late 1930s. In later sections I characterize the view of normativity of Wittgenstein's later philosophy as a nonpsychologistic pragmatism that preserves the distinction between empirical propositions and normative laws or principles. I will try to show that, far from collapsing the normative and the empirical, Wittgenstein's mature view of rule following provides an account of how a sharp (though always contextual) distinction between the normative and the empirical is instituted in linguistic practices and transmitted through learning processes. As we shall see, in order to avoid a crude psychologism that reduces our normative practices to mere regularities, Wittgenstein will rely heavily on the view of learning as a process of enculturation hinted at in the *Brown Book* and elaborated in later writings.

6.1. Psychologism and "Logical Madness"

In the preface to *Grundgesetze,* Frege criticizes the psychologistic conception of the laws of logic. He contends that logical laws are "not psychological laws of *holding as true*, but laws of *being true*" (BLA xvi). Given that what is true is utterly independent of being recognized as such by anyone, he argues, the laws of truth have an absolute character: they are universal and eternal ("boundary stones set in an eternal foundation"; BLA xvi). The psychologistic logician, however, rejects the universality and eternal validity of the laws of logic and "wants to restrict them to our thought as it is at present." (BLA xvi). According to psychologism, logical laws are empirical generalizations that have only a restricted validity: they are valid only for "the kind of being whose thought is empirically governed by them" (BLA xvi). This view opens the possibility of beings of a different kind who think according to different logical laws: "logical aliens," to borrow Conant's expression.[199] Thus in his critique of psychologism Frege is led to the following thought experiment: "What if beings were even found whose laws of thought flatly contradicted ours and therefore frequently led to contrary results even in practice?" (BLA xvi). If we found such logical aliens, Frege replies, "I would say: here we have *a hitherto unknown kind of madness*" (BLA xvi; my emphasis); whereas, the psychological logician would have to say "Here is a new kind of logic" (my wording). In Frege's eyes this reveals the incapacity of psychologism to account for the normativity of logic. For, according to Frege, anyone who takes seriously the prescriptive character of logic cannot regard the conflict between incompatible logical laws as final:

> Anyone who understands logical laws as prescribing how one should think, as laws of *being true*, not as natural laws of human beings' *holding as true*, will ask: who is right? Whose laws of *holding as true* are in accord with the laws of *being true*? The psychological logician cannot ask this. (BLA xvi)

Psychologism makes room for a plurality of logics and this undermines the normativity of logic. But why? Frege's thought seems to be that the prescriptive character of our logical laws would be lost if it were possible to think according to alternative laws, because then anything we say could, in principle, count as the expression of a thought. Indeed, according to psychologism, all that is required for the linguistic expression of thoughts is the congruity of our words with *some* regularity or pattern in linguistic usage. By treating the laws of logic as empirical generalizations that describe how we think, the psychological logician cannot rule out the fragmentation of logic into a plurality of independent systems of logical laws. But Frege warns us that if logical laws were relativized in this way, logic could not carry out its function, which is to provide *objective* standards for communication and correct inference. He insists that if logic is to retain its normative function, its laws cannot be made dependent on how we think as a matter of fact; they must be conceived as governing "everything thinkable" (cf. FA §14), as setting the "boundary stones" of thought (cf. BLA xvi). For Frege, logical laws define thought, not just for us, not just here and now, but *sub specie aeternitatis*. The fact that the psychological logician must allow for the possibility of logically alien thought is, on Frege's view, a *reductio ad absurdum* of psychologism. According to Frege, there cannot be such a thing as logically alien *thought*, for the primitive laws of logic are *constitutive* of what is thinkable and expressible in language: we could not communicate with someone who rejected, for instance, the law of identity; we would be able to make no sense of his utterances and hence there would be no reason for us to think that they expressed any thoughts.[200] Given their constitutive role, logical laws cannot be relativized to a restricted domain of thought (ours as opposed to other possible ones).

Frege's remarks on logical "madness" constitute an important theme in Wittgenstein's writings and lectures from 1937–39 (RFM I.143–153 and LFM pp. 201–207). In the lectures Wittgenstein introduces this theme in connection with the distinction between logical and psychological propositions. Agreeing with Frege, he remarks that it is a "fact that logical propositions are not psychological propositions" (LFM pp. 201). He then brings up the question raised by Frege in the preface to *Grundgesetze*: "What should we say if we found people who made judgments contrary to our logical propositions?" (LFM p. 202). Should we say that we found a new kind of logic or a new kind of insanity? Wittgenstein does not immediately side with either the psychological logician or Frege. His first reaction to Frege's claim about "a hitherto unknown kind of madness" is to say: "This is queer. We wouldn't call a man mad who denied the law of contradiction—or would we?" (LFM p. 202). At this point Wittgenstein's discussion, both in the *Lectures* and in the *Remarks*, takes an interesting turn: instead of addressing the issue of logically alien thought directly, he tries to make it more specific by discussing a series of thought experiments that are supposed to illustrate what it would be like to encounter such logical aliens. He criticizes Frege for not doing this himself: "He never said what this 'insanity' would really be like" (RFM I.152).

The first thought experiment Wittgenstein discusses is also the most celebrated: *the wood sellers*.[201] He asks us to imagine people who calculate the price of piles of wood by measuring the area they occupy, disregarding completely the height of the piles. This practice cannot be said to consist of random and meaningless exchanges, for its practitioners follow a very definite rule: "The rule is to pay according to the product of length and breadth" (LFM p. 202; cf. also RFM I.149). And yet this practice of wood selling certainly seems incoherent to us, for it is based on an utterly inadequate method of measuring piles of wood and calculating their price, a method that leads to contradictory results unless the height of the piles is maintained fixed. What would we do if we encountered these peculiar wood sellers? Well, we would certainly try to show them that the quantity of wood contained in a pile is not determined by the area covered by the pile, but by its volume or its weight. We would try to *show* them the inadequacy of their current method and *teach* them a method for measuring volume or weight. We would try to convince them that, according to their method, the *same* amount of wood would be priced differently if it is distributed in piles that cover different areas. But how? We could do this not only by means of verbal explanations but also by means of demonstrations, by *doing* things in such a way that the incoherence of their method and the need to refine it are highlighted: "I take a certain pile which they price at three shillings, and make it longer by making it less high" so that "the heap piled differently amounted to £1" (LFM p. 202; cf. also RFM I.150). They may be convinced by this. If so, we would have to conclude that the practice of these height-blind wood sellers was not as alien to ours as we thought, but just a little bit confused. But they may not be convinced. They may fail to see what remains the *same* in the heap of wood after it is piled differently and say: "Well, he's buying more now, so he must pay more" (LFM p. 202).

What should we say about these stubborn wood sellers? Should we declare them logically insane in Frege's sense? Or should we simply say that our methods and standards are not applicable to their practice? No primitive law of logic is directly violated by their practice: they just sell wood by the area (not by volume or by weight), and there is nothing logically repugnant in that. Their method yields contradictory results only when we assume that it is used to price quantities of wood that remain constant however piled. But what they mean by "the amount of wood contained in a pile" just is the product of the length and the breadth of the pile. So it seems that, as Wittgenstein remarks, we should conclude: "they simply do not mean the same by 'a lot of wood' and 'a little wood' as we do" (RFM I.150). We may still think that there is something wrong with their practice, for they are selling wood according to an absurd method that allows one to buy as *much* wood (by our standards) as one can pile up in a surface worth one's money. "We might call this a kind of logical madness. But there is nothing wrong with giving wood away. So what is wrong with this? We might say, 'This is how they do it'" (LFM p. 202). This seems to put Wittgenstein in agreement with the psychological logician, for it suggests that our normative standards and those of the wood sellers are simply different; they do not touch. But this agreement is only apparent. Saying "They mean something different" or "This is how they do it" is simply to notice a *conceptual* gap between our practice and theirs. But the recognition of this conceptual difference is not the end of the story; rather, it is just the beginning. The point of the "wood sellers thought experiment" is not to defend the point of view of the psychological logician against Frege, but to change the terms of the dispute.

To begin with, Wittgenstein's imaginary case does not even contain the necessary elements to enable him to adjudicate in the dispute between Frege and the psychological logician. The crucial difference between the practice of the wood sellers and ours is not a difference in logic but a difference in the concepts involved. So it is not clear that Frege should have any problem with Wittgenstein's wood sellers and that he should feel inclined to call them mad. For as long as the primitive laws of logic are not violated by their practice, as long as these laws are applicable to their concepts (never mind how peculiar they are), Frege should regard them as fine-thinking and calculating beings, as beings we could (in principle) communicate with and understand. They just have different concepts! For this reason too, the psychological logician could not claim to have found a different logic in their practice. Neither logical madness nor a different logic. So what is the point of this thought experiment? Is Wittgenstein simply changing the topic? No, the topic remains the same (though it is generalized a bit): the question is still whether there are principles (logical *or otherwise*) that are constitutive of what we call "thinking," "speaking," "inferring," or "calculating" (cf. LFM p. 203; RFM I.96), whether there are limits (logical *or otherwise*) to the intelligibility of linguistic practices. Wittgenstein sets out to investigate how we could run up against these limits, that is, what it would be like to encounter a linguistic practice we cannot understand. In this investigation he finds practices (such as that of the wood sellers) that seem unintelligible to us, but what renders them unintelligible is not (strictly speaking) their different logics but the different *techniques* employed in these practices, the different ways of *doing* things in which these practices consist (cf. esp. RFM I.143).

As Wittgenstein puts it, the crucial question that the thought experiment of the wood sellers raises is: "How do we know that a phenomenon which we observe when we are observing human beings is what we ought to call a language? or what we should call calculating?" (LFM p. 203). Well, how do we know? Wittgenstein remarks that if we saw people making "articulated noises" at each other, we would be inclined to say they are talking, and if we saw people making "marks" on a piece of paper in an orderly fashion, we would be inclined to say they are calculating. In order to render their behavior intelligible to us, we would regard these noise- and mark-making people as speakers and calculators, and we would subject their behavior to our normative standards; that is, we would take them into our practices. We would form certain *normative expectations* about what they are doing. We would expect them to use their "articulated noises" and "marks" in certain ways, according to certain techniques (cf. LFM p. 203). But these people may not live up to our expectations. What if their behavior did not lend itself to be subject to our normative standards? What if what they actually do violated our expectations, not just occasionally but systematically? We would then have to withdraw our judgment that these people are talking and calculating (based on the behavioral clues initially available), and we would be at a loss to understand what they are doing. This is precisely what happened in the case of the wood sellers.

In Wittgenstein's description of our imaginary encounter with the wood sellers, there was an initial presumption of intelligibility warranted by the striking similarities between how things were done in their practice and how they are done in ours. The structured behavior of the wood sellers closely resembled the things we do in our everyday commercial practices: taking measurements, calculating prices, and exchanging goods for money. So we expected them to measure, price, buy, and sell piles of wood according to a quantitative notion we are familiar with (e.g., by their volume). This expectation was not the result of an inadmissible ethnocentrism on our part; it was just a necessary assumption we needed to make in order to make sense of their practice. But this expectation was violated by their practice. And this violation created a gap between their practice and ours, calling into question the intelligibility of what they are doing: "We say we can't understand these people—because we *expect* something which we don't find. (If someone came into the room with a bucket on his shoulders, I'd say, 'That bucket must hide his head.')" (LFM p. 203; my emphasis). The practice of the wood sellers does not seem to contain an intelligible concept of *quantity* because what they call "more" or "less wood" runs contrary to the principle of the conservation of quantity (i.e., that the quantity contained in a pile remains constant no matter how the pile is arranged). This principle is an essential part of our quantitative techniques of measuring and calculating the price of goods; it is something that we *hold fast* in what we do, a norm that regulates our interactions. And when we recognize that the practice of the wood sellers violates this norm, we are unable to understand what they do as a meaningful commercial practice. Wittgenstein remarks that we may even feel inclined to call these people mad.[202] He explains this name calling as follows:

> The madness would be like this: (a) The people would do something which we'd call talking or writing. (b) There would be a close analogy between our talking and theirs, etc. (c) Then we would suddenly see *an entire discrepancy between what we do and what they do—in such a way that the whole point of what they are doing seems to be lost*, so that we would say, "What the hell's the point of doing this?" (LFM p. 203; my emphasis)

The "madness" Wittgenstein talks about is not, strictly speaking, a *logical* disease. For it is not necessarily caused by deviations from logical laws, but, more generally, by radical departures from what Wittgenstein calls our *techniques*, that is, our structured ways of doing things. On Wittgenstein's view, the laws of logic are indeed a crucial part of our techniques; they are principles that we hold fast in many (if not all) of our practices, and their denial would certainly call into question the intelligibility of what we are doing. But in this, logical laws are not different from other constitutive components of our practices, such as the principle of the conservation of quantity or the expectation that people have heads on their shoulders. Even when we call into question the intelligibility of a linguistic practice on logical grounds, the rationale is not that what is intelligible (i.e., thinkable and expressible in language) is determined by the sempiternal laws of logic, as Frege thought. For Wittgenstein, the rationale is, rather, that we cannot recognize something as an intelligible linguistic practice other than by its *similarity* with our techniques of language use, and these techniques are inapplicable to a practice that contradicts the logical laws embedded in ours. On Wittgenstein's view, the ground for attributing unintelligibility and madness is always the recognition of a fundamental discrepancy in techniques or ways of doing things, which is revealed by the violation of normative expectations and principles (logical laws among them) that regulate our practices. We base our assessments of intelligibility not on logical laws that define the essence of language and thought *sub specie aeternitatis* but on normative presuppositions that underlie our actual practices.

Take, for instance, the law of noncontradiction. Whether this logical law is criterial for the intelligibility of a linguistic practice depends on whether linguistic constructions of the form "p and not-p" are excluded from that practice. No role is given to commands of this form (e.g., "Sit and don't sit") in our practice of giving and obeying orders (cf. Wittgenstein's discussion in pp. 205–206); nor are assertions of this form ("It is raining and it is not raining") admitted in our reporting practices. We simply cannot act on commands and reports of this form. As Wittgenstein puts it, our practices are "jammed" when constructions of the form "p and not-p" occur (cf. LFM pp. 190–91). But, he insists, it would be a mistake to think that what causes the "jam" is something external to our practices, some supernatural normative force that constrains our practices from without: "The phenomenon of jamming *consists* in the fact that we say it jams: that we say, 'Oh, it's a contradiction and we cannot do anything with it', etc." (LFM p. 191).

In his discussion of "logical madness," Wittgenstein asks us to imagine a General who received two contradictory reports from the battlefield and, without being puzzled, acted on these reports and won the battle. We would say: "What does he do with these reports? Perhaps he does not regard them as reports at all" (LFM p. 205). We are inclined to say that because the law of noncontradiction is presupposed by our reporting use of language, and we cannot see how someone can give up this law and still be engaged in reporting practices. But what is the relation between this logical law and our reporting techniques? Is what we call "reporting" defined by logical laws in such a way that we have, first of all, the logical laws of reporting and then practices that conform to these laws? Or are these laws in fact derived from our reporting techniques, remaining parasitic on what we actually do and say in those linguistic practices we call "reporting"? In the reporting use of language we hold the tacit conviction that an assertion and its denial exclude each other *necessarily*, not just because we never find them combined in our practices. The uncompromising conviction of the law of noncontradiction that characterizes our reporting practices is not the product of an empirical generalization about our peculiar ways of doing things; it is, rather, a normative presupposition about how things *ought* to be done. But, Wittgenstein asks, what is the source of this inexorable conviction? "How do we get convinced of the law of contradiction? In this way: *We learn a certain practice, a technique of language*; and then we are all inclined to do away with this form—on which we do not naturally act in any way" (LFM p. 206; my emphasis).

On Wittgenstein's view, logical laws are bound up with our ways of doing things and using language, with our "techniques": they do not have any intrinsic normative force *independent* of our actual practices. But what is it about our practices that gives normative force to maxims and principles such as the law of noncontradiction? Why does it matter whether or not a norm is enforced by an actual practice? Isn't "not-(p and not-p)" still a norm even if it is not in use? Norms have a regulatory function: they regulate how things are to be done. But they cannot carry out this function unless they have a determinate content, that is, unless they prescribe a particular way of doing things. And the content of a norm cannot be fixed by the mere formulation and interpretation of rules. As already established by the regress arguments of the early 1930s, rule formulations and their interpretations cannot determine a particular course of action because they "can be reinterpreted in any way whatsoever" (LFM p. 183). But in the 1939 lectures Wittgenstein does not simply rehash earlier regress arguments; he introduces a new idea—namely, that what gives definite normative content to a rule is how *we all* use it in *actual* practice: "*the point is that we all make the SAME use of it*" (p. 183) For Wittgenstein, the indeterminacy of rules is irrevocable as long as they are considered independently of particular practices of application. But there is nothing indeterminate about a rule when it is considered against the background of a practice: we are "to use it *in the same way* as other people do" (p. 183). The normative content of a rule is utterly indeterminate when considered in the abstract, but it becomes contextually determinate when viewed against the background of situated activities. This idea of *contextual determinacy* will be further elaborated in Wittgenstein's discussions of meaning and rule following in the

Investigations. But in these lectures he already points out that it is only the agreement of the members of a practice that can properly constrain the applicability of a rule and make its normative content as determinate as it needs to be. He argues that even the determinacy of logical laws rests on the agreement underlying our practices. This agreement, he emphasizes, is not "a consensus of opinions" but "a consensus of *action*: a consensus of doing the same thing, reacting in the same way" (LFM pp. 183–84). This agreement in ways of doing things, this "consensus of action," is prerequisite for rule following: only against the background of this agreement can our norms be regarded as regulating behavior, and our actions as complying with norms.

Wittgenstein's appeals to this requisite agreement in action also convey a *contextualist point about intelligibility*: what we do and say acquires significance only against a *background* or in a *context*; namely, the background or context provided by a *practice*, a shared way of doing thing. Wittgenstein now thinks that the whole in which an action or an utterance is to be inserted to become meaningful and subject to normative assessments is not an inferential network or a calculus of rules but a structured activity and the particular circumstances in which it is typically carried out. Wittgenstein's claim that our assessments of intelligibility are necessarily holistic and context dependent underscores that understanding can only be achieved within a community of actual practices. It is precisely "a consensus of action" that was lacking between us and the wood sellers, or between us and the general who acted on contradictory reports. This is why we could not understand them: because we found "an entire discrepancy between what we do and what they do" (LFM p. 203), and we couldn't find a context in which we could make sense of their behavior. So the point of Wittgenstein's thought experiments is not to assert or deny our capacity to understand practices radically different from ours but, rather, to show that this capacity is *context dependent*, for understanding is something that can only be achieved against the background of a 'consensus of action' which *may or may not* obtain. It is only against the background of a complicated network of activities (such as pricing, buying, selling, making profit, etc.) that an action can be understood as an instance of measuring or calculating. Removed from these surroundings, detached from such connections, it is not clear at all how the action is to be understood.[203] Since the encounter with the wood sellers remains underdescribed, since we know so little about their activities, about the contexts of their actions, we cannot determine how their actions are to be understood and, therefore, the issue of whether they are measuring and calculating or doing something entirely different remains undecided. And this is precisely Wittgenstein's point: that we cannot pass judgment on the intelligibility of actions that we cannot properly situate. For, as he will put it a few years later (circa 1943–1944): "What, in a complicated surrounding, we call 'following a rule' we should certainly not call that if it stood in isolation" (RFM VI.33).

According to Wittgenstein, Frege's mistake was to consider the intelligibility of our actions and utterances in abstract terms, independent of particular contexts of actions. For what makes an action or an utterance unintelligible is not the violation of logical laws *in and by itself*, as Frege thought, but the violation of logical laws or other normative principles *in the context of a practice* in which those laws and principles are fixed by a consensus of action. As Wittgenstein emphasizes, there is nothing intrinsically wrong with giving wood away (RFM I.148; LFM p. 202) except in the context of a commercial practice. Similarly, there is nothing intrinsically wrong with finding a use for an inscription of the form "p and not-p", as the general did. But everything is wrong with using "p and not-p" in the context of a linguistic practice (such as reporting) in which we coordinate our actions by excluding linguistic constructions of that form. Given their discrepancies with our practices, the "commercial" practice of the wood sellers and the "reporting" practice of the general and his officers seem unintelligible: "the whole point" of these practices "seems to be lost" (LFM p. 203). We wouldn't know how to begin if we had to sell our goods as the wood sellers do, or if we had to go on in our reporting practices being undisturbed by contradictions as the general and his officers are.

Wittgenstein emphasizes that it is "immensely important" that our uses of language have "a *point*" (LFM p. 205), that is, that they play a role in regulating our dealings with the world and with each other, that they be integrated in our forms of life. But having a point is always "a matter of degree" (p. 205), and the extent to which a use of language has a point depends on the context in which that use figures. For instance, the intelligibility of a ceremonial act such as the coronation of a king is crucially dependent on an institutional context: whether (and to what extent) the point of this ceremony is transparent or esoteric to us depends on what role (if any) the monarchic institution and its practices play in our lives. What people say and do in the coronation of a king may seem quite absurd to an outsider watching the ceremony; and he "might ask, 'What is the point of all this?'" (LFM p. 204; cf. also RFM I.153). But the point of this ceremony may be explained to him. Similarly, we cannot see any point in a practice of "selling"' piles of wood by the area or in a practice of "reporting" that admits contradictions, but Wittgenstein contends that we cannot rule out the possibility that the point of these activities "might be explained to us" (LFM p. 205). In the case of the wood-"sellers," for instance, we may learn that "these people don't live by selling wood, and so it does not matter much what they get for it"; we may learn that, contrary to appearances, what they do is not part of a commercial practice at all, but of a ceremonial custom instituted by "a great king long ago" (LFM p. 204). "Then what is wrong? They do this. And they get along all right. What more do you want?" (p. 204).

According to Wittgenstein, we cannot determine *sub specie aeternitatis* whether a linguistic practice is composed of judgments that express thoughts or of articulated noises that express nothing, for there is no *absolute and fixed* threshold of intelligibility established by logical laws or other sempiternal principles. By saying that a practice is intelligible or unintelligible *to us* we do not fix the logical status of that practice once and for all; we simply make a remark about *our* relationship with that practice, about *our* capacity to understand it. Indeed, a collection of utterances and actions is not intelligible or unintelligible *in itself*, but relative to a linguistic community and its epistemic situation. And the horizon of understanding of a linguistic community may be broadened or narrowed as its epistemic situation changes, as the range of techniques available in its practices becomes enriched or impoverished. Accordingly, on Wittgenstein's view, our assessments of intelligibility are not absolute and final, but *context dependent and open to revision*. For Wittgenstein, the intelligibility of actions and utterances is a contextual matter (what makes sense in one context may not make sense in another), and a matter of degree (actions and utterances are intelligible or unintelligible up to a point). This *contextualist* view tries to overthrow the *constitutive* view of norms characteristic of transcendental approaches such as Frege's view of logic. These approaches emphasize the *fixity* of normative principles that function as conditions of possibility that define the limits of an activity (e.g., the way in which Frege thought the laws of logic defined once and for all what counts as thought). For Wittgenstein, this fixity is illusory: we cannot impose fixed limits on a practice, for, in order to do that, we would have to be able to survey the entire practice (past, present, and possible futures) from an external (omniscient) standpoint. According to Wittgenstein's contextualism, the relation between normative principles and the practices they regulate is fluid and always changing; and there cannot be inviolable principles that predetermine a priori what counts as thinking, speaking, or calculating.[204]

The main idea concerning intelligibility that the view I am describing as *pragmatic contextualism* elaborates is that our capacity to understand presupposes a practical context constituted by a consensus of action or a community of practices. Since understanding requires a consensus of action, when we try to understand others it is only natural to fall back on the practices we have already mastered and to try to bring our interlocutors into our practices. However, as we saw, our interlocutors may prove to be quite stubborn and they may not tolerate their assimilation into our practices. When this assimilation is not possible, should we conclude (according to

Wittgenstein) that we have run up against the limits of our understanding? No. On the contrary, Wittgenstein's discussion suggests that in most cases, where there is no consensus of action readily available to understand an alien practice, one can be brought about. He considers two ways in which an initial lack of consensus can be repaired: by learning more about the practice of our interlocutor (in particular, its history); or, alternatively, by being trained (or acculturated) in it. First, when we fail to bring people into our practices, we can try to understand their behavior in its own terms by learning more about the particular context in which it takes place. Despite our initial puzzlement when we encounter alien behavior, a context of action in which this behavior makes sense may be recreated for us through historical or anthropological decriptions. As Wittgenstein puts it: "if you wish to give the point [of a practice], you might tell the history of it" (LFM p. 204). But we may fail to make sense of an alien practice by learning about its history and the normative context in which it is conducted. In that case what we need is to "go native," to become children as it were and undergo a process of acculturation. In the lectures (e.g., LFM p. 204) Wittgenstein insists that when we cannot understand a linguistic practice by relating it to those already available to us, what we need is *training*. It is through training that a new consensus of action is formed. Through repeated practice in doing the *same* thing under the guidance of competent practitioners, new forms of behavior become second nature. As we shall see in the next section, for Wittgenstein, this process of acculturation is a process of *concept formation* that shapes our standards of similarity (cf. RFM IV.29ff). If we were successfully acculturated into the practice of the wood sellers, we would share their standards for what counts as the *same* amount of wood and it would become natural for us to use the expressions "more wood" and "less wood" as they do; we would then see the point of doing things as they do.

The upshot of Wittgenstein's thought experiments is that our encounters with alleged logical aliens do not have a predetermined outcome. When we recognize a normative and conceptual gap between our practices and the practices of our interlocutors, a number of different things can happen. We may achieve understanding with these aliens by training them in our practices, or by being ourselves trained in their practices. Alternatively, we may enter into a process of negotiation and mutual clarification with the aliens, which (if successful) can bring our practices closer together and provide a common ground for communication. Of course it is also possible that none of this will happen. It is possible that all our attempts to communicate with the aliens will fail. But even in this case, even if we have no clue as to how we can bridge the gap between our practices, we are not forced to withdraw the presumption of intelligibility on a priori grounds. After all, the recognition of a gap that we have been so far unable to bridge does not warrant the conclusion that the gap is *in principle* unbridgeable. Wittgenstein's contextualism suggests that even in the worst case scenario, even when we encounter beings whose behavior exhibits radical deviations from our concepts and normative priciples and we are at a loss to understand them, even then we can still treat these aliens as potential interlocutors, as thinkers and speakers who are minded in a different way. We can, but why should we? Is there any reason to think that Wittgenstein's contextualism recommends this liberal attitude? I think there is. The adoption of a stingy attitude in our assessments of intelligibility only make sense if we think that it is possible to impose fixed limits on what can be thought and expressed in language. This is what Wittgenstein thought until the mid 1930s; it is the view of intelligibility that derives from the logical realism about *possibilia* that he shared with Frege (cf. chapter 1 and chapter 4). However, Wittgenstein now thinks that there are no hard and fast limits to what is intelligible, that all we have to go by in our assessments of intelligibility is the techniques of rule following available in our historical and changing practices: "We take it as a matter of course that people—'if they can think correctly'—go *this* way. We have now given a *road*, as it were by means of the footsteps of those who have gone this way. And the traffic now proceeds on this road—to various purposes" (RFM I.163) Does this mean that we are imprisoned in a tradition of rule-governed practices? No. For Wittgenstein, our practices do not constitute a straitjacket for thought and language; they impose contextual constraints on what is intelligible for us, but not fixed limits. As Wittgenstein puts it, we are "always building new roads for traffic; by extending the network of the old ones" (RFM I.166). On Wittgenstein's view, what can be considered intelligible in a practice depends on how we extend the techniques employed in that practice, and "there may be many different techniques, any one of which we might decide to call the continuation of the old technique" (LFM p. 69). Our techniques *constrain but do not determine* what is intelligible for us. This contextualist view recommends that we adopt a liberal attitude toward what counts as an intelligible action or an intelligible utterance. For the more liberal we are in our assessments of intelligibility, the more room we make for our horizon of understanding to be expanded in unforeseen ways. Wittgenstein's contextualist view of intelligibility underscores the plastic and open-ended nature of language and thought: "The line between what we include in 'thinking' and what we no longer include in 'thinking' is no more a hard and fast one than the line between what is still and what is no longer called 'regularity'" (RFM I.116).[205]

Is this a regularistic and psychologistic view? Is Wittgenstein reducing our normative practices to empirical regularities? Is he falling into some sort of psychologism by depicting what is thinkable and expressible in language as constrained only by our actual and situated practices? Frege could reply to Wittgenstein that he is simply talking about the limits of intelligibility *in practice*, not about the limits of what is intelligible *in principle*. For Frege, the former is a psychological issue of no interest to philosophy, the latter a logical one. So, by making the bounds of significance dependent on actual practices, Wittgenstein seems to be naturalizing a logical issue. And isn't this just what the psychological logician does? According to Frege's depiction, the psychological logician holds that there are no universal logical limits to what is intelligible for everybody at all times; but he does not deny that there are *natural limits* to what is intelligible *for us*. Wittgenstein also talks about these "natural limits":[206] "Thinking and inferring (like counting) is of course bounded for us, not by an arbitrary definition, but by *natural limits* corresponding to the body of what can be called the role of thinking and inferring in our life" (RFM I.116; my emphasis). However, it would be a mistake to understand Wittgenstein's contextualism as a form of psychologism.

A psychologistic reading would misconstrue Wittgenstein's view of the relationship between normative and empirical propositions. Wittgenstein can hardly be accused of collapsing the logical and normative into the psychological and empirical. Echoing Frege, he writes: "We cannot find out the truth of the propositions of logic by means of a psychological investigation—they do not depend on what we think" (LFM pp. 201–202). Far from dissolving the distinction between normative and empirical propositions, Wittgenstein is trying to give an account of how this distinction is established and maintained in our practices. He repeatedly emphasizes that logical and mathematical laws (as well as other normative principles) are to be sharply distinguished from empirical propositions. As he puts it, these are propositions that have been "hardened [. . .] into a rule," propositions that have been "withdrawn from being checked by experience" and have become "a paradigm for judging experience" (RFM VI.22–23). According to Wittgenstein, it is a mistake to view the laws of logic and mathematics as describing how we think, for their role is not descriptive but *prescriptive*: they regulate how we *ought* to think. However, unlike Frege, Wittgenstein does not conclude that these laws are, therefore, independent of anything actual. On the contrary, he maintains that they are crucially dependent on our actual practices, for they can only play their prescriptive role against the background of a consensus of action.[207] It is because we all agree in what we do that we can lay down rules governing our practices. If there were no consensus of action in our practices, there would be no room for normative regulations. So agreement in action is a necessary condition for a rule-governed practice; but the rules governing our practices *do not describe* our agreement, they are not mere codifications of the ways of thinking and behaving that we share as a matter of empirical fact.[208]

Thus Wittgenstein rejects Frege's strong dichotomy between the logical and the psychological without thereby falling into a crude psychologism: the logical and psychological elements of our linguistic practices cannot be radically separated à la Frege, nor conflated à la psychological logician; neither the logical nor the psychological *separately* are sufficient for a normative practice to get off the ground. However, the crucial dependence of logical laws (as well as other normative principles) on our contingent practices seems to be at odds with the *necessity* of these laws. As Wittgenstein puts it, the contextualization of logical laws in "the natural history of man" does not seem to be "combinable with the hardness of the logical 'must'" (RFM VI.49). Far from denying the necessity or "inexorability" of logic, Wittgenstein regards it as a cultural phenomenon that needs to be elucidated: "We talk of the 'inexorability' of logic; and think of the laws of logic as inexorable, still more inexorable than the laws of nature" (RFM I.118). What is the source of this inexorability?

6.2. Learning and Necessity

A crucial point of continuity in Wittgenstein's philosophy is the attempt to articulate a deflationary account of necessity that does away with the metaphysical view of necessity imagined as fact. As in the *Tractatus*, in his later view Wittgenstein attacks the idea that there are superstrong facts that make certain statements (such as the laws of logic and mathematics) necessary. However, Wittgenstein now thinks that the proper route to deflate the notion of necessity is not the analysis of the logical structure of our statements but, rather, the elucidation of the normative structure of our practices. On Wittgenstein's later view, what is necessary does not derive from the hidden logical form of our symbolisms but, rather, from the normative attitudes of rule followers that are exhibited in their actions and utterances. Wittgenstein sets out to determine the genesis of these atitudes by examining the learning processes through which we are initiated in rule-following practices. In what follows I will analyze Wittgenstein's genetic account of necessity in the *Remarks on the Foundations of Mathematics*. My analysis will draw on the interpretation of Meredith Williams, which underscores the normative significance of learning in Wittgenstein's later philosophy.[209]

What accounts for the necessity of logical and mathematical propositions? Wittgenstein emphasizes that it is a mistake to think that there is something hidden in the propositions themselves that makes them inexorable. According to Wittgenstein, these propositions are not inexorable in and of themselves; what makes them inexorable is the way we use them: "It is *we* that are inexorable in applying these laws" (RFM I.118). We apply the laws of logic and mathematics "blindly" (RFM I.109), without allowing for alternatives. So, for Wittgenstein, the inexorability of logical and mathematical laws resides, as Williams puts it, in the "alternative-blindness"[210] that characterizes our application of these laws. When we carry out an arithmetical operation, we do not consider alternative results as possible outcomes, we are blind to alternatives: "One can only *see* that 13 ¥ 13 = 169" (RFM I.109).[211] This blind obedience is also what characterizes the application of logical laws in our inferential practices: "So long as one thinks it can't be otherwise, one draws logical conclusions" (RFM I.156). We stick to the laws of logic and mathematics come what may, "whatever the facts may be" (RFM I.121); but our special adherence to these laws is not the product of our belief in a special kind of truth.[212] For Wittgenstein, the application of logical and mathematical laws is nothing like acting on a belief; it is more like following an order blindly: "Here is the rule, like an order! And like an order too in its *effect*" (RFM VII.39). He emphasizes that this peculiar *attitude* toward logical and mathematical laws is the result of the techniques of use enforced by our actual practices. On Wittgenstein's view, it is our techniques that are ultimately responsible for "the peculiar inexorability of mathematics" (RFM I.4). As he puts it, the mathematical "must" is "the expression of an *attitude* towards the technique of calculation, which comes out everywhere in our life. The emphasis of the *must* corresponds only to the inexorableness of this attitude both to the technique of calculating and to a host of related techniques" (RFM VII.67).

How do we acquire this *attitude* toward logical and mathematical principles? According to Wittgenstein, the explanation lies in the *education* we have received, in the *training* into techniques we have gone through. Take, for instance, the discussion of the rule of squaring that opens Book I of the *Remarks*. We express this rule with the formula "$y = x^2$" and we think that "the way the formula is meant determines which steps are to be taken" (RFM I.2). But "the criterion for the way the formula is meant" is "the way we always use it, the way we are taught to use it" (RFM I.2). What determines the steps of our calculation is the technique of squaring we use in our practice, and our feeling of inexorability is the product of the training we have received in this technique: "People are brought by their education (training) so to use the formula $y = x^2$" (RFM I.1). Similarly, Wittgenstein remarks, the inexorability with which numbers are regarded to follow one another in the series of natural numbers can only be explained by the fact that "we learn to count as we do: with endless practice, with merciless exactitude," that "it is inexorably insisted that we shall all say 'two' after 'one', 'three' after 'two' and so on" (RFM I.4). There would be nothing inexorable about the series of natural numbers "if everyone said the numbers one after another *anyhow*" (RFM I.4). Similarly, there would be no necessity in our inferential practices if people were allowed to "infer *any*how!" (RFM I.116).

The source of our blind obedience to logical and mathematical laws, and hence of their inexorability, is the training we have received in the application of these laws. But how can I produce an inexorable "mathematical conviction" in someone by training him? "*I impress a procedure on him*"; "And this procedure can *as a matter of fact* always be carried out again. And he can be rightly convinced of that" (RFM I.39). Our logical and mathematical convictions are the product of the training we have received into certain techniques. But how can we achieve through this training anything more than an empirical certainty, which will always fall short of the hardness of the logical "must"? What is needed is an account of learning that distinguishes the training into techniques conducive to inexorable convictions from inductive learning. For if our training into techniques were to be conceived as a process of inductive generalization, then the question would arise: but "how can the picture (or procedure) that you shew me now oblige me always to judge in such-and-such a way? If what we have here is an experiment, then surely *one* is too little to bind me to any judgment" (RFM I.55). Experiential learning is not enough for the acquisition of normative standards that characterizes mathematical learning (cf. RFM I. 164–65).

The obvious alternative to the inductive model of learning is the behaviorist view of learning as conditioning and habit formation. On this view, learning consists in establishing causal connections between stimuli and responses, not in producing convictions with varying degrees of certainty. What the learner acquires through conditioning is a set of automatic responses. This view of learning seems to be closer to Wittgenstein's view, for it seems to underscore the blindness characteristic of the training into techniques he emphasizes. However, the similarity is only apparent. For the blindness of stimulus-response learning and its products (behavioral dispositions) is not the alternative-blindness of how things *ought* to be done discussed above. It is more akin to the blindness of reflexes or causal mechanisms that operate quite independently of normative considerations.

As discussed above (cf. 5.2), in the early and mid 1930s Wittgenstein provided forceful arguments against the normative significance of learning conceived as a causal process (as the process of "installing an electric connection between a switch and a bulb"; BLB p. 12). Although the process of learning now acquires crucial significance in Wittgenstein's discussions of rule following, his earlier arguments against a purely causal acount of learning still hold. A causal account of the training we receive in logical and mathematical practices cannot explain the normative role that logical and mathematical propositions come to play in what we do: "If calculation reveals a causal connexion to you, then you are not calculating. [. . .] What I am saying comes to this, that mathematics is *normative*" (RFM VII.61). Wittgenstein is decidedly opposed to naturalizing the hardness of the logical (or mathematical) "must" in causal terms. But his attempt to ground the necessity of logic and mathematics in our training into techniques may obscure this point. For his remarks about learning could be seen as an attempt to unmask our logical and mathematical compulsion as a psychological one ("It looked at first as if these considerations were meant to shew that 'what seems to be a logical compulsion is in reality only a psychological one'"; RFM I.118). But that's not what Wittgenstein's emphasis on learning is intended to show. He emphasizes that, through training processes, our behavior becomes, not causally determined, but normatively structured; that is, we acquire the ability to engage in *self-regulating* behavior.[213]

As Wittgenstein puts it, "the point" of a training exercise in arithmetic is not to show the pupil one way (among other possible ones) in which things *can* be done, but rather, to teach her "the *kind of way*" in which things are done in our arithmetical practices, the path she has to go through if she is to engage in these activities (RFM I.86). The learning process is successfully completed, the mastery of a technique achieved, when the learner adopts that "kind of way" of doing things, that learned procedure, as *the* way things *ought* to be done. In arithmetic, Wittgenstein emphasizes, the very results of our calculations are incorporated into our calculation procedures. That is, the results are not regarded as contingent outcomes, but as constitutive parts of our techniques, criterial for their correct application: we do not accept alternative results; and if we obtain a different result, we say "I must have made a mistake; the *same* kind of way would always have to produce the same result" (RFM I.86). According to Wittgenstein, this response is indicative of the mastery of a technique: it "shows that you are incorporating the result of the transformation into the kind of way the transformation is done" (RFM I.86).

So, for Wittgenstein, our training into techniques is more than an inductive process or a process of conditioning: it is a process of structuring behavior until it becomes self-regulated. Learning processes of this kind endow us with more than behavioral dispositions or empirical certainties. These processes lead to the adoption of normative standards; or, as Wittgenstein puts it in the early 1940s, 'the adoption of concepts': "'It must be so' means that this outcome has been defined to be essential to this process. This *must* shews that he has adopted a concept" (RFM VI.8–9; cf. also VII.67). What we gain through this training process (if successful) is a new concept or criterion of identity: "I form a new concept. One involving something that was not there before. [. . .] I am making something into a criterion of identity" (RFM IV.30). The account of learning as a normative process of concept formation sketched in the *Remarks* provides the crucial background to understand Wittgenstein's mature philosophy and to distinguish it from psychologism.

In the *Remarks* Wittgenstein repeatedly draws a contrast between the empirical and the conceptual. He writes: "The limit of the empirical—is *concept-formation*" (RFM IV. 29). He characterizes the process of concept formation as "the transition that I make from 'It will be like this' to 'it *must* be like this'" (RFM IV.29). This transition is what gives rise to the alternative-blindness characteristic of our rule-following behavior, for "'it will be like this' chooses between one possibility and another. 'It must be like this' sees only *one* possibility" (RFM IV.31). "The word 'must' surely expresses our inability to depart from *this* concept. (Or ought I to say 'refusal'?)" (RFM IV.30). But what do we acquire through the process of concept formation that makes us see how things must be? When I form or "adopt" a concept, "I am making something into a criterion of identity. So I am recasting my concept of identity" (RFM IV.29). For Wittgenstein, the acquisition of concepts is the acquisition of criteria of identity or standards of similarity. It is only through these criteria or standards that we can see, not just how things are done as a matter of fact, but how things must be done *as a norm*: "Our way of seeing is remodelled" (RFM IV.30). By "adopting" a concept I commit myself, blindly, "to see things like *this*" and "to act in such-and-such a way" (RFM VI.7). For instance, only when we acquire the concept of addition (that is, when we learn what counts as adding two figures by being trained into calculating techniques), "we see as a *norm* that 3 things and 2 things make 5 things" (RFM VI.9).

Wittgenstein emphasizes that the ability to follow a rule presupposes the ability to grasp what counts as doing the *same* thing: "Acting according to a rule presupposes the recognition of a *uniformity*" (RFM VI.44). But, on the other hand, he also emphasizes that the recognition of uniformities requires the ability to engage in uniform activities, "for only through a technique can we *grasp* a regularity" (RFM VI.2). So it appears that we have run into a circle. But circles are fine as long as they are not vicious. And there is nothing vicious in the claim that our capacity to follow rules and our capacity to grasp similarities are interdependent, that we cannot have one without the other. But how do we get into this circle? Someone cannot follow a rule if he does not yet have the appropriate standards of similarity; but his inability to engage in rule-following behavior makes it impossible for him to grasp what he should count as the same. How can we bring him to see that? How can we make someone sensitive to similarities and able to follow rules simultaneously? "I can train someone in a *uniform* activity" (RFM VI.17). For instance, I can train someone in writing the pattern "_.._.._.._.." I do that by showing him what to do first, and "he is always to go on as I have shewn him" (VI.17) He will first follow my lead mechanically, without seeing the pattern. But through repeated practice, through his actually writing down the pattern countless times, I establish a regularity in his behavior. And then he can go on on his own. He then sees the pattern; he sees what counts as doing the same thing.

So is the point of our training into techniques simply to produce behavioral regularities? No, that is only part of the point. The regularity produced in the learner's behavior is only a prerequisite for the formation of a concept, for coming to see and do things in a certain way *as a norm*. The learner has to move from an empirical regularity to a law, from seeing how things are done to seeing how they *must* be done:

> When I write down a bit of a series for you, that you then see *this regularity* in it may be called an empirical fact, a psychological fact. But, if you have seen *this law* in it, that you then continue the series in *this* way—that is no longer an empirical fact. (RFM VI.26; my emphasis)

The learner now sees "how things *must* be done"; and, as Wittgenstein remarks, "this 'must' shews that he has gone in a circle" (RFM VI.7). The "circle" created by the process of training into a technique consists in the following: that what the learner is trained to do, blindly, becomes the criterion of identity for what he is doing. Thus the end of the process becomes the beginning: what is obtained by the learned procedure becomes criterial for having followed that procedure. The actual applications of the rule thus fix the normative standards of similarity that define what counts as following the rule.[214]

By adopting a learned procedure as the criterion of identity for what one does, certain propositions are "hardened" into rules (cf. RFM VI.22). The way we are trained to proceed, the learned technique, becomes a "rule-grounding proceeding," "a proceeding that we assume as *decisive* for the judgment of other proceedings" (RFM VI.16). As a result, the outcomes yielded by the application of this procedure are no longer regarded as results obtained regularly, determined by one's experience: "That 4 + 1 makes 5 is, so to speak, *overdetermined*. Overdetermined by this, that the result of the operation is defined to be the criterion that this operation has been carried out" (RFM VI.16). When the learner "has gone in a circle" in this way, "he has read off from the process, not a proposition of natural science, but, instead of that, the determination of a concept" (RFM VI.8). Obtaining 5 from 4, for instance, becomes criterial for having applied the rule + 1; and thus the proposition "4 + 1 = 5" acquires a special normative status: "The proposition rests on too many feet to be an empirical proposition. It will be used as a determination of the concept 'applying the operation + 1 to 4'. For we now have a new way of judging whether someone has followed the rule" (RFM VI. 16).

So, by viewing learning as the source of normativity, Wittgenstein does not fall into a crude psychologism that reduces normative standards to empirical regularities. Wittgenstein's account of normativity in terms of learning processes does not involve the dissolution of the distinction between the normative and the empirical or psychological; rather, it constitutes a genetic account of how this distinction comes to be established in the first place. So the normative and the empirical are not conflated on Wittgenstein's view: the crucial role that the process of learning plays in his view consists precisely in establishing a sharp distinction between them. The news is not that the normative is a mere psychological illusion in a world of contingent, empirical facts. The news is that the normative is not something self-subsistent or given, but something created in and by our actual practices.

By fixing standards of similarity and "hardening" propositions into rules, the process of training into techniques *initiates* the novice into rule-following practices. But how can this process of *initiate learning* turn anomic behavior into behavior regulated by norms? According to Wittgenstein, this is possible only through highly structured and constrained training processes that impose different demands and responsibilities on the participants. To begin with, teaching a technique requires that certain physical and psychological preconditions be satisfied, for there are always "physical and psychological facts that make the technique *possible*" (RFM VII.1). On the one hand, initiate learning requires an appropriate physical environment. For example, we cannot teach *our* measuring practices in an environment in which rulers and the objects to be measured with them expand and contract randomly (cf. RFM I.5). On the other hand, once the appropriate physical environment is available, certain psychological facts about the trainee must obtain: the learner must exhibit certain *natural reactions*. These natural reactions include basic discriminations (such as that of elementary colors, shapes, etc.) and automatic responses to certain stimuli (such as to a scream, a smile, etc.) [cf. e.g., RFM VI.35]. The natural reactions of the novice constitute the requisite starting point of the training. They feed the learning process with raw material. The goal of this process is to broaden the learner's "natural" reactions, to make new, acquired responses become *second nature*. By the end of the learning period (if successful), the novice will share new matter-of-course reactions with others in virtue of her membership, not in the same species but in the same learned practice. So, for Wittgenstein, being the member of a practice or sharing a form of life involves sharing certain unlearned reactions and learned procedures, as well as an appropriate environment in which these reactions and procedures can be exercised.[215]

There are both domain-specific and domain-general natural reactions that are condition *sine qua non* of initiate learning. For instance, having perceptual sensitivity to colors is prerequisite for learning color words. On the other hand, having the capacity to react positively or negatively to interpersonal stimuli such as shouting or smiling is a multipurpose, spontaneous response required for many learning processes—where these stimuli are used as signs of approval or disapproval that serve to structure the behavior of the novice normatively[216] (until they are replaced with more sophisticated means of sanctioning such as a mere yes/no, or right/wrong). As Wittgenstein puts it, "instruction effects [. . .] agreement in actions on the part of pupil and teacher" (RFM VI.45). But this agreement must start somewhere; and if pupil and teacher share no natural reactions whatsoever, they have no means to achieve agreement, and they can only "part company," to use Wittgenstein's phrase (cf. e.g., RFM I.61). The availability of certain natural reactions in the initiate learner thus constrains her capacity to be trained in rule-governed practices.

Closely related to the learner's natural reactions is her attitude in the training process. An indispensable condition of initiate learning is that the novice have a *receptive attitude*, that is, that she accept the authority of the teacher *blindly*: "Can the pupil contradict and say: 'How do you know that?' [. . .] Well, we do not assume that the pupil can say that" (RFM VII.26). In fact, we assume that the novice's attitude will be that of total submission to the authority of the master, of blind obedience to her commands. For, without this passive collaboration of the novice, the learning process cannot take place. A constant questioning of the teacher's directions as to how to proceed would leave the process of training in an impasse at every turn, making learning impossible. In fact, in initiate learning, there is not even the requisite logical space for this kind of questioning. The context of initiate learning is structured so that the teacher has the prerogative of determining how things are to be done. The novice, therefore, is not in a position in which she can protest the teacher's disapproval, or challenge the responses sanctioned by the teacher as correct, going on obstinately in alternative ways. The role of the novice in initiate learning is to follow the lead of the master.

This structure of differential authority is what characterizes not just the interactions between children and adults but, more generally, any joint activity in which participants exercise differential responsibility by virtue of their differential expertise. The teacher is invested with a special authority by virtue of her competence in the practice at issue. Her mastery of the rule-following practice makes her a representative of the community of rule followers; and, as such, the teacher has the capacity and authority to bring the behavior of the novice into harmony with the behavior of the rule-following community. The goal of the training process is to bring the pupil into the practice, and this is achieved by effecting an "agreement in actions" between the pupil and the teacher (RFM VI.45) and hence, by the same token, between the pupil and the community of practitioners.

The process of learning is, therefore, not only crucially dependent on an appropriate physical environment and on the receptive attitude and natural reactions of the novice, but also, and more importantly, on the competence of the teacher or master who directs and structures the training. It is the teacher's competence in the practice at issue that provides the scaffolding for the *bootstrapping* process. In this regard, Wittgenstein emphasizes that the initiate learning of language games requires "stage-setting"—that is, a context structured by norms governing the correct use of words (cf. PI §257). This normative context is not provided by the physical environment *alone* or by the mind of the learner *alone*. Rather, it is set up by an experienced adult who frames, selects, and feeds back the learner's use of words. This crucial *structuring role* of the teacher is often ignored in contemporary accounts of language learning, which regard the learner as possessing conceptual competence from the start.[217] On Wittgenstein's view, by contrast, the conceptual development of the initiate learner or novice is made possible by the guidance of a teacher or master who provides the requisite background for concept use.

This relation of cognitive dependence is particularly radical in the early stages of initiate learning, where the learner's utterances and actions acquire conceptual significance only by virtue of a "courtesy" extended to the learner by the teacher or master (cf. Williams 1994). This incipient competence extended to the learner by courtesy is crucial for structuring his behavior normatively. For Wittgenstein, an essential part of the training into a rule-governed practice is treating the learner as if she were (already) a member of the practice, as if she could not only conform to the rules of the practice but actually follow them. The teacher treats the pupil's *correct* responses as indicative of an incipient competence and her *incorrect* responses as "mistakes" (cf. RFM VII.61). But the learner's reactions to the training are invested with normative significance only when viewed against the background of the whole rule-governed practice (cf. RFM VII.47). And this is something which, by definition, the initiate learner cannot yet do by herself. Because of her lack of competence, the initiate learner does not yet exhibit *self-corrective* behavior; her behavior is subject to the check and correction of the teacher (cf. Williams 1999, chapter 7). These evaluations and corrections of the pupil's responses are essential for structuring her behavior normatively: "The words 'right' and 'wrong' are used when giving instruction in proceeding according to a rule. The word 'right' makes the pupil go on, the word 'wrong' holds him back" (RFM VI.39).

The normative background that the teacher brings to bear upon the behavior of the novice is progressively made available to the learner through the training, up to the point where the learner's behavior becomes regulated by norms without the assistance of the teacher, thus becoming an autonomous practitioner. In other words, by interacting with masters who structure and regulate the learning environment, novices come to adopt structuring and regulatory activities of their own. The process of initiate learning is, therefore, a process of acquiring autonomy or gaining control in normative practices. What characterizes this process is a gradual shift of responsibility and authority, a developmental progression *from other-regulation to self-regulation*. Initiate learning is thus conceived as a process of *enculturation* or *apprenticeship*:[218] we learn norms by being acculturated into rule-following practices, by mastering their techniques.

This cultural account of learning explains how the behavior of the initiate learner becomes normatively structured. On this account, the criteria for the correct application of a rule are established by training. So one might think that the normative significance of learning consists in fixing the interpretation of rules. But this would be a mistake. As Wittgenstein puts it, one might wonder: "How then does the teacher interpret the rule for the pupil? (For he is certainly supposed to give it a particular interpretation.)" (RFM VII.47). But he argues that the teacher does *not* interpret the rule for the pupil *in any way*. What the teacher provides are not interpretations but demonstrations: she *shows* the pupil how to follow the rule by means of examples. The training process is not, therefore, the locus of privileged interpretations; it is, rather, where "interpretation comes to an end" (VII.47). So Wittgenstein does not appeal to the training process as a *deus ex machina* that solves the regress of rules and interpretations. The appeal to learning is not a solution but a *dissolution* of the regress problem, an attempt to go beyond the realm of interpretations, to show that rule following does not consist of interpretations all the way down.

On Wittgenstein's view, competence in a rule-following practice is not acquired by being handed down the interpretation of a rule but by having one's *behavior* shaped so as to agree with that of other practitioners, and by being inculcated into a normative *attitude* toward how things are to be done. The two crucial components of the process of initiate training are *drilling and instilling a normative attitude*. In the first place, training someone into following a rule involves creating a regularity in her behavior with repeated practice. This is the behavioristic aspect of Wittgenstein's account of learning. For drilling certainly involves conditioning processes that establish behavioral patterns. However, the creation of these patterns is only one step toward the "consensus of action" that is the goal of the training. Wittgenstein's account of initiate training also contains a *normative* element: it involves, in the second place, infusing a normative *attitude* toward actions and utterances (cf. RFM VII.61). The novice is taught not only to do things in a certain way, but also to react approvingly when things are done that way and disapprovingly otherwise, to discriminate between correct responses and mistakes: "Our children are not only given practice in calculation but are also trained to adopt a particular attitude towards a mistake in calculating [towards a departure from the norm]" (RFM VII.61). The mastery of a rule is achieved when the learner is bound by a technique in what she does and says: "If I have once grasped a rule I am *bound* in what I do further. [. . .] I am *bound* in my judgment about what is in accord with the rule and what not" (RFM VI.27; my emphasis). As in the early 1930s, Wittgenstein emphasizes that rule following involves *commitments*. But notice that these commitments are no longer said to derive from the rule itself but from our training into its use, from an actual practice of application: they do not spring from the grasp of an internal relation but from blind obedience. For Wittgenstein, the process of learning is completed when the learner becomes *blindly* committed to a particular way of acting and talking (cf. RFM VI.7). By the end of the training period, the course of action sanctioned as correct by the teacher is viewed by the learner as the *necessary* outcome of applying the rule. As Wittgenstein puts it, this attitude signals that the learner "has gone *in a circle*": "he does not say: I realised that *this* happens. Rather: that it must be like that. This 'must' shews the kind of lesson he has drawn from the scene" (RFM VI.7; emphasis preserved and added).

Learning is where the distinction between correct and incorrect is forged. As Wittgenstein puts it, learning is the process by which a particular way of doing things is established as the "How of 'making'" (RFM VI.4). It follows from this view that learning is, therefore, *indispensable* for rule following. "Doesn't the technique (the *possibility*) of training someone else in following it belong to the following of a rule?" (RFM VII.53). For Wittgenstein, normatively structured training techniques are indeed the characteristic mark of a rule-following activity.[219] It is the presence of training processes that enable us to distinguish between rule-following and rule-conforming behavior. This is underscored by Wittgenstein's discussion of the behavior of chimpanzees. He argues that whether we can see in the patterned behavior of chimpanzees a rule-following activity or a mere regularity depends, crucially, on whether we can identify learning processes through which they coordinate their behavior and distinguish between correct and incorrect actions:

> If one of a pair of chimpanzees once scratched the figure |--| in the earth and thereupon the other the series |--| |--| etc., the first would not have given a rule nor would the other be following it, whatever else went on at the same time in the mind of the two of them. If however there were observed, e.g., *the phenomenon of a kind of instruction, of shewing how and of imitation, of lucky and misfir-*

> *ing attempts, of reward and punishment and the like*; if at length the one who had been so trained put figures which he had never seen before one after another in sequence as in the first example, then we should probably say that the one chimpanzee was writing rules down, and the other was following them. (RFM VI.42; my emphasis)

Insofar as it provides the logical space required to draw a distinction between correct and incorrect applications, learning is the condition of possibility for acting according to a rule. And, since learning to follow a rule is a process of enculturation into a practice, to say that learning is indispensable for rule following is to say that rule following has an intrinsic *social* dimension. Indeed, for Wittgenstein, the indispensability of learning goes hand in hand with the essentially social character of rule following:[220] "Suppose one day instruction no longer produced agreement? Could there be arithmetic without agreement on the part of calculators? Could there be only one human being who calculated? Could there be only one who followed a rule? [. . .] 'Can one man alone engage in commerce?'" (RFM VI.45). (In the last section of this chapter I will examine the sense in which rule following has an intrinsic social dimension according to Wittgenstein.)

What we acquire in initiate learning is a set of regulatory activities, a technique or procedure that cannot be captured in a list of rules or in an interpretation. A technique of rule following remains crucially dependent on the process of learning through which it was acquired. And if we want to *show* this technique to someone unfamiliar with it, we "bring him to a mastery of it by training"; "someone who is a master of it, I may remind of the kind of training" (RFM VI.31).[221] However, we have the intuition that the way we learn to follow rules is only *accidentally* related to our capacity to follow rules. We are under the impression that our rule-following skills stand on their own, independent of their history: that they are what they are, *however* they are acquired, and even *whether or not* they are acquired. Thus the process of learning appears as irrelevant to what one learns. As Williams has argued (1996, 1999), this sense of irrelevance is in fact an illusion created by the very process of learning. For when the way one is taught to do things is adopted as the way things *must* be done, the training appears as an ancillary process. As Wittgenstein puts it: when the learner comes to see "the How of the following as something that is a matter of course," he is "under the impression that he has only followed a thread that is already there" and he accepts only "*one* explanation of his actions: how the thread runs" (RFM VII.4). But, Wittgenstein continues, "isn't it the *application* that elicits that conception: that it is not we, but the calculation, that takes a certain course?" (RFM VII.5). This diagnosis is further elaborated in the *Investigations*, where Wittgenstein argues at length that a rule seems "to produce all its consequences in advance" only when (and because) we "draw them as a *matter of course*" (PI §238).

For Wittgenstein, learning is the *invisible* ground of our normative activities. This ground becomes invisible because the training that leads to the mastery of rules falls into oblivion as soon as this mastery becomes "second nature." Wittgenstein warns us that this oblivion is likely to foster philosophical misconceptions,[222] for it creates "the illusory image of a greater depth" beneath the ground (RFM VI.31). Wittgenstein sets out to unmask these philosophical illusions by presenting the training we receive in rule-following practices as the ground for what we do: "The difficult thing here is not, to dig down to the ground; no, it is to recognize the ground that lies before us as the ground" (RFM VI.31).

On Wittgenstein's view, the normative standards of a practice become available only to those who have been trained in it. This is an *internalist* view of normativity that privileges the insider's perspective: in order to know what counts as following a rule, we have to adopt the perspective of practitioners, of those who have been *trained* in following the rule; for only then do we have "a How of 'making'" (RFM VI.4), only then does a particular "proceeding" appear "as *decisive* for the judgment of other proceedings" (RFM VI.16). What counts as correct in the application of a rule is determined—in fact, "overdetermined"—by the training received in following the rule. Therefore, if we break the connection between learning and rule following, indeterminacy will ensue: what is "overdetermined" from within will appear utterly indeterminate from without. Learning provides the link between rule-following practices and the actions and utterances of the individuals trained in those practices. When this link is cut off, the normative background of an actual practice is no longer available, and there is no fact of the matter as to what counts as correct and, hence, as to whether one is following a rule correctly, or even following a rule at all.

As we saw in chapter 5, the motivation for severing the connection between learning and rule following is to establish the self-sufficiency of the normative ("the autonomy of the grammatical," in Wittgenstein's terms). Paradoxically, however, this separation ultimately results in the dissolution of normativity, making it impossible to draw an objective distinction between correct and incorrect. This, I will argue, is what the indeterminacy arguments of the *Investigations* try to show. *Pace* Kripke (1982), Wittgenstein's indeterminacy arguments concerning meaning and rule following do not reveal something final about our epistemic situation, some sort of neo-Humean skeptical insight into the nature of normativity.[223] Rather, what these arguments show is the deep flaws of the philosophical pictures we use to explain normativity. Wittgenstein attacks the philosophical misconceptions that arise when we lose sight of "the ground that lies before us" and search for "a greater depth," for firmer foundations (RFM VI.31). In the *Investigations* he tries to unmask these unassailable foundations beneath our practices as philosophical illusions: there are no invisible "rails" on which our practices run (cf. PI §§218ff; also RFM VI.66). But, on Wittgenstein's view, our rule-governed judgments and actions are not intrinsically and unavoidably indeterminate; on the contrary, they are "overdetermined" (RFM VI.16). The upshot of Wittgenstein's arguments is that rule following becomes indeterminate only when viewed as a frictionless activity, unaffected by anything actual. "So we need *friction*. Back to the rough ground!" (PI §107).

6.3. Back to the Rough Ground!

In this section I will examine some of the central arguments of the *Philosophical Investigations*: the critique of ostensive definition (PI §§1–38) and the rule-following arguments culminating in the Paradox of Interpretation (PI §§139–219). My examination of these arguments will gather support for the developmental account of Wittgenstein's philosophy I have offered so far. As we saw in previous chapters, skeletal versions of the critique of ostensive definition (cf. 3.3.1) and of the rule-following considerations (cf. 4.2) already appeared in the early 1930s. However, the very different discursive contexts in which these arguments now appear and the interesting ways in which they are modified will reveal that, in the *Investigations*, they are at the service of the practice-based view of normativity that Wittgenstein developed in the late 1930s. The account of learning elaborated in the *Remarks* seems to have been what gave Wittgenstein the motivation and guidance to rework his previous arguments concerning normativity.

6.3.1. The Indeterminacy of Ostension: Definition versus Training

As in *Philosophical Grammar*, in the opening sections of the *Investigations* Wittgenstein uses the critique of ostensive definition to attack the denotational approach to meaning that he refers to as "the Augustinian picture of language." As before, Wittgenstein starts by emphasizing that an ostensive definition is always ambiguous: it "can be variously interpreted in *every* case" (PI §28). One may reply, Wittgenstein suggests, that the indeterminacy of ostensive definition can be dispelled by specifying what *sort* of thing the word defined is supposed to name (PI §29). But the information that ostensive definitions then convey to us is parasitic on our mastery of the classificatory terms used. These terms, Wittgenstein remarks, are not self-explanatory; and if they are not understood, "they just need defining [. . .] by means of other words!" (PI §29). So we are thus led to a regress: "And what about the last definition in the chain?" (PI §29). This regress of definitions can only be stopped if (and when) we reach words that the learner can already understand. But how was that mastery of these first words attained? This question is precisely what the appeal to ostensive definitions was supposed to answer; but it can't, for an ostensive definition that does not rely on previously acquired linguistic competence remains wholly indeterminate. What this argument shows is that ostensive definitions cannot explain the acquisition of linguistic competence, that they are not at all what gives us primitive access to language; they are in fact quite sophisticated linguistic acts: "The ostensive definition explains the use—the meaning—of the word when the overall role of the word in language is clear" (PI §30), when the learner has already mastered the language "up to this last point" (PI §31).

Both in *Philosophical Grammar* and in the *Investigations* the critique of ostensive definition is used to convey a key *holistic* point; namely, that in the ostensive definition of words "a great deal" is presupposed (cf. PG §24 and PI §§30–31). However, the kind of holism developed from this point is different in each case, for *what is presupposed* is understood differently. In *Philosophical Grammar* it is argued that an ostensive definition presupposes all the other rules or conventions that apply to the word and fix its grammar. Each of these rules settles one aspect of the use of the word, and it is only *all the rules taken together* that can establish the role of the word in the calculus and hence its meaning (cf. PG §27 and Lectures 1932–35, p. 3). These "rules for use," Wittgenstein remarks, are "*explanations* of meaning" that comprise both "verbal definitions and ostensive definitions" (PG §24). So, on this view, the proper context in which an ostensive definition can carry out its function is provided by a system of rules or network of definitions; this is what lies in the background when we ostensively define a word. By contrast, in the *Investigations* Wittgenstein emphasizes that what is presupposed in an ostensive definition is *not more of the same*, more definitions or rules.[224] The linguistic competence required in order to understand ostensive acts is not provided by "explanations of meaning"; what is needed is *training*: "The teaching of language is not explanation, but training" (PI §5). As he puts it in *Zettel*: "Any explanation has its foundation in training. (Educators ought to remember this.)" (Z §419). The ostensive definition of a word is, therefore, crucially dependent on linguistic skills acquired through training. These background skills are not fully expressible in definitions or explanations of meaning (which can always be variously interpreted); they can only be exhibited in the actual employment of words in practice (cf. PI §29).

These different versions of the critique of ostensive definition have a quite different scope. In the early 1930s what this critique establishes is that an ostensive definition is *insufficient* to fix the use (and hence the meaning) of a word: "Ostensive definition is one rule only for the use of a word. And one rule is not enough to give the meaning" (Lectures 1932–35, p. 45). It is suggested that the indeterminacy problem of ostensive definition is to be solved by adding definitions until all the rules governing the use of the word in question are specified. On this view, definitions are fine as long as they come in clusters, the more the merrier. The illusion that this critique of ostensive definition tries to dispel is that there is a privileged kind of definition that can singlehandedly determine the meaning of words—namely, those that connect language with reality by correlating words with objects, as if these objects could identify themselves, independently of language, and determine what our words ought to mean. By undermining the primacy attributed to ostensive definition, Wittgenstein is trying to make room for a different picture of language: language as an *autonomous* calculus of rules, utterly independent of anything outside itself. According to this picture, word-object relations are established holistically, by an entire network of definitions or grammatical rules. Thus Wittgenstein concludes the discussion of ostensive definition in *Philosophical Grammar*: "The connection between 'language and reality' is made by *definitions* of words, and these belong to grammar, so that language remains *self-contained* and *autonomous*" (PG §55; my emphasis).

In the *Investigations* Wittgenstein's critique of ostensive definition also undermines the idea that word-object relations can be fixed with bare pointings. But he no longer holds that what fixes these relations is a set of arbitrarily stipulated definitions (for these, by themselves, would remain indeterminate). Word-object relations are established in and by a *practice* of language use in which we have to be *trained* to acquire linguistic competence. And a practice, in contrast with an arbitrary stipulation, is in no way independent of the environment in which it is exercised. On this pragmatist view, language, far from being autonomous, is crucially dependent on worldly contingencies: on there being certain uniformities in the environment, on there being speakers who use language in regular ways in their interactions with the environment, and on their having the capacity to be trained and train others in these regular activities.

The critique of ostensive definition in the *Investigations* is more radical than in *Philosophical Grammar* and the lectures: it establishes that definitions (of whatever kind and however many) are *not the kind of thing* that can bring about an initial mastery of language, for the indeterminacy of the definiendum cannot be eliminated by adding to the definiens. The upshot of this critique is that there must be something more primitive than definitions and explanations in the acquisition of linguistic competence. Wittgenstein is thus compelled to outline an alternative account of language learning (cf. PI §§5–7; see below). Notice that, by contrast, in *Philosophical Grammar* and the lectures no alternative was offered. There, the indeterminacy problem was allegedly solved by appealing to the holism of the calculus view of language; but this view left us at a loss to determine how the language learner can access the holistic systems of interrelated definitions that determine the meaning of words. However, this is not surprising, for in the early 1930s Wittgenstein's primary concern was not to develop an account of language learning (which, after all, he considered "mere history"; cf. e.g., PG §43); it was, rather, to elucidate what determines the normativity of language (however this is acquired). In the writings from the 1940s, however, genetic questions acquire a new significance and Wittgenstein sets out to determine how the normative use of language comes to be established in the first place.

There is a more primitive way of learning language than by means of definitions—namely, learning by practice, by being trained in linguistic activities (cf. PI §§5–7): "Children are brought up to perform *these* actions, to use *these* words as they do so, and to react in *this* way to the words of others" (PI §6). But what does this training consist in? Wittgenstein remarks that "an important part of the training," though only one part, "will consist in the teacher's pointing to the objects, directing the child's attention to them, and at the same time uttering a word" (PI §6). This is what Wittgenstein calls the "ostensive teaching of words," which is to be distinguished from "ostensive definition."[225] The ostensive teaching of a word—for instance, "slab"—will consist in simple exercises or drills such as the following: the pupil "utters the word when the teacher points to the stone"; or a "still simpler exercise: the pupil repeats the word after the teacher" (PI §7). With these drills the pupil learns to articulate certain sounds and to utter them in the presence of certain objects. In these exercises, Wittgenstein remarks, we can see "processes *resembling* language" (PI §7; my emphasis).

These processes resemble but are not yet language, for a language involves more than articulate sounds repeated in certain contexts and after certain signals. What we have here is a *protolanguage*, a language that we extend by courtesy to the primitive behavior of the initiate learner. *We* say "the learner *names* the objects" (PI §7), even though he does not yet have the requisite capacity to do so. Wittgenstein's italics here underscore that this is a special use of the verb "name," for in this case the term can only be used by courtesy, by assimilating the learner's behavior to our practice despite his lack of competence in it. It is the teacher's competence that provides the requisite context, the "stage setting," in which what the learner does can be regarded as *naming*. Thus Wittgenstein emphasizes the structuring role of the teacher in the learning situation and the crucial dependence of the novice's actions on the teacher's competence. The starting point of language learning consists, therefore, in patterned activities structured by a competent speaker or teacher. Under the guidance of the teacher, these drills are used as *bootstrapping devices* that exploit the natural reactions of the pupil to bring him to a mastery of the language. However, these preliminary exercises are simply processes of habituation (not very different from stimulus-response conditioning) that can only produce regularities in the learner's behavior. These behavioral regularities are indispensable for the acquisition of linguistic competence; but, by themselves, they cannot yield the mastery of language. As Wittgenstein remarks, what the ostensive teaching of a word achieves is "to establish an association between the word and the thing" (PI §6). But this association does not amount to an understanding of the word, although it is a crucial step toward it: "Am I to say that [the ostensive teaching] effects an understanding of the word? [. . .] Doubtless the ostensive teaching helped to bring this about; but only together with a *particular training*. With different training the same ostensive teaching of these words would have effected a quite different understanding" (PI §6; my emphasis). So beyond the ostensive teaching of words, language learning requires training into the practice in which those words are used. And only a competent member of that practice can provide this training. The teacher acts as a representative of the practice, and therefore the stage setting he provides is also a *social* setting. What the teacher has to inculcate in the novice is the normative standards of the linguistic community. The required training consists in getting the novice to use words as others do and also in getting him to see that they *should* not be used otherwise.

The process of language learning is thus presented as having an essential social dimension: the teaching of a language is a process of enculturation into linguistic practices. This cursory account of language learning that supplements the critique of ostensive definition consitutes the key background of the rule-following discussion of the *Investigations* (§139ff). As we shall see, this discussion presents striking structural similarities with the critique of ostensive definition.

6.3.2. The Indeterminacy of Rule Following: Interpretations versus Actual Applications

As we saw in chapters 4 and 5, the rule-following considerations of the 1930s were developed around the regress of rules and interpretations. In the 1930s it was the Regress Argument *alone* that supported Wittgenstein's conclusions about rule following; namely, (a) the *negative* conclusion that there is *no intermediary* we can interpose between rule and application that can determine what counts as correct and incorrect rule-following and (b) the *positive* conclusion that rule and application stand in an *internal relation*, that is, that they define each other. Wittgenstein further argued that the way a given rule and its range of possible applications define each other is determined by a particular "method of application" fixed by an entire system of grammatical conventions. He emphasized that this "method" was not to be understood as an extra thing besides the rule and the application but, rather, as the very relation in which rules and applications stand to each other (cf. 4.2).

A different picture of normativity emerges from the rule-following discussion of the *Investigations*. In this discussion the Regress Argument plays a comparatively minor role and serves to establish different conclusions. As before, this argument is used to undermine any inflationist account that postulates an intermediary between rule and application to explain the normativity of rule following: these intermediaries are unmasked as suspect entities, as "idle wheels." But in the *Investigations* the Regress Argument paves the way for quite different positive conclusions: it is used to underscore that rule following cannot be isolated from particular contexts and histories of use. Wittgenstein now argues that what determines the correct applications of a rule is not a "method" but a "technique" of application (cf. PI §150, §199)—that is, the standard procedures or ways of going on of an actual practice. As we shall see, Wittgenstein's conclusions about rule following in the *Investigations* are not drawn from the Regress Argument alone. He uses a whole battery of arguments to draw a practice-based picture of normativity: the Regress Argument is complemented with the Paradox of Interpretation, and the insights these two arguments provide are further elaborated in the Manifestation Argument.

In the *Investigations* the Regress Argument appears in two different contexts: first, in the discussion of what determines the correct use of a word (e.g., "cube"; §§139–42); and second, in the discussion of what determines the correct application of a rule (e.g., in the continuation of a numerical series; esp. §§186–98). In both discussions the Regress Argument is used to establish the same point: that there are no privileged representations (pictures, schemas, rule formulations, or interpretations) which, *by themselves*, can univocally determine what counts as correct; and hence we are led from one representation to another indefinitely in the attempt to fix the correct use of a word or the correct application of a rule by means of representations alone. Representations (of whatever kind, whether physical or mental) are not enough to determine correctness because they can always be interpreted and applied in different ways. So, for instance, the correct use of the word "cube" cannot be fixed by a representation of the object designated by this word, by a picture or drawing of a cube. For, even if we suppose that this picture "comes before our mind" every time we use the word, it is still up for grabs what accords with this representation and what doesn't: "In what sense can this picture fit or fail to fit a use of the word 'cube'?" (PI §139). One may think that if you apply the word to a triangular prism, "then this use of the word does not fit the picture" (PI §139). But this is a mistake, for whether it fits or not depends on how the picture is to be interpreted and projected onto the prism, and "it is quite easy to imagine a *method of projection* according to which the picture does fit after all" (PI §139). So Wittgenstein concludes that although the picture of a cube can "indeed *suggest* a certain use" of the word, it is always "possible for me to use it differently" (PI §139).

One might reply that the indeterminacy problem caused by the multiple projectability of the picture can be solved by fixing the *method* of projection. Perhaps it is the picture together with its method of projection that "comes before our mind": "Perhaps I see before me a schema shewing the method of projection: say a picture of two cubes connected by lines of projection" (§141). But this does not "really get me any further," for: "Can't I now imagine different applications of this schema too?" (§141). The method of projection, insofar as it is a further representation (a schema that "comes before our mind"), is also subject to different interpretations and we need to appeal to something else to determine how it is to be applied. The conclusion that Wittgenstein draws from this Regress Argument is that representations cannot play a normative role in our linguistic activities when detached from particular contexts and histories of use. Pictures and schemas can indeed have normative power, but only against the background of a regular activity of use. As Wittgenstein puts it, what is important is that "people in general apply *this* picture like *this*"; and against this background we can say "we have here a *normal* case, and abnormal cases" (§141). This is what I called above the idea of *contextual determinacy* (cf. 6.1). On the one hand, it is not the case that the use of the term "cube" is radically indeterminate and one can mean by it anything one wants à la Humpty Dumpty. On the other hand, it is not the case either that the term has a fixed range of applications which can be specified *sub specie aeternitatis*. The normative use of words is crucially dependent on actual regularities of use; and these in turn depend on certain constancies in the environment and in our natural reactions:

> *It is only in normal cases that the use of a word is clearly prescribed* [. . .]. And if things were quite different from what they are—if there were for instance *no characteristic expression of*

> *pain, of fear, of joy*; if rule became exception and exception rule; or if both became phenomena of roughly equal frequency—*this would make our normal language-games lose their point.*—The procedure of putting a lump of cheese on a balance and fixing the price by the turn of the scale would lose its point if it frequently happened for such lumps to suddenly grow or shrink for no obvious reason. (PI §142; my emphasis)

Similar argumentative moves and similar conclusions can be found in the discussion of the continuation of a numerical series according to the rule "+ 2" (esp. §§186–98). We are under the impression that the rule determines its applications and that an algebraic representation of the rule can fix the correct continuation of the series. But an algebraic formula (like a picture, or a schema) can be variously interpreted, and hence different continuations of the series can be regarded as correct applications of the same formula (§146). We are likely to reply that it is not the mere expression of the rule (the algebraic formula) but its *meaning* that determines correct usage. For we are "inclined to use such expressions as: 'The steps are *really* already taken . . .' as if they were in some *unique* way predetermined, anticipated—as only the act of meaning can anticipate reality" (§188). So it may appear that if we fix the interpretation of the rule, we thereby fix its meaning and hence its applications. We may think that how the formation rule "+ 2" is to be applied to the series of natural numbers can be fixed by giving the following interpretation: "Write the next but one number after *every* number" (§186). To this suggestion Wittgenstein responds: "But that is just what is in question: what, at any stage, does follow from that sentence. Or, again, what, at any stage we are to call 'being in accord' with that sentence (and with the *mean*-ing you then put into that sentence—whatever that may have consisted in)" (§186). The interpretation of the rule does not really get us any further, for it can in turn be understood in different ways: it is in fact just another formulation of the rule, like the algebraic formula, and it can also be variously interpreted. So Wittgenstein concludes at §198 that "any interpretation still hangs in the air along with what it interprets, and cannot give it any support. Interpretations *by themselves* do not determine meaning" (my emphasis).

As with pictures and schemas, Wittgenstein's point is not that rule formulations and interpretations can have no normative power over our actions but, rather, that "by themselves" they do not determine what we do: far from prescribing a single course of action, they can always be interpreted in countless ways. So, Wittgenstein asks, "what has the expression of a rule—say a signpost—got to do with my actions? What sort of connexion is there here?" (§198). The connection cannot possibly be effected by another representation that gives expression to the rule (for, again, what has *this* expression of the rule got to do with my actions?). So Wittgenstein suggests that the connection is "perhaps this one: I have been trained to react to this sign in a particular way, and now I do so react" (§198). But he emphasizes that this is not to suggest that there is a "causal connexion" between the representation of the rule and its application, between the signpost and my action. "On the contrary; I have further indicated that a person goes by a signpost only insofar as there exists *a regular use* of signposts, *a custom*" (§198; my emphasis). For Wittgenstein, the normative significance of being trained into a custom does not lie in the causal aspects of the training but in the fact that this training provides the link with a regular way of going on, with a canonical procedure for doing things, which functions as the standard for judging the correctness of one's actions.

So, in short, the upshot of the Regress Argument is that interpretations and the like are *not sufficient* to determine correctness, that something else is needed. And this conclusion is accompanied by the suggestion that what is needed is a background of actual practices, of regular activities of use: rule-following activities "are customs (uses, institutions)"; "obeying a rule" is not something that it is "possible for only *one* man to do, and to do only *once* in his life" (PI §199). It is at this point that Wittgenstein resorts to the Paradox of Interpretation. For it is this argument that leads to the definite and *unqualified* rejection of interpretations as the ground for rule following, and that establishes conclusively that the normativity of rule following depends on *actual* practices of application. The Paradox of Interpretation builds on the Regress Argument but it exploits another aspect of the indeterminacy problem created by the multiplicity of interpretations, a *more radical* one.[226] The Paradox shows that the fact of multiple interpretations not only poses the threat of a regress but, ultimately results in *the dissolution of normativity*. As Wittgenstein puts it:

> This was our *paradox*: no course of action could be determined by a rule, because every course of action can be made out to accord with the rule. The answer was: if everything can be made out to accord with the rule, then it can also be made out to conflict with it. *And so there would be neither accord nor conflict here.* (§201; my emphasis)

A rule can be interpreted in countless ways; hence it can be conceived as prescribing any course of action whatsoever and therefore no course of action in particular. Interpretations make the relation between rule and action purely arbitrary, thus depriving rules of their prescriptive power. So the appeal to interpretations is not only idle (as the Regress Argument showed), but in fact *self-undermining*: the very thing that was invoked to explain the normativity of rule following does away with it. What the Paradox of Interpretation shows is not simply that interpretations are insufficient to determine correctness but, rather, that they are *not the kind of thing* in which the normativity of rule following can be grounded. The requisite background for rule following cannot be something akin to an interpretation; it must be something of a completely different nature. Thus Wittgenstein concludes: "What this shews is that there is a way of grasping a rule which is *not* an *interpretation*, but which is *exhibited* in what we call 'obeying the rule' and 'going against it' in *actual* cases" (§201; emphasis preserved and added). The normative relation between rule and application cannot be something susceptible of codification because then it would be subject to multiple interpretations. This relation can only be exhibited in practice, in what we actually do. Furthermore, what counts as the correct application of a rule is not something that can be shown in the isolated actions of a single individual, for then whatever the individual does would be in some way in accord with the rule. A richer context is required: the normative standards for the application of a rule are exhibited in what *we* (competent rule followers) regard as "obeying the rule" and "going against it" in actual cases.

In §202 Wittgenstein makes more explicit the implications of the Paradox of Interpretation: "'Obeying a rule' is a practice. And to *think* one is obeying a rule is not to obey a rule. Hence it is not possible to obey a rule 'privately'." It is important to notice that the claim that "'obeying a rule' is a practice" serves to convey two distinct points: first, that to follow a rule is not something we can do *only in thought,* that it must be *public*; and second, that to follow a rule is not something we can do *only in private*, that it must be *social.* The public *and* social character of rule following is substantiated with two different arguments: the Manifestation Argument and the Private Language Argument. These arguments support and elaborate the conclusions of the Paradox of Interpretation,[227] emphasizing the crucial dependence of the normativity of our actions on our actual and shared practices of rule following.

6.3.3. *The Importance of Being Manifest*

As we have seen, the critique of ostensive definition and the rule-following discussion contain similar argumentative moves and similar conclusions: both underscore the crucial importance of background skills and of the background practices in which these skills are acquired and exercised.[228] Just as the critique of ostensive definition established that there must be a more primitive way of learning language than by means of definitions, the rule-following discussion establishes that there must be a more primitive way of following a rule than by means of interpretations: this is what Wittgenstein calls following a rule "*blindly*" (PI §219) or "as a *matter of course*" (PI §238). The crucial argument that supports this view of rule following is the so-called Manifestation Argument.

In the *Investigations* the Manifestation Argument has a twofold significance. In the first place, it is used to establish a thesis about the nature of understanding; namely, that understanding is not a hidden mental process but a know-how that has to be displayed in actions (§§146–71). As we saw (cf. 2.3.2), Wittgenstein had already defended this conception of understanding in *Philosophical Grammar*. But the Manifestation Argument of the *Investigations* has another, deeper side: it applies not only to our understanding of rules, but also to the rules themselves. This version of the argument shows that rules are immanent in *actual* practices of rule application, that there is *no autonomous* realm of rules distinct and apart from our de facto rule-governed activities (cf. esp. PI §190; but also §§204–38). I will try to show that Wittgenstein's Manifestation Argument in the *Investigations* acquires a new significance because it is supplemented with a discussion of initiate learning. This discussion of learning introduces crucial differences: first, it puts the Manifestation Argument concerning understanding in an entirely new light; and second, it substantiates a similar Manifestation Argument concerning rules, while at the same time avoiding a crude naturalism or regularism that Wittgenstein always regarded as destructive of normativity. So I will argue that the main insights of the Manifestation Argument of the *Investigations* cannot be understood if we disregard Wittgenstein's discussion of initiate learning, as most commentators have done.[229]

The Manifestation Argument concerning understanding is clearly expressed at §146. There Wittgenstein contends that it is a mistake to think of the understanding of a rule as something prior to and independent of actual applications, as "a state which is the *source* of the correct use" (§146). Such a state cannot guarantee correct use, for however this state is conceived (as an algebraic formula appearing in one's mind, as the grasp of an interpretation, etc.), it does not determine one single course of application (§146). So independently of what state one is in, whether or not one understands the rule is to be judged according to what one does: the postulation of a mental state as the source of correct use "does not get us any further. The application is still a criterion of understanding" (§146). Whether the expression "Now I can go on!" indicates understanding does not depend on any mental event concerning the person who utters it but on the context of the utterance (§154); and this context is a temporal one: it includes the subject's prior use of the rule (§179) as well as "what he goes on to do" with it (§180). So far there is no substantial difference with the Manifestation Argument of *Philosophical Grammar*: there too it was emphasized that the only warrant for the attribution of the mastery of a rule is its correct use over time. The differences arise when Wittgenstein considers how a regularity of use is to be determined and how it is produced. Wittgenstein emphasizes that the application of a rule on multiple occasions is not a regularity unless the rule is always applied *in the same way*. And he raises the following problem: any collection of applications—no matter how unlike each other these applications may seem—can be regarded as a regularity, as the manifestation of a pattern, given the appropriate criteria of similarity; and this pattern, in turn, can be seen as being in accord with the rule under some interpretation. Regularities *by themselves* do not solve the indeterminacy problem posed by the Regress Argument and radicalized by the Paradox of Interpretation. So how can regular use then be the proof of understanding? Actual use would indeed be an empty criterion if whatever we do could be counted as the manifestation of understanding. But this appears to be so only when we consider the applications of a rule in isolation. We cannot distinguish between regular and random behavior in a decontextualized series of actions. Nor can we single out among all the possible ways of going on which one instantiates the *right* regularity, the pattern of *correct* use. We need a broader context than the actions of an isolated individual strung together. The normative context required is provided by "what *we* call 'obeying the rule' and 'going against it' in actual cases" (§201; my emphasis). The normative criteria for what counts as doing the *same* thing are to be found in a shared practice of application. Only against the background of a shared practice can we recognize the relevant similarities and distinguish between correct and incorrect ways of going on. These considerations put the Manifestation Argumet concerning understanding in an entirely new light: understanding is manifested not just in what the individual in isolation does on multiple occasions but in what she does, repeatedly, *against the background of a shared practice*. As Wittgenstein puts it, understanding requires the "'mastery' of a technique" (§150)—that is, the skilled use of a common procedure, the participation in a shared way of going on.

Wittgenstein's discussion of initiate learning makes perspicuous the crucial dependence of rule-following regularities on shared practices and their techniques of application. In the learning situation the teacher, as a competent rule follower and hence as a representative of the practice, has the capacity and authority to distinguish between "a normal and an abnormal learner's reaction" (§143). Wittgenstein invites us to consider how we would teach someone to write down the series of natural numbers. At the beginning "series of numbers will be written down for him and he will be required to copy them" (§143). And it is only the teacher who can determine whether the learner copies the numbers in the right order, in the wrong order, or in no order at all. If the pupil writes down numbers at random, he has not understood and further training is required, for "the *possibility of getting him to understand* will depend on his going on to write down [the series] independently" (§143). And here, Wittgenstein remarks, the pupil's capacity to learn may come to an end if he does not exhibit the appropriate reactions to the training.[230] The upshot of this discussion is that the attribution of understanding to the learner is only warranted when he habitually "continues the series *correctly, that is, as we do it*" (§145; my emphasis).[231] So what is required for the understanding or mastery of a rule is not a behavioral regularity of whatever kind, but the kind of regularity that is established through training processes. To understand a rule is to be a member of a practice, to participate in the 'consensus of action' that sustains the use of the rule. It is only in the light of that consensus, against the background of a shared practice, that the behavioral regularities of the pupil acquire normative significance and can be considered as indicative of his understanding or lack thereof.

So far I have tried to show that Wittgenstein's discussion of learning in the *Investigations* gives a peculiar twist to the Manifestation Argument concerning understanding[232] already defended in *Philosophical Grammar*. But it does more than that. With this discussion the Manifestation Argument is extended to establish a more radical idea; namely, that the rules that govern our actions must be manifested in actual practices. A rule can only provide standards of correctness for what we do if there is an actual practice of application that is the manifestation of it. Detached from actual practices, a rule could not have prescriptive power, for there would be no fact of the matter as to what it commands: anything whatever could be counted as following the rule. As Wittgenstein remarks, the normative criteria for the application of a rule are manifested in "the kind of way we always use it, the way we are taught to use it" (PI §190). In the *Remarks* he emphasizes that what is important about a rule governing our practices is "that it is usable, and, above all, *it is used*" (RFM I.4). We can of course see the normativity of a game as contained "in the list of rules of the game," but only when we know how the rules of the game are employed "in the teaching of it, in the day-to-day practice of playing" (RFM I.130). "What is it that compels me?—the expression of the rule?—Yes, once I have been *educated* in this way" (RFM VII.27; my emphasis). So the rules that we can understand and follow presuppose the existence of previously established practices of application. We can indeed introduce new rules that have never been applied before, but they can be understood and followed only when (and insofar as) they are assimilated to the techniques of application available in actual practices. Rules that have never been used can only be the exception, and their intelligibility requires their assimilation to rules embedded in actual practices. Wittgenstein emphasizes this point both in the *Remarks* and in the *Investigations*:

> What surrounding is needed for someone to be able to invent, say, chess? Of course I might invent a board-game today, which would never actually be played. I should simply describe it. But that is possible only because there already exist similar games, that is because such games *are played*. [. . .] I may give a new rule today, which has never been applied, and yet it is understood. But would that be possible, if no rule had *ever* actually been applied? (RFM VI.32)

> As things are I can, for example, invent a game that is never played by anyone.—But would the following be possible too: mankind has never played any games; once, however, someone invented a game—which no one ever played? (PI §204)

On Wittgenstein's mature view, a rule can only be followed when it is embedded in an actual practice of use that constrains its possible applications. By contrast, as discussed above (cf. 3.3.2), in *Philosophical Grammar* Wittgenstein explicitly rejected the dependence of the normativity of rules on our actual practices. He thought that doing so would commit him to an unacceptable regularism that ultimately results in the dissolution of normativity. Indeed, the identification of what a rule prescribes with an actual regularity or pattern of use would make rule following utterly indeterminate, for any given set of performances may be regarded as the manifestation of infinitely many regularities. And this indeterminacy underscores that mere regularities cannot provide standards of correctness: take any pattern of actions and for anything you might go on to do, there is some regularity with respect to which your action counts as "going on *in the same way*." So how can Wittgenstein assert the necessary dependence of rules on actual practices and yet avoid this unacceptable regularism?

For Wittgenstein, there is more to the manifestation of a rule in a practice than mere behavioral regularities. Manifestation involves two interwoven elements: behavior and attitude. The manifestation of a rule in a practice requires regularity in the actions of practitioners as well as uniformity in their reactions to each other's actions. A rule is manifested in a practice only when, by and large, practitioners agree in what they do *and* in how they assess their actions. Rule following thus involves a twofold consensus: rule followers must share not only a particular way of doing things but also a normative attitude toward what is done. A mere regularity in behavior is not sufficient for the manifestation of a rule; behavioral regularities have to be accompanied by expressions of approval and disapproval, of acceptance and rejection.

The manifestation of normative attitudes becomes perspicuous in the process of learning, where the behavior of the pupil is constantly assessed by the teacher. Thus it is not surprising that Wittgenstein appeals to the teacher-pupil interactions when he tries to distinguish his Manifestation Argument from a crude regularistic view of rules. He asks "am I defining 'order' and 'rule' by means of 'regularity'?" (§208). His answer is that "order," "rule," "regularity," and "sameness" are interrelated normative terms whose meaning we grasp by being acculturated in particular practices of rule following. In these processes of enculturation what becomes perspicuously manifested is not only a particular way of going on, but also a particular *attitude* toward how to go on: "I do it, he does it after me; and I influence him by *expressions of agreement, rejection, expectation, encouragement*. I let him go his way, or hold him back; and so on" (§208; my emphasis).

On Wittgenstein's view, the behavioral regularities and the normative attitudes of practitioners are the mutually supporting elements of which rule-following practices are made. As discussed above, only when the learner has acquired behavioral mastery in the use of a rule can she exhibit a normative attitude toward what she does. On the other hand, the learner's regular use of the rule is initially established through the guidance provided by the normative attitude of the teacher, and it is subsequently sustained by the learner's own attitude when she becomes a competent practitioner. So Wittgenstein's account of rule following does *not* involve a naturalistic reduction of normativity. For, in this account, the normative is not reduced to something else, a more primitive, nonnormative element (such as causal connections or mere behavioral "regularities"). On the contrary, the normative attitudes of practitioners are an essential component of what Wittgenstein calls the "bedrock" of our rule following practices (cf. PI §217). A practice of rule-following requires from its members that they act as a matter of course and refuse any other path; that is, it requires an attitude of "blind obedience" (cf. PI §219).

I have argued that, on Wittgenstein's view, we become rule followers by being acculturated in rule-following practices, thus acquiring the normative procedures and attitudes of a community. This may suggest that my interpretation ascribes to Wittgenstein an impoverished view of normativity in which what is correct is what the community decides to count as such. Simon Blackburn (1984) has argued that this is the mistake of all community interpretations. According to Blackburn, there is no satisfactory community reponse to the rule-following arguments of the *Investigations*. As we saw, the isolated individual cannot follow rules because she cannot distinguish between what is correct and what seems correct to her; but similarly, the community cannot provide the appropriate normative context for rule following if there is no distinction between what is correct and what the community regards as correct. So the community does not seem to offer a firmer ground for the normativity of rule following than the individual. Just as an individualistic view of rule following makes the individual infallible, a community view precludes collective mistakes; and where there is no room for mistakes, there is no genuine distinction between correct and incorrect. Thus Blackburn's challenge to community interpretations is to make sense of the possibility of the community being wrong.[233] This challenge is just a formulation of the threat of relativism that haunts community views. When norms are said to be embedded in particular practices, it may seem to follow that different practices will have not just different but *incommensurable* norms. But can normativity be relativized in this way? Can't our assessments of correctness transcend particular communities? In what follows I will argue that my contextualist version of the community view of rule following does not entail relativism and makes room for the possibility of collective mistakes. The trick will be to show how community agreement can provide the requisite context for normative assessments without thereby determining the outcome of those assessments.

To conclude this chapter I also want to address another challenge that arises for my reading of Wittgenstein's later view. Recent interpretations have emphasized the *quietism* of Wittgenstein's philosophy, calling attention to the antitheoretical attitude of his metaphilosophical reflections (cf. esp. Diamond 1991, Minar 1995, McGinn 1997, and Crary and Read 2000). These quietist interpretations issue a challenge to any reading that attributes to Wittgenstein a positive philosophical view. The quietist challenge is to explain how Wittgenstein can hold any positive view without betraying the antitheoretical attitude of his metaphilosophy.[234] It may appear that I have sinned against the quietism of Wittgenstein's philosophy, for I have attributed to the later Wittgenstein a contextualist and practice-based view of normativity centered around the notion of community agreement. In what follows I argue that my reading is not insensitive to Wittgenstein's antitheoretical attitude and is in fact perfectly compatible with his metaphilosophical reflections (cf., esp., PI §§89–133). My discussion will focus on the quietist interpretation of Edward Minar, who criticizes those commentators who depict Wittgenstein as offering a new philosophical picture of language and rule following based on community agreement.

So in the next section I will try to kill two birds with one stone. My elucidation of the role of community agreement in Wittgenstein's view of normativity will try to meet both the relativist challenge (as posed by Blackburn) and the quietist challenge (as posed by Minar).

6.4. The Role of the Community: Contextualism and Quietism in Wittgenstein's Later Philosophy

In "Feeling at Home in Language" Edward Minar (1995) argues that the goal of Wittgenstein's reflections in the *Philosophical Investigations* is purely therapeutic; namely, to achieve the dissolution of philosophical "pictures" by going to the very roots of philosophical thinking and blocking the path to theory construction. These pictures are the product of a metaphysical or essentialist impulse that compels the philosopher to search for foundations. In this search we are forced to bracket the familiar and ordinary, to forget our lives in language. As Minar puts it, what goes into the elaboration of a philosophical picture is "an *effort* of forgetfulness":[235] "We act *as though* we have forgotten what language is."[236] Wittgenstein tries to repair this forgetfulness by "assembling reminders" (PI §127) that call attention to aspects of language which have fallen into oblivion. Minar insists that these reminders do not convey new philosophical insights; they have only a therapeutic value: they help us recover our lost innocence, the "natural attitude" we had before our lives were touched by philosophy.[237] So, according to Minar, it is a mistake to derive any positive philosophical view from Wittgenstein's arguments as the defenders of community interpretations do.

Norman Malcolm (1989) has argued that for Wittgenstein a common agreement in action is a *necessary condition* for rule following. Barry Stroud (1990) has ascribed to Wittgenstein the view that what *determines* the meaning of an expression is the way it is used by a community of speakers. And Meredith Williams (1991) has attributed to Wittgenstein the thesis that the presence of an actual community is *indispensable* for language and rule following. Minar argues that these claims misrepresent Wittgenstein's position. But what exactly is wrong with the community view of language and rule following? Minar's diagnosis of the community view is that it rests on a misunderstanding of the role that ordinary language plays in Wittgenstein's arguments.[238] According to this diagnosis, the crucial mistake that motivates community interpretations is the idea that Wittgenstein's appeals to our everyday practices yield a philosophical picture of language and rule following. For Minar, to say that Wittgenstein's elucidations of meaning and normativity in terms of ordinary practices of use amounts to a philosophical picture is to say that the *essence* of meaning and normativity are contained in ordinary language. Once this essentialist picture is in place, it stands in need of justification; and the natural place to look for the *foundations* of this picture is in the consensus of action underlying our ordinary practices. In what follows I will try to refute this diagnosis. First, I will argue that Minar focuses on a very radical version of the community view and that, even if his critique is fair to some of the authors he criticizes, it is not the case that every version of the community view is necessarily committed to an essentialist picture of language and rule following. Second, I will argue that Minar's critique does not apply to the *antiessentialist and contextualist* picture of language and normativity that I have attributed to the latter Wittgenstein. I will try to show that community agreement does play a crucial role in this picture, though not a foundational role.

What is the essentialist misunderstanding concerning the role of ordinary language that Minar denounces? He describes this misunderstanding in two different ways. First, Minar argues that commentators have taken Wittgenstein to hold that ordinary language provides "an accurate conceptual map of reality," that it functions "as a standard against which to measure the way things really are."[239] There is no commentator I know of who has ascribed to Wittgenstein this kind of metaphysical realism grounded in ordinary language; and, at any rate, it is certainly not the view of the authors who are the main target of Minar's critique (Malcolm, Stroud, and Williams). These authors claim that, for Wittgenstein, our ordinary practices of language use fix the grammar of our concepts; but they do not suggest that these concepts are absolutely the right ones or that they carve reality at the joints. On the contrary, they call attention to Wittgenstein's explicit rejection of this metaphysical view.[240] The second way in which Minar describes the essentialist misunderstanding concerning the role of ordinary language is more felicitous. He observes that commentators have ascribed to Wittgenstein the view that "possibilities are somehow projected or created by linguistic usage."[241] Indeed, despite crucial differences in their interpretations, Malcolm, Stroud, and Williams all agree that, for Wittgenstein, the possible uses of a term and the possible employments of a rule are to be grounded in an actual practice of application. But in what sense is this an *essentialist* claim?

The idea that ordinary language can determine what makes sense *sub specie aeternitatis* certainly invokes an essentialist picture. The Kantian interpretation of Wittgenstein's later philosophy put forth by Bernard Williams and Jonathan Lear seems to indulge in this picture, depicting Wittgenstein's later philosophy as a transcendental view of language that concerns itself with the a priori limits of intelligibility.[242] According to this interpretation, in Wittgenstein's later view ordinary language plays the same role that logical form played in his earlier view: it draws sharp boundaries around what can be thought and expressed in language. Although

Minar does not refer to the Kantian interpretation, it is really the transcendental reading that he is criticizing when he argues that the notion of "the limits of intelligibility" cannot find a place in Wittgenstein's later view.[243] Minar is right in arguing that there is no room in this view for imposing a priori restrictions on the possible uses of a term or the possible applications of a rule since all we have is an irreducible plurality of linguistic practices in constant change. But the fact that the possible applications of a term or a rule are openended does not mean that they are up for grabs (cf. my discussion of "contextual determinacy" in 6.1 and 6.3). On Wittgenstein's view, our ordinary practices of language use do *constrain* our speech and rule-following behavior by providing the requisite normative *background* for our utterances and actions. But, as discussed above (6.1), this does not mean that the practices of ordinary language constitute a straightjacket for our thought and speech, for these practices are not static structures that are fixed once and for all, but dynamic activities that are always in the making. As we saw, in the *Lectures* from 1939 Wittgenstein emphasizes that our speech and normative behavior are constrained by the techniques of language use and rule following available in our practices, but he also points out that what can be considered intelligible in a practice depends on how we extend the techniques employed in that practice; and "there may be many different techniques, any one of which we might decide to call the continuation of the old technique" (LFM p. 69). So, on Wittgenstein's view, the actual practices of ordinary language in which we are trained *constrain but do not determine* our ways of thinking and talking.

On my interpretation, Wittgenstein's appeals to ordinary language convey a contextualist point about language use; namely, that it requires a normative *context* in which standards of correctness are exhibited, a context that can only be provided by the actual practices of ordinary language. The crucial essentialist move behind the traditional philosophical pictures that Wittgenstein criticizes is precisely the decontextualization of language. When language is detached from ordinary contexts of use, its normativity appears mysterious and only explicable by appealing to metaphysical fictions. On this picture of language, grammar appears as a free-floating structure that needs to be grounded in secure foundations. Decontextualized pictures of this kind which incite foundationalist ambitions are the target of Wittgenstein's critique. He urges us to resist those philosophical pictures that compel us to look for explanations behind the phenomena and to elaborate theories: "We may not advance any kind of theory. There must not be anything hypothetical in our considerations. We must do away with all *explanation*, and description alone must take its place" (PI §109). But does it follow from this that we must do away with *all pictures*? Would it be admissible to use a picture of language that does not call for explanation and theory building? As Charles Crittenden (1970) has argued, Wittgenstein has nothing against "pictures" as such and he himself makes use of pictures in his discussions (cf. e.g., PI §144). As Crittenden remarks, for Wittgenstein a "picture" (*Bild*) is simply a "way of looking at things" (PI §144). A picture is not necessarily theoretical, for it may or may not lead to the elaboration of a theory (*Theorie*).

Wittgenstein attacks the theoretical pictures that depart from our ordinary practices and distort them. But when these pictures are dissolved, we are not left emptyhanded; we are left with a more accurate picture: "the picture of our ordinary way of speaking" (PI §402). Wittgenstein wants us to look at language afresh as we encounter it in our everyday lives. In the process of debunking various philosophical pictures he calls attention to features of language that have been overlooked in philosophy and thus he suggests a new way of looking at language: an antiessentialist and contextualist picture (or set of pictures)[244] that is in perfect harmony with our ordinary linguistic practices because it never departed from them. As Wittgenstein puts it, the point of his discussion is "to establish an order in our knowledge of the use of language: an order with a particular end in view; one out of many possible orders; not *the* order." (PI §132). This pluralistic and contextualist view of language that Wittgenstein offers is a non-theoretical picture (or set of pictures) that needs no grounding. As Crittenden puts it, Wittgenstein "has advanced a 'conception' of language, but there is no question of its being *true* or being *proved* right (or probable) by argumentation or evidence: it is a way of looking at language and does not purport to be a *thesis* to be established or falsified."[245]

On Wittgenstein's view, pictures (unlike theses and theories) are neither true nor false; they are simply ways of looking at things that can be more or less useful and more or less appropriate to the task at hand. His own critical enterprise relies on a picture (or set of pictures) of language which he uses to undercut metaphysical impulses and to block the path to theory construction. Now, by claiming that the ascription of a positive view or picture to Wittgenstein is an act of hubris, Minar seems to overlook the Wittgensteinian distinction between pictures and explanatory theories. He assumes that when we ascribe a picture of language to Wittgenstein, we depict him as indulging in theses and theories that try to explain the phenomena instead of describing them. Hence he concludes that Wittgenstein's arguments do not rely on any positive view. But, of course, we cannot understand Wittgenstein's reflections as a *presuppositionless* critical activity. It would be a mistake to think that Wittgenstein voices his criticism from nowhere, that he carries out his critical enterprise without taking a stance. As Minar himself points out: "There is no neutral stance, no 'nothing' from which to begin" (p. 446). But Minar emphasizes that Wittgenstein tries to undermine philosophical pictures from within by exploiting their internal tensions and contradictions without presupposing anything *philosophical*.[246] Although it is certainly true that the critical reflections of the *Investigations* do not presuppose philosophical theses and theories that would stand in need of grounding, they do express Wittgenstein's *philosophical commitment* to a particular way of looking at things: the situated perspective of ordinary language. Wittgenstein wants us to go "back to the rough ground" of our ordinary linguistic practices (PI §107), to look at language from the perspective of the engaged practitioner who finds herself *in media res*. This is the contextualist picture of language that emerges from Wittgenstein's discussions. Now, what is the role of the community in this picture?

Minar argues that community interpretations of Wittgenstein's philosophy assign a *foundational* or *constitutive* role to the agreement of the community. According to Minar's diagnosis, commentators assume that Wittgenstein's appeals to what we normally say and do in our ordinary practices stand in need of justification and they find this justification in community agreement, which is thought to be the ultimate ground of normativity, something *constitutive* of meaning and rule following. In this way, Minar remarks, interpreters create the illusion that "Wittgenstein's appeals to what we say have been *justified*, in the sense that the community view has shown agreement in (our) use to be the *only source* of (our) standards of correctness."[247] Some commentators have construed the role of community agreement in this way (cf. esp. Wright 1980 and Kripke 1982). And Minar is right that this radical construal of the community view rests on a foundationalist picture. But this is not the contextualist picture I have ascribed to Wittgenstein. In this picture, community agreement plays a crucial role, but not a justificatory and foundational one. In Wittgenstein's contextualist view the agreement of the community is not the foundation or the ultimate ground of normativity; it is simply part of the requisite background against which we use language and follow rules. The upshot of Wittgenstein's arguments is that language use and rule following cannot take place in a vacuum; they are situated activities which require a context: an important *part* of this context is the agreement in action of the members of a community of speakers or rule followers; another important part consists in what Wittgenstein calls "very general facts of nature" (e.g., PI p. 230). Community agreement and facts of nature play a similar role in Wittgenstein's view. An analogy between these elements of the contextualist picture can be illuminating.

Consider, for example, our ordinary practices of measuring. There are certain general facts of nature that constitute the background conditions of these practices. Our practices of measuring are crucially dependent on physical contexts in which the weight and length of objects remain (more or less) constant. As we have seen, Wittgenstein brings these background conditions to the fore by means of thought experiments. In these thought experiments he asks us to imagine what would happen if the background conditions that make up the physical contexts of our practices did not obtain. For instance, he remarks that our ordinary practice of measuring length with rulers would lose its point if we started to use elastic rulers made of soft rubber (cf. RFM I.5). In the same vein, Wittgenstein emphasizes that our practices of measuring are crucially (*but not foundationally*) dependent on our agreement in action and in form of life. We can distinguish between correct and incorrect results in these practices because we all take measurements in similar ways and by and large we all get the same results: "What we call 'measuring' is partly determined by a certain constancy in results of measurement" (PI §242). If there were no agreement whatsoever in the results we obtain in our measuring practices ("if rule became exception and exception rule; or if both became phenomena of roughly equal frequency"), these practices would "lose their point" (PI §142). The point of a practice depends (among other things) on the consensus of action of its practitioners (cf. my discussion of the *wood sellers* thought experiment in 6.1). This consensus of action makes the practice *contextually* determinate but, given its openended nature, it allows for certain amount of indeterminacy, leaving room for change. Two important points about this consensus should be noted. First, the agreement in action of a community *constrains but does not determine* the normative behavior of the members of that community, for (as discussed above) this consensus can be extended, transformed, and even replaced by a different one if need be. Second, the practical agreement of a community functions as the *background* of the normative assessments of its members, not as the guarantor and ultimate ground for the correctness of what the say and do.

For Wittgenstein, a normative activity requires a consensus of action. But this does not mean that the normativity of a practice has to be *grounded* in the consensus of its practitioners, that what counts as correct in the practice has to be determined and justified by reference to the common behavior of the majority. As Wittgenstein puts it, our agreement "is the *pre-condition* of our language-game, it is not affirmed in it" (RFM VII.9; my emphasis). This explains why Wittgenstein wants to emphasize, on the one hand, that the laws of logic and mathematics are crucially dependent on our agreement in forms of life and, on the other hand, that these laws "are not propositions of human natural history" which say "Human beings agree with one another in such and such ways" (RFM VI.49). For instance, in what sense is an arithmetical law governing the computations of a group of people dependent on their agreement? Not in the sense that the principle is adopted as a norm by majority vote; that is, not in the sense that it is "established by their all agreeing that it's true—as if they were witnesses of it" (LFM p. 107). The sense of this dependence is more indirect: it is a *precondition* of their following an arithmetical rule that "they agree in what they do," that they all get the same results in their calculations. "*Because* they all agree in what they do, we lay it down as a rule, and put it in the archives" (p. 107). More generally, it is a *precondition* of a rule-following practice that its practitioners agree in what they do, that by and large they all do the same thing, that their actions exhibit a sufficient degree of uniformity.

Community agreement plays a positive role in Wittgenstein's view, but not an explanatory or justificatory role. The role of our agreement in action and form of life is analogous to the role of "certain very general facts of nature": these are crucial elements of the contexts in which our practices take place, elements without which our practices would not be what they are, elements that we cannot neglect if we want to understand the normativity of our practices. But this contextualist picture does not have foundationalist implications. By stressing the importance of "certain very general facts of nature" Wittgenstein is not suggesting that these natural facts constitute the source of normativity, that nature somehow determines our standards of correctness. And just as Wittgenstein's appeals to natural facts do not entail a crude naturalism, his appeals to community agreement do not entail a naive majoritarian view of normativity. In Wittgenstein's view the community does not function as a last court of appeal for settling normative disputes, as an unchallengeable tribunal that, like on oracle, dictates what is right and what is wrong. Rather, the practical agreement of a community provides a horizon of understanding, a situated perspective for normative evaluations; but this horizon, far from being a straightjacket, can always be expanded and transformed in unforeseen ways. This view does not preclude, but in fact invites the possibility of a radical critic who calls into question and tries to transform the established normative standards accepted by a community. As we saw, the consensus of action of a community is always in the making; and the conscious attempt of practitioners to contribute to the formation or transformation of this consensus in order to improve the practice based on it, making it more open and fair, is certainly to be welcome. But Wittgenstein's view does issue a warning to the social critic; namely, that for her activity to be genuinely transformative, it cannot be limited to words, but it must be directed toward actions. Words can only bring about superficial changes. If we want to change not only the appearance (or wording) of a practice but its normative structure, we need to change the consensus of action of its practitioners. As discussed above (cf. esp. 6.2), this would involve instituting new processes of training through which the members of the practice are acculturated and acquire new normative attitudes.

According to the contextualist view I have ascribed to Wittgenstein, the member of a practice can call into question any aspect of the existing consensus of action that sustains the practice, but she cannot question *every* aspect of the existing consensus without becoming an outcast, that is, without ceasing to be a participant in the practice. However, this does not curtail the possibility of criticism. For, on this contextualist view, it is perfectly possible to challenge the correctness of an entire practice from the perspective of another practice. So my contextualist version of the community view can meet the challenge raised by Blackburn, which was the following: if our normative assessments depend on community agreement, how can we make sense of a whole community of rule followers being mistaken, or of an entire practice being wrong? I hope to have shown that my interpretation of Wittgenstein's view of normativity does not exclude the possibility of collective mistakes or incorrect practices, which can be assessed as such from the standpoint of some other community of practices. What this contextualist view does exclude is the possibility of assessing our actions and practices from an *absolute perspective* or a *view from nowhere*. Wittgenstein's contextualism rejects the idea that there is a single correct perspective that can be invoked in all contexts and for all purposes (as metaphysical realists claim); but it does not follow from this that any perspective is as good as any other.[248] As far as I can tell, there is nothing in Wittgenstein's view that entails relativism[249] and the thesis of the incommensurability of normative standards. As suggested above (cf. 6.1), whether the standards of different practices are commensurable or incommensurable is not something that can be established a priori. For there are no a priori facts that determine whether or not the norms of different practices are combinable; this is a historical issue: it depends on what practitioners do, on whether or not they can find a common ground in which the two practices can be evaluated against each other. Even when we encounter two radically different practices that appear to be mutually exclusive, we cannot rule out a priori the possibility that their practitioners might eventually form a consensus of action that brings the two practices close enough to be compared. So there is no room in Wittgenstein's view for incommensurability *in principle*.[250]

When the role of community agreement is properly understood within this contextualist view as constraining (but not determining) our normative behavior, relativism is no longer a threat. On the other hand, I hope to have shown that my contextualist version of the community view also meets the quietist challenge raised by Minar. As argued above, the contextualist appeal to community agreement as part of the requisite *background* of our normative assessments does not invoke an essentialist or foundationalist picture and, therefore, Minar's worry about attributing a positive role to community agreement is unfounded. My contextualist reading of Wittgenstein's later view is perfectly compatible with the antitheoretical spirit of his philosophy. For Wittgenstein's ferocious attack on philosophical theorizing is aimed against a particular way of doing philosophy: systematic philosophy and its essentialist and foundationalist assumptions,[251] and the philosophical picture I have attributed to Wittgenstein is certainly not part of a philosophical system that purports to solve philosophical problems in a traditional way. But the arguments of the later Wittgenstein put philosophical issues concerning language and rule following under a new light, suggesting a new way of thinking about them; and this is what I have called his contextualist and practice-based view of normativity. On this view, norms are embedded in particular contexts of action; but these contexts, far from being sealed off from each other, are interconnected and exhibit a (degree of) porosity that allows for traffic to flow across them. From a contextualist point of view, the norms of a practice do not have a fixed and constitutive character but, rather, a fluid and openended nature and, therefore, they are always open to criticism and change.[252]

I think that the contextualist account of normativity I have attributed to the later Wittgenstein is the most deflationary story about normativity that one can tell. But, of course, the quietist would reply that there is a much thinner story—namely, no story at all. However, this won't do. The silence treatment won't be enough for those who are struggling with philosophical problems. According to Wittgenstein, in order to deflate philosophical notions (such as "meaning," "necessity," and "correctness") and dissolve philosophical problems, we need to provide "perspicuous representations" that can produce the kind of "understanding which consists in 'seeing connexions'" (PI §122). As Wittgenstein remarks, the "perspicuous representations" that his discussions offer take a particular "form"—namely, the contextualization of philosophical issues and concepts. Wittgenstein's contextualism has a methodological significance: it is a method for tackling philosophical problems, a deflationary way of looking at things, a strategy that enables us to put things in perspective, "to bring words back from their metaphysical to their everyday use" (PI §116). This is the deflationary strategy that Wittgenstein was developing and perfecting throughout his philosophical career.

I hope to have shown in this chapter that Wittgenstein's deflationary method acquires maturity with the *pragmatic contextualism* he developed in the late 1930s and early 1940s. This view constitutes the framework within which Wittgenstein's subsequent works were drafted. Most (if not all) of his later writings can be read as showing in various ways how decontextualization breeds philosophical illusions. From the late 1930s on, what unifies the Wittgensteinian corpus is the attempt to show how in a variety of areas (psychology, mathematics, ethics, aesthetics, religion, etc.) philosophical thinking can go astray by removing concepts and claims from their everyday practical contexts, that is, by assessing their significance and validity in abstraction from their connections with ordinary activities, independently of the role they play in our lives.[253] Most notably, in *On Certainty* Wittgenstein discusses in detail how the philosophical assessment of our epistemic practices can become idle when philosophical reflection is so removed from all practical contexts that it leaves our lives untouched.[254] This and other themes in Wittgenstein's later philosophy call for a separate treatment that remains beyond the scope of this work. But I hope that my account of Wittgenstein's contextualist view of normativity can be used as a springboard for futher studies.

If my developmental story has shed some light on what unifies Wittgenstein's philosophy throughout its changes, it has achieved its goal. I wish I could have offered a less abstruse story. But I would like to think that the entangled nature of my story reflects not only the limitations of its narrator but also the complexity of the development of Wittgenstein's thought.

Notes

Introduction

1. There were of course some exceptions. The most important one was the developmental account of A. Kenny (1972), which was a pioneer in emphasizing points of continuity in Wittgenstein's thought.

2. Important steps in this direction were already taken in the 1980s by commentators who have reconstructed interesting lines of continuity in the evolution of Wittgenstein's thought: Baker and Hacker (1985); Hintikka and Hintikka (1986); and D. Pears (1987 and 1988). More recently, there have been careful examinations of the previously overlooked intermediate period of Wittgenstein's philosophy which stress the continuity of his thought. See D. Stern (1995) and D. Jacquette (1998).

3. Later writings such as *On Certainty* (from 1950–51) will remain beyond the scope of this work. I will assume that there are no substantive changes in Wittgenstein's view after he completed the composition of the rule-following discussion in part 1 of the *Philosophical Investigations* by 1945. Since no one in the literature argues that there are such changes, the attempt to show the continuity of Wittgenstein's philosophy after 1945 seems superfluous. Therefore, the goal of this book will be simply to show the unity in the development of Wittgenstein's thought from the *Tractatus* to the *Investigations*. An examination of the rule-following discussion will bring my developmental account to a conclusion.

4. In my opinion the newly formed orthodoxy in the Wittgenstein literature sometimes goes too far in denying any new development or change in Wittgenstein's thought throughout his career. Although I reject this extreme formulation of the continuity thesis, I take my developmental

account to be in line with and give support to the recent trend in the literature. As Alice Crary puts it in her introduction to *The New Wittgenstein*, what is characteristic of the new line of interpretation that originates in Diamond's and Conant's work is not the idea that Wittgenstein never changed his mind but, rather, the idea that Wittgenstein's philosophy "is unified in its fundamental aim, in its characteristic modes of criticism and even, to some degree, in its methods" (Crary and Read [2000], p. 13). However, I do not want to overstate the general convergence between my developmental account and the recent trend in the literature. For my interpretation of Wittgenstein will also be critical of certain aspects of this trend. See my critical remarks on Diamond (1991) in chapter 1 (section 1.1; though I do rely heavily on her work); my arguments in response to Minar (1995) in chapter 6 (section 6.4); and my arguments against Cerbone (2000) in notes 159, 200, and 204.

5. As we shall see, these different kinds of contextualism draw on different conceptions of the holistic aspects of language.

6. See M. Dummett, "Frege and Wittgenstein," in I. Block (1981), pp. 31–42; and Baker (1988).

7. See Diamond (1991), esp. chapters 2–4, pp. 95–144; Conant (1991a); and Reck (2000).

Chapter 1. Necessity and Intelligibility in the Tractus

1. Cf. A. Kenny (1972), chapter 6, pp. 103–119; E. B. Allaire, "*Tractatus* 6.3751," in S. Shanker (1986) vol. 1, pp. 202–206; J. Austin, "Wittgenstein's Solutions to the Color Exclusion Problem," also in S. Shanker (1986) vol. 1, pp. 207–12; and S. Shanker (1987), p. 6.

2. See esp. D. Jacquette (1990).

3. Diamond (1991), p. 195.

4. Wittgenstein makes this remark about the truth of a tautology when he writes: "It is the peculiar mark of logical propositions that one can recognize that they are true from the symbol alone" (6.113). He could have said the same thing about the falsity of a contradiction.

5. Diamond (1991), p. 196.

6. For a fuller account of what I have termed "the deontologization of necessity," I refer the reader to her exposition in "Throwing Away the Ladder: How to Read the *Tractatus*," in Diamond (1991), pp. 179–204.

7. Diamond (1991), p. 193.

8. In the normal case of a significant proposition, its logical form shows which possibility is depicted by the proposition. By contrast, the logical form of tautologies and contradictions shows that there is no possi-

bility whatsoever that they depict. "Propositions show what they say: tautologies and contradictions show that they say nothing" (4.461).

9. Diamond gives an account of why Wittgenstein's remark that there is only logical necessity (6.37 and 6.375) is nonsensical (and not merely empty). As she puts it, this remark "is itself ironically self-destructive. It has the form, the syntactic form, of 'There is only this sort of thing,' i.e., it uses the linguistic forms in which we say that there are only thises rather than thises and that's. It belongs to its syntax that it itself says something the other side of which can be represented too" (1991, p. 198).

10. Diamond (1991), p. 192.

11. This is how Diamond explains the Tractarian view of truth-functionality : "We make entirely clear what sentence a sentence is, what its functionality is, if we are able to write it so that its truth-valuedness can be clearly seen to be independent of the truth or falsity of any other sentence *and* of its own truth or falsity: independent of the truth or falsity of *any* sentence" (1991, p. 191).

12. D. Pears, for one, talks about "a latent possibility of conflict between the separatism and the holism of the *Tractatus*" (1987, p. 134). See also his "The Logical Independence of Elementary Propositions" in I. Block (1981), pp. 74–84.

13. Diamond (1991), p. 194.

14. Diamond (1991), p. 194.

15. Wittgenstein's remarks on logic emphasize the intimate connection between necessity and logical syntax. He characterizes logic as "a field [. . .] in which the nature of the absolutely necessary signs speaks for itself. If we know the logical syntax of any sign-language, then we have already been given all the propositions of logic" (6.124). Wittgenstein's discussion of logic also underscores that all logical propositions are tautologies and, therefore, the necessary truths of logic are entirely empty: "The propositions of logic [. . .] have no subject-matter" (6.124).

16. F. P. Ramsey (1923), p. 473.

17. Shanker (1987), p. 6.

18. H. Ishiguro (1969), pp. 20ff.

19. Ishiguro (1969), p. 34. Note that, according to Ishiguro, there is no difference between the sense of a proposition and its truth conditions, for the distinction between intensional and extensional contexts collapses in Wittgenstein's view. By contrast, in his realist reading of the *Tractatus*, Pears (1987) argues that Wittgenstein distinguishes between the truth conditions of a proposition (which capture what the proposition says) and its "sense conditions" (which "are ineffable"; p. 71).

20. Ishiguro (1969), p. 34.

21. See B. McGuinness (1981), esp. pp. 65–68.

22. A full defense of this realist reading (in a qualified form) can be found in D. Pears (1987), chapter 5, pp. 88–114. He writes: "Once a name has been attached to an object, the nature of the object takes over and controls the logical behavior of the name, causing it to make sense in some sentential contexts but not in others" (p. 88).

23. Pears (1987) argues that the Ishiguro-McGuinness interpretation misrepresents the "direction of fit" between a name and its referent by assuming that the propositional contexts in which the name figures set the "standard of fit," and that the referent is "whatever object meets the standard" (p. 111). Pears contends that the direction of fit is in fact the opposite one: "When a name has been attached to an object, the object is the dominant partner in the relationship, and its inherent possibilities decide whether the name thereafter represents it" (ibid.). But this objection does not seem to do justice to the Ishiguro-McGuinness interpretation. It is misleading to suggest that this interpretation involves a thesis about the "direction of fit" between name and object, for this makes it seem as if name and object could exist independently of each other and had to be put in a proper relation. But this is precisely what the Ishiguro-McGuinness interpretation denies. What is at the core of this interpretation is the thesis that the identity of a name and the identity of the object it designates are inseparable, since they are simultaneously constituted by the semantic role the name plays in sentences. So, on this interpretation, names and objects cannot be independently identified and therefore the issue of the "direction of fit" cannot even arise: it makes literally no sense to ask "What is the relation in which name and object stand to each other?" and "What is the 'dominant partner' in the relation?"

24. Cf. Pears (1987), pp. 108–109.

25. McGuinness (1981), p. 73.

26. McGuinness (1981), p. 63.

27. Diamond (1991), pp. 197–98.

28. Ramsey (1923), p. 473.

29. Ramsey (1923), p. 473.

30. J. Hintikka and M. B. Hintikka (1983), p. 164.

31. Wittgenstein (1979), p. 81.

32. Hintikka and Hintikka (1983), p. 163.

33. See J. Hintikka and M. B. Hintikka (1986), chapter 3.

34. G. E. M. Anscombe (1959), pp. 25–28.

35. M. Black (1964), ad loc.

36. Shanker (1987), p. 6.

37. In Wittgenstein (1993), pp. 29–35.

38. See esp. Wittgenstein (1993), p. 35; and PG, pp. 210–11.

39. Diamond (1991), p. 193.

40. Hintikka and Hintikka (1983), pp. 163–64.

41. This very idea is echoed in the *Philosophical Investigations*: "It is clear that every sentence in our language 'is in order as it is'" (§98).

42. Hintikka and Hintikka's interpretation not only goes against the thesis that ordinary language is "in perfect logical order," but also fails to do justice to the thesis that the simultaneous attribution of different colors to a point in the visual field is a *logical* impossibility. For this thesis does not simply require that it should be possible to construct a language in which incompatible color attributions would have the form of truth-functional contradictions. The import of this thesis is, rather, that *every* language of color attribution *must* display color incompatibilities truth-functionally, whether in their surface form or in their hidden structure. What counts as a logical impossibility in color attributions is an a priori requirement on any language, and not just something to be shown in a logically perfect notation. Those statements that are necessarily true or false must have the truth-functional form of a tautology or a contradiction, if not in their surface structure, then in their underlying structure.

43. PG, p. 210.

44. PG, p. 210.

45. D. F. Gottlieb (1983), p. 242.

46. "I used to think [. . .] that it is the task of logical analysis to discover the elementary propositions. I wrote: 'We are unable to specify the form of elementary propositions' [. . .]. Yet I did think that the elementary propositions could be specified at a later date" (WWK, p. 182).

47. See esp. McGuinness (1981), p. 73; and Diamond (1991), pp. 202–203.

48. In the 6s Wittgenstein develops the deflationary implications of his account of logic and uses this account to attack the traditional conception of philosophy as a body of doctrine. According to Wittgenstein, philosophy is to become a critical activity of logical analysis whose goal is to unmask the absurdity of metaphysical propositions by showing that no meaning has been assigned to them (cf. esp. 6.53).

49. McGuinness (1981), p. 69.

50. Diamond (1991), p. 193.

51. The logical realism I attribute to Wittgenstein does not depend on anything that cannot be put into words and, therefore, it does not involve the kind of "chickening out" that Diamond sees implicit in traditional realist interpretations. Unlike these interpretations, mine takes seriously the Tractarian idea that philosophical thinking ought to be replaced by logical analysis; and it is for the most part compatible with Diamond's deflationary reading.

52. This realism about logical possibilities is to be distinguished from a metaphysical realism about possible worlds á la David Lewis (1986), which does indeed involve an inflated ontology.

53 According to my interpretation, even elementary propositions have this "logical scaffolding." As discussed in section 1, elementary propositions are logically independent from each other, but they are crucially dependent on logical truths and falsehoods. That is, even elementary propositions have a *hidden body*, but their *hidden body* is entirely composed of tautologies and contradictions.

54. Even Diamond's interpretation, which emphasizes the strong continuity from the *Tractatus* to the *Investigations*, recognizes that the Tractarian notions of logical form and logical analysis do not survive in Wittgenstein's later view. (See esp. Diamond (1991), p. 184 and p. 193.) In his discussion of logical analysis in the *Investigations* Wittgenstein seems to be warning us against the logical realism and monism of the *Tractatus* when he writes: "It may come to look as if there were something like a final analysis of our forms of language, and so a *single* completely resolved form of every expression [. . .] as if there were something hidden in [our usual forms of expression]" (PI §91).

Chapter 2. From Pictures to Yardsticks

55. On generality and infinity in mathematics. See G. E. M. Anscombe's note published with a reprint of this piece in I. Copi and R. Beard (1966).

56. Notice that the order of my analysis will be the opposite of Wittgenstein's exposition's. On my interpretation, the order of exposition of SRLF is in fact misleading. This paper goes from a reformulation of the notions of logical analysis and logical form to a new treatment of the problem of color exclusion, as if the former had been independently established and the latter were only a mere application of the improved version of these notions. But in fact the impulse to reformulate these notions came from the problem of color exclusion. As we shall see, this reformulation is precisely what was required for its solution.

57. D. Pears, "The logical independence of elementary propositions," in I. Block (1981), p. 83.

58. Wittgenstein's ephemeral adoption of phenomenalism in SRLF may reflect the influence of the Vienna Circle. He had already been in contact with some of the members of the Vienna Circle during 1927–28, before he wrote SRLF. Wittgenstein had several conversations with Schlick, Waismann, Herbert Feigl, and Maria Kasper (occasionally joined by Rudolf Carnap as well). Unfortunately, there are no systematic notes available from any of the participants in the conversations from these years. See WWK, pp. 14–16.

59. In 1929–30 Wittgenstein repeatedly emphasized the logical nature of necessity: "'Red and green *cannot* be in the same place'. Here I would

ask, What does the word '*can*' mean here? The word 'can' is obviously a grammatical (logical) concept, not a material one" (WWK, p. 67); "'Red and green won't fit into the same place' doesn't mean that they are as a matter of fact never together, but that you can't even say they are together" (PR §78).

60. For Kripke's discussion of identity statements, see especially (1972), pp. 122–33. For his account of "necessary *a posteriori* truths," see also (1972), pp. 35–38 and 158–160.

61. Kripke (1972), p. 125.

62. Note that in the *Tractatus* it was entirely clear what Wittgenstein meant when he emphasized the tautological character of all necessities: this point was supposed to convey the idea that necessity resides in the purely formal features of language and does not belong to the *ordo essendi* or the *ordo cognoscendi* but rather, to the *ordo linguae*. By contrast, it is no longer clear what the tautological character of necessity means in SRLF since here what is said to be necessary is the structure of "the actual phenomena." Although in SRLF Wittgenstein still emphasizes the logical nature of necessity, he now seems to hold that necessity has also epistemic and metaphysical aspects, since it concerns the very identity of the contents of our experience.

63. As Wittgenstein put it in 1930, "It would be odd if the human race had been speaking all this time without ever putting together a genuine proposition" (PR §3).

64. Cf. M. Dummett (1981), pp. 360–427.

65. In the introduction to *Foundations of Arithmetic* Frege remarks that one of his "fundamental principles" is "never to ask for the meaning of a word in isolation, but only in the context of a proposition" (p. X). As we saw in chapter 1, Wittgenstein endorsed this Fregean principle in the *Tractatus* (cf. 3.3).

66. P. Winch, "Im Anfang war die Tat," in I. Block (1981), p. 160.

67. Cf. G. P. Baker and P. M. S. Hacker (1985), pp. 37–40.

68. Baker and Hacker (1985), p. 37.

69. Shanker (1987), p. 7 and p. 9.

70. I borrow this expression from A. Kenny, who also emphasizes the continuity in Wittgenstein's view from 1930 on; cf. Kenny (1972), p. 114.

71. Shanker (1987), p. 9.

72. On Wittgenstein's view, metaphysical realism and phenomenalism involve similar misconceptions about language. The common root of these views is made explicit below.

73. Kenny (1972), p. 119.

74. In SRLF, however, Wittgenstein offers the phenomenalistic correlate of the idea that language must be "kept in bounds" by the reality it describes. As discussed above, in the 1929 paper Wittgenstein argues that it

is the logical form of "the actual phenomena" that sets the limits of significance that constrain language. He remarks that what makes a combination of signs a nonsensical pseudoproposition is a clash with the logical structure of the phenomena that are the object of our description.

75. Although I contend that the thesis of the autonomy of grammar does not survive in Wittgenstein's mature philosophy, there are aspects of this thesis that will be maintained in Wittgenstein's later view of rules: in particular, the idea that the rules for the use of our terms do not stand in need of justification and that we do not have an epistemic relation to them (the idea of "bedrock" in PI §217). But, as we shall see in later chapters, the ideas retained from the autonomy thesis will have a very different significance in Wittgenstein's mature view.

76. This idea is part of the logical realism and monism of the *Tractatus* discussed in 1.4 above.

77. There is a striking similarity between this argument and Davidson's argument in "On the Very Idea of a Conceptual Scheme." Cf. D. Davidson (1984), pp. 183–98.

Chapter 3. The Calculus of Language

78. See D. Stern (1995), pp. 99–102. See also Shanker (1987), p. 8.

79. I borrow this contrast between different kinds of holism and the term "radical holism" from Michael Williams (1991); cf. esp. pp. 272–79.

80. For a brief discussion of the Tractarian notions of *meaning* and *object*, see chapter 1, esp. 1.2.

81. As Max Black has noticed, Wittgenstein's identification of meaning with use during this period led him to treat *all* words as syncategorematic. See M. Black, "Verificationism and Wittgenstein's Reflections on Mathematics," in S. Shanker (1986), vol. 3, pp. 68–76.

82. See S. Shanker (1987), p. 8. The argument that follows is based on Shanker's suggestion. Portions of it have appeared in Medina (2001).

83. M. Black (1986), p. 75.

84. Even in the *Philosophical Investigations*, verification will retain certain grammatical significance: "Asking whether and how a proposition can be verified is only a particular way of asking 'How d'you mean?' The answer is a contribution to the grammar of the proposition" (PI §353).

85. In his inferentialist account of semantic content Brandom emphasizes that there are two central aspects of the content of a proposition: its "circumstances of application" and its "consequences of application" (1994, pp. 116–32). He argues that "verificationists, assertibilists, and reliabilists make the mistake of treating the first aspect as exhausting content" (p. 121). Interestingly enough, this criticism does not apply to Wittgenstein's methodological verificationism, which is used to link the content of a proposition

with the propositions from which it follows *and* with the propositions that follow from it (cf. Lectures 1932–35, pp. 19–20). What this shows is that Wittgenstein tries to derive from the method of verification of a proposition all the elements required for an inferentialist analysis of its content and, as a result, he talks about verification conditions in a nonstandard way.

86. M. Black (1986), p. 69.

87. M. Black (1986), pp. 70–71.

88. J. A. Coffa (1991), pp. 244–58; cf. esp. pp. 249–50.

89. A. Gargani, "Schlick and Wittgenstein: Language and Experience," in in Shanker (1986) Vol. I, pp. 275–286.

90. F. Waismann, "The nature of mathematics: Wittgenstein's standpoint," in Shanker (1986), vol. 3 (pp. 60–67); cf. pp. 60–61.

91. Coffa (1991), p. 260.

92. G. E. Moore, "Wittgenstein's Lectures in 1930–33," in his (1962), p. 266.

93. Anscombe reports that when someone in Cambridge attributed the "verification principle" to Wittgenstein, he repudiated his authorship "in a tone of outrage"; cf. Anscombe (1995), pp. 405–406.

94. G. E. Moore (1962), p. 266; my emphasis.

95. However, in the course of the same lecture Wittgenstein is reported as saying that verification "gives" the meaning of propositions (Lectures 1932–35, p. 30; cf. also p. 20, quoted above). It seems unlikely that he would defend and reject the distinction between *giving* and *determining* meaning in the course of the same lecture. So this is presumably only a terminological conflict to be attributed to Wittgenstein's careless language or to that of the people taking notes.

96. Forget about verification methods if you like, and replace them with, say, methods of learning. According to D. A. T. Gasking and A. C. Jackson, Wittgenstein remarked at the Moral Science Club: "I used at one time to say that, in order to get clear how a certain sentence is used, it was a good idea to ask oneself the question: 'How would one try to verify such an assertion?' But that's just one way among others of getting clear about the use of a word or sentence. For example, another question which it is often very useful to ask oneself is: 'How is this word learned?' 'How would one set about teaching a child to use this word?'" ("Wittgenstein as a teacher," in K. T. Fann, ed., 1967; p. 54). As we shall see in subsequent chapters, replacing the question "How can one verify this assertion?" with the question "How does one learn to use these words?" is a major step in the development of Wittgenstein's thought. But if learning were to play the same methodological role that verification played in the inferentialist account of meaning of 1930–32, it would also result in semantic proliferation: words learned in different ways would have different meanings.

97. See N. Chomsky (1972).

98. Cf. Chomsky (1972), pp. 115–17.

99. Wittgenstein remarks that grammar does not give an abstract description of language in the same way that "physics gives a simplified description of a natural phenomenon, abstracting from secondary factors" (PG §36).

100. In the early 1930s Wittgenstein referred to grammar as "the geometry of signs" (cf. e.g., PG §14).

101. G. P. Baker and P. M. S. Hacker (1985), p. 38 and p. 40. Baker and Hacker also think that this thesis is one of the central tenets of Wittgenstein's mature view. In chapter 5 I will argue that this is not the case.

102. See C. Wright (1987), esp. pp. 16–23; and Me. Williams (1991), esp. p. 108.

103. Cf. G. P. Baker and P. M. S. Hacker, "Critical Notice: *Philosophical Grammar*," in S. Shanker (1986), vol. 1, pp. 323–51.

104. "Ostensive definition is one rule only for the use of a word. And one rule is not enough to give the meaning" (Lectures 1932–35, p. 45).

105. See P. Geach (1957), Section 16.

106. The question that immediately arises for this holistic view of meaning is the following: How do we learn the meaning of a word? How do we get into that complex network of interrelated rules that determines the meaning? After all, in the Augustinian picture of language, ostensive definition was not only a way of fixing the meaning of words, but also the way in which word meaning was supposed to be learned. However, Wittgenstein does not seem to pay much attention to the issue of learning. Interestingly enough, the critique of ostensive definition in *Philosophical Grammar* is not supplemented with an alternative account of language learning. When Wittgenstein was under the sway of the calculus view of language, he was not genuinely interested in the genetic issue of the acquisition of word meaning; his only interest was in the semantic issue of what determines the meaning of words (however this is acquired). He remarks, for instance, that we could learn the meaning of a sign by a verbal definition, by an ostensive definition, or "by a drug"; but "the way we actually learn its meaning drops out of our future understanding of the symbol—the drug drops out" (Lectures 1930–32, p. 23). The significance of learning will be discussed at length below in 5.2 and 6.2–6.3.

107. Cf. PR §164; PG p. 213; Lectures 1930–32, pp. 67–68; Lectures 1932–35, p. 90.

Chapter 4. The "Unbridgeable Gulf" between Rule and Application

108. This chapter has benefited enormously from the careful reading of a previous draft by my colleague Jeffrey Tlumak. Some of the notes

below as well as modifications in the text are the result of his critical remarks.

109. This is Hilbert's reply to Frege's objections against the possibility of an axiom defining a primitive sign, in "Frege-Hilbert Correspondence," p. 6; in Frege (1971).

110. J. Thomae was a nineteenth-century formalist mathematician. He was a colleague of Frege at Jena, where they engaged in a lifelong debate about the foundations of arithmetic.

111. WWK, pp. 103–105, 130–41, and 150ff; PR Appendix pp. 320–22 and 325–33; PG II pp. 289–95 and 319–20; Lectures 1932–35, pp. 43–44.

112. The similarities and differences between Frege's and Wittgenstein's view that my analysis will uncover should be taken *cum grano salis*, given the very different motivations that led these philosophers to take an interest in the issue of the applicability of rules: in Frege, this issue is part and parcel of his attempt to construct the *science* of arithmetic from the bottom up; in Wittgenstein, this issue constitutes the core of his elucidation of the normativity of language use.

113. J. A. Coffa (1991) has drawn a contrast between Kant's and Frege's view of logic and arithmetic, considering the latter as ground-breaking work in the semantic tradition (cf. chapter 4, pp. 62–82). J. Weiner, however, has argued that what unifies Frege's work is an epistemological project in the Kantian tradition. See J. Weiner (1984), (1986), and (1990), chapter 1, pp. 17–44. See also the account of the relationship between Kant's and Frege's projects in Benecerraf (1981). For other perspectives on this issue (including that of Tyler Burge) I would refer the reader to the volume edited by Haaparanta and Hintikka (1986).

114. J. Weiner (1990), p. 80.

115. Note that Kant would agree with the claim that arithmetical truths are constitutive of what is thinkable while denying their analyticity. For a discussion of the different construals of the analytic/synthetic distinction in Kant and Frege, see Weiner (1990).

116. M. Dummett (1991), p. 258, emphasis preserved and added.

117. "If arithmetic is to be independent of all particular properties of things, this must also hold true of its building blocks: they must be of a purely logical nature" ("On Formal Theories of Arithmetic," p. 96; in G. Frege, 1984).

118. According to Frege, arithmetical truths about particular numbers can be derived from the definitions of numbers, for "the properties of numbers follow from their definitions" (FA §10). Since all numbers can be defined from their predecessors using the notion of increased-by-one, we only need to define the number one and the notion of increased-by-one, and then derive particular truths about particular numbers from their "method

of generation": "from the way in which a number, say 8, is generated through increasing by one all its properties can be deduced" (FA §10). On the other hand, from the definitions of the concept of number and of the arithmetical functions, we can derive the general laws of arithmetic, for example, the commutative law of addition (cf. BLA II §64).

119. G. Frege (1979), p. 244 and p. 208.

120. The other two are (1) the consistency requirement: a definition must not lead to contradictions (cf. FA ix); and (2) the "fruitfulness" requirement: a definition must be usable in inferences (cf. FA viii, §81). For a full discussion of Frege's criteria for adequate definitions, see Weiner (1990), pp. 86ff.

121. For Frege, this demand is a logical requirement of decidability (in principle, if not in practice), which is intimately related to the law of excluded middle: "The law of excluded middle is really just another form of the requirement that the concept should have a sharp boundary" (BLA II §56).

122. Frege (1984), pp. 362–63; my emphasis.

123. Ricketts (1986), p. 71.

124. Frege (1984), p. 368.

125. See esp. her (1995), pp. 363–82; and chapters 4–5 of her (1990), pp. 133–224.

126. See T. Burge (1992).

127. Frege (1984), p. 376.

128. Weiner (1995), p. 369.

129. Weiner (1995), p. 378.

130. Frege (1979), p. 179.

131. Weiner (1995), p. 364.

132. Weiner (1995), p. 368.

133. See Weiner (1995), p. 367.

134. See also Frege (1979), p. 133; and (1984), p. 368.

135. Weiner (1995), p. 370; emphasis added.

136. Weiner (1995), pp. 370–71.

137. Weiner (1995), p. 366. Weiner discusses an interesting passage which seems to suggests this realist picture: "what we see into or single out from amongst other things is already there and does not come into existence as a result of these activities" (Frege [1979], p. 137). As Weiner points out, the English phrase "single out from amongst other things" suggests that reality is already divided up into self-identifying objects that determine the conceptual choices we can make (or, worse yet, that there is no room for such choices). Weiner emphasizes that this suggested implication is, in fact, the product of the translators' reading of what Frege said and not of what he actually said, for "Frege talks of reading something out of a *Gemange*—a mixture or jumble" (p. 366). According to Weiner, what the passage in question in fact suggests (although this is obliterated by the English translation)

is that "*whatever* we read out of a mixture is *really there*" (p. 366). So, on Weiner's interpretation, Frege's view of the objectivity of science does not imply that there is just one correct way of conceptualizing reality and just one correct scientific theory in each domain, as one would expect from a metaphysical realist. On the contrary, it implies that any domain of scientific inquiry admits alternative conceptualizations and theoretical descriptions.

138. I have limited my discussion to Burge's Platonist reading of Frege, but there are other ways of construing the possible ontological implications of Frege's view. See in this connection the pioneer work of Alonzo Church (1973 and 1974). I am inclined to think, however, that the objections I have considered here against Burge's reading of Frege also have critical force against the realist reading of Church.

139. In Geach and Black (1952).

140. On this reading of Frege, the objects, concepts, and laws discovered in science have objective reality not insofar as they are denizens of a separate realm but insofar as they are *possible* objects of thought, communication, and scientific inquiry. Indeed, for Frege, if something is, not just unrecognized by us and unexpressed in our languages but *in principle* unrecognizable and inexpressible in language, then that thing is simply not a possible object of scientific inquiry.

141. The restriction here to scientific contexts is important because it is far from clear that Frege would be willing to extend this claim to the ordinary contexts in which natural languages are used. Weiner (1990), for one, has argued that Frege's logical views apply exclusively to scientific contexts.

142. As we saw, Frege argues that when the signs of mathematics are defined piecemeal, they lack designation (see esp. BLA II §64). But the reasons Frege gives for the lack of designation of signs so defined are not ontological, but logical. He does not claim that there is nothing in the Platonic world of mathematical entities corresponding to piecemeal definitions (e.g., fuzzy mathematical concepts and objects). His claim is, rather, that the procedure of piecemeal definition does not satisfy the logical requirements for admissible definitions in science.

143. Frege (1979), p. 137. One could raise the following question: "What is on this view the place of the necessary? For the necessary seems to occupy an objective domain that is not reducible to the merely physical or psychological. Yet (*a fortiori*) this cannot be a domain of possibilities. Doesn't the necessary then belong to a third realm that is not merely the realm of logical possibilities?" The most plausible suggestion here (the one that supports the deflationary reading) is to think of the necessary not as constituting an independent realm but, rather, as the scaffolding of the realm of what is possible. This suggestion reinforces the convergence between Frege and the early Wittgenstein that has been observed in the recent literature by a number of commentators: esp. Diamond (1991),

Conant (1991a and 2000), and Ricketts (1986). I comment on this convergence, as I see it, in the next paragraph.

144. Cf. Brandom (1994), pp. 18–26.

145. Cf. Brandom (1994), pp. 26–30.

146. J. McDowell (1984), p. 342. Brandom (1994, p. 29) also borrows this image from McDowell in his discussion of Wittgenstein.

147. This is what Brandom calls the "gerrymandering" argument. Cf. Brandom (1994), p. 28.

148. Brandom (1994), p. 23.

149. Brandom (1994), p. 22.

150. Cf. Baker and Hacker (1985), p. 103.

151. Wittgenstein's remarks about "internal relations" and "methods of projection" are an explicit elaboration of ideas that were already contained in the *Tractatus*. There Wittgenstein argued that the significant use of language involves a "method of projection" (3.11) that creates the "internal relation of depicting that holds between language and the world" (4.014). However, in the *Tractatus* Wittgenstein was naïve in assuming that there is a single method of projection underlying all language use that can simply be taken for granted. In *Philosophical Grammar* he remarks that in the *Tractatus* he had confused the "method of projection" with the "lines of projection" (pp. 212–14). He says that what he called "a picture" was "the blueprint plus the method of its application," and he thought of "the method as something which is attached to the blueprint" as "the projection lines" that are "part of the picture" (p. 213). This led him to believe "that the difference between proposition and reality is ironed out by the lines of projection belonging to the picture, the thought, and that no further room is left for a method of application, but only for agreement and disagreement" (p. 214). The method of projection is thus conceived as something already contained in the underlying structure of a proposition, as projection lines built into the picture which "reach out" to reality. But this is a mistake, for the picture *together with the lines of projection* can be variously applied: "The picture *plus* the projection lines leaves open various methods of application" (p. 213).

152. Note also that in the course of this explanation Wittgenstein makes a parenthetical reference to Frege. Cf. PR §154.

153. For instance, Wittgenstein argues that in arithmetic "what first gives the system a foundation" is "a rule of calculation" (PR §168). The foundational status of the rules of arithmetic resides in that they define the meaning of the arithmetical signs by prescribing how we are to use them (cf. esp. PR §163).

154. These remarks could be taken to echo Carnap's view of "linguistic frameworks" and his distinction between *internal* and *external* questions. Coffa (1991), for one, has emphasized the convergence between Wittgen-

stein's and Carnap's views. However, this convergence has been called into question by some commentators; see, for instance, Witherspoon (2000).

155. However, the factual emptiness of grammatical statements (unlike that of the logical propositions of the *Tractatus*) cannot be explained in terms of their *tautological form*, but only in terms of the special place they occupy within an inferential system.

156. Frege said that the objects of mathematical inquiry ought to be sharply delimited by definitions and accurately described by laws, just as seas and islands must be sharply defined and accurately described in geography (cf. BLA Preface xiii and (1979), p. 133).

157. H. Putnam, "Rethinking Mathematical Necessity," in his (1994), pp. 245–63.

158. J. Conant (1991a), esp. pp. 137–50.

159. David Cerbone (2000) sees a different tension in Frege's view of logic. According to Cerbone, Frege is of two minds in his accounts of logical laws. On the one hand, he holds a *constitutive* view according to which logical laws are the conditions of possibility of thought. But, Cerbone argues, he also holds a weaker, *normative* view according to which logical laws are prescriptions for adequate thinking. According to Cerbone, the core of Wittgenstein's critique of Frege consists in exposing this tension and attacking the latter view. I disagree with Cerbone's interpretation. The weak "normative yet not constitutive" view of logical laws he attributes to Frege is not warranted by the textual evidence. If Frege thought of the laws of logic as prescriptions of a regular kind, it would be a mystery why he saw in them a special kind of normativity. Moreover, as we shall see in chapter 6, this interpretation is self-undermining because it forces us to attribute to Frege two incompatible views. See note 200 below.

160. BLA §12; cf. Conant (1991a), p. 138.

161. Cf. Frege (1979), p. 128.

162. Putnam (1994), p. 248.

163. Ibid.

164. Ibid.

165. Frege (1984), p. 351.

166. Burge (1992), p. 646.

167. Weiner (1995), p. 373.

168. Weiner (1995), p. 374.

Chapter 5. Internal Relations in Action

169. G. P. Baker and P. M. S. Hacker (1985), pp. 158–59.

170. According to the editor of *Philosophical Remarks*, Rush Rhees. See his footnote 1 on page 171.

171. G. P. Baker and P. M. S. Hacker (1985), p. 104.

172. G. P. Baker and P. M. S. Hacker (1985), p. 156 and p. 155 respectively; my emphasis.

173. In the *Investigations* Wittgenstein criticizes the idea that intentions have the intrinsic power to confer a special quality to our actions. He argues that this idea derives from "a misleading picture of 'intending'" (PI §337). Intentions are misconceived if they are thought of as the foundations upon which we build our normative practices, for our intentions are in fact crucially dependent on prior practices of rule following: "An intention is embedded in its situation, in human customs and institutions" (PI §337). The agent's intention, therefore, cannot constitute a difference *internal* to her act of rule-following, for intentions are not simply acts of the will that accompany isolated actions, they refer to a larger context, to a complete practice.

174. Wittgenstein's appeals to insights and decisions as the basis of our rule-following actions are nothing more than tentative proposals that he tried out in the early 1930s. In the following passage from the *Lectures on the Foundations of Mathematics* (1939), he summarizes and rejects his prior intuitionistic and decisionistic tendencies: "Intuitionism [. . .] requires that we have an intuition at each step in calculation, at each application of a rule [. . .]. We might as well say that we need, not an intuition at each step, but a *decision.*—Actually there is *neither*. You don't make a decision: *you simply do a certain thing. It is a question of a certain practice*" (LFM p. 237; my emphasis).

175. As Baker and Hacker (1985) put it, criticizing this transitory view of rule following that Wittgenstein held around 1933: "Most instances of carrying out computations or calculations do not involve any consultation or formulation of the rules of a calculus, just as competent chess players seldom advert to any rules of chess in playing games" (p. 158).

176. Cf. Lectures 1930–32 p. 23, p. 54, p. 116; PR §6, §23; PG §3, §39, §43; and BLB p. 14.

177. "It is a *hypothesis* that the process of teaching should be needed in order to bring about these effects. It is conceivable, in this sense, that *all* the processes of understanding, obeying, etc., should have happened without the person ever having been taught the language" (BLB p. 12).

178. As Wittgenstein puts it, using a different analogy: "The bolt of a lock is caused to slide by this particular combination [of notches and teeth], but we should not say that the movement of the bolt was guided by the way in which we combined teeth and notches, i.e., we should not say that the bolt moved *according* to the pattern of the key bit" (BRB p. 118).

179. See Kripke (1982), pp. 22–37.

180. Kripke (1982), p. 24. Kripke also argues that our dispositions are not fit to give the guidance required for rule following because they are

always finite, while most rules (e.g., those of arithmetic) have infinitely many applications (cf. esp. pp. 26–27). This could suggest that our dispositions for the use of a rule can at least give us guidance for the application of the rule in a finite number of cases, namely, those previously encountered during training. But Kripke's criticism goes deeper. He argues that behavioral dispositions do not succeed in drawing a distinction between correct and incorrect behavior *in any case*.

181. See esp. Kripke (1982), pp. 28–30.

182. G. P. Baker and P. M. S. Hacker (1985), p. 156; emphasis preserved and added.

183. Wittgenstein remarks that the sharp contrast between motives and causes is obscured by the ambiguous use of words such as "why" and "because" which designate both causes and reasons. The systematic ambiguity of these terms is what leads us to think of motives as a special kind of causes: it "gives rise to the confusion that a motive is a cause of which we are immediately aware, a cause 'seen from the inside', or a cause experienced" (BLB p. 15).

184. S. Toulmin (1970), p. 11.

185. S. Toulmin (1970), p. 18.

186. Keep in mind that in his later writings Wittgenstein will characterize rule-following actions, not as deliberate acts, but as acts of *blind obedience*: "When I obey a rule, I do not choose. I obey the rule *blindly*" (PI §219). Me. Williams (1991) has contrasted this model of blind rule following with the intellectualist model of "'sighted' rule following" which requires the explicit "recognition of a rule or standard" (p. 120). It is this latter model that is underscored in Wittgenstein's discussions of rule following in the early 1930s.

187. The radical construal of the distinction between reasons and causes results in false dichotomies. Given this radical construal, we feel forced to choose between two extreme alternatives: intentionalistic and mechanistic accounts of human actions. Unfortunately, this dichotomy is still very much alive today.

188. S. Toulmin (1970), p. 4.

189. S. Toulmin (1970), p. 21.

190. Toulmin examines the example of blinking, a paradigmatic case of behavior triggered by physiological mechanisms which is normally explicable in purely causal terms. But even this mode of behavior can be qualitatively transformed with a simple learning manipulation. After certain ear operations (e.g. fenestration), patients experience severe attacks of giddiness and they are taught to blink more often than normal as a means of stabilizing the visual field and controlling their giddiness. As a result of this training, the patient's blinking acquires a normative dimension. Blinking is something that can now be done correctly or incorrectly; and the question

'Why are you blinking like that?' acquires a different meaning: it can no longer be answered in causal terms, it is a request for reasons. Toulmin argues that the normative dimension that the patient's blinking has acquired "is directly associated with the fact that the action is an application of a learned procedure" (1970, p. 14).

191. A review of some of this evidence can be found in Gentner and Medina (1998).

192. See also his celebrated discussion of the word "game" ion p. 17. Wittgenstein's notion of "family resemblances" undergoes development. In the early 1930s it was *exclusively* applied to the formal concepts of the *Tractatus* ("language," "proposition," "word," "meaning ," "sense," etc.), not to ordinary concepts. E.g., "Propositions do not all have something in common, but are a family of things having overlapping likenesses. We can make subgroups of this family" (Lectures 1932–35, p. 67; cf. also PG §69 and §§73–74). In the *Blue Book* and later lectures (cf. Lectures 1932–35, p. 96). Wittgenstein began to give a wider application to the notion of "family resemblances," arguing that the meaning of a word is constituted by overlapping similarities rather than by a single defining feature or set of features.

193. Cf. BRB pp. 95–98; cf. also BLB pp. 33–34 and Lectures 1932–35, pp. 107–10.

194. These different holistic views have been examined in chapters 1 through 3. According to my analysis, the main difference between the inferential holism of the *Tractatus* and that of the early 1930s is that the former is based on the model of formal inference and the latter on the model of material inference.

195. Cf. M. Williams (1998), chapter 8, "The Etiology of the Obvious: Wittgenstein and the Elimination of Indeterminacy"; esp. pp. 227–28. Williams uses the distinction between *homogeneous* and *heterogeneous* holism to underscore the differences between Quine's idea of a *network* of interconnected propositions and Wittgenstein's concept of *background*.

196. Baker and Hacker (1985), p. 38. On Baker and Hacker's interpretation, the thesis of the "autonomy of grammar" is an important part of the stable core of Wittgenstein's view from 1930 onward. According to Baker and Hacker (1985), this thesis was "Wittgenstein's most fundamental principle" (p. 164).

Chapter 6. Normativity in Practice

197. In later writings the references to "internal relations" virtually disappear, and what Wittgenstein emphasizes as the cornerstone of norma-

tivity is what is "held fast" in our linguistic practices (cf. RFM VI.47; VII.73).

198. This is strongly suggested by Kripke's skeptical reading of the *Philosophical Investigations*, which presents Wittgenstein's arguments as indeterminacy arguments that support psychologistic conclusions à la Hume. See S. Kripke (1982), esp. chapter 3.

199. See J. Conant (1991a), esp. pp. 146–50.

200. For a full discussion of this point, see J. Weiner (1990), pp. 74–76; and J. Conant (1991a), pp. 146–50. According to both Weiner and Conant, Frege does not think that there can be "logical aliens," but he uses them as rhetorical figures for polemical purposes. On this interpretation, Frege's goal is to show that the possible existence of "logical aliens" is illusory, that the possibility of "logically alien thought" is self-undermining, oxymoronic, and must be rejected. Cerbone (2000) disagrees with this interpretation, arguing that it captures only one strand in Frege's view of logic and is therefore at best incomplete. According to Cerbone, the strand that is overemphasized in the afore-mentioned interpretation is "the *constitutive* strand," according to which logical laws are constitutive of thought and the possibility of "logically alien thought" is spurious. But Cerbone argues that there is a weaker, "*normative* strand" in Frege's view according to which logical laws are prescriptions that can be violated and, therefore, "logical aliens are, in some straightforward sense, a genuine possibility: such unfortunate creatures would forever be wrong in their judgments" (p. 297). I think the textual evidence does not support Cerbone's interpretation, for the statements he takes as evidence for the weaker "normative strand" are not statements of Frege's own positions but statements he makes in setting the premises of his thought experiment. These premises, however, can't be taken at face value because they are subverted in the thought experiment, whose conclusions Cerbone takes to be as revealing of Frege's view as its premises. As a result, Cerbone depicts Frege as holding two contradictory claims—namely, that logical aliens *can and cannot* exist. This alone, I take it, tips the balance in favor of Weiner's and Conant's interpretation, which does not attribute inconsistent views to Frege. For further criticisms of Cerbone's interpretation, see note 159 above and note 204 below.

201. An analysis of this thought experiment can be found in Cavell (1979), chapter 5, pp. 86–125. More recent accounts include Cerbone (2000) and Risjord (2000). Some commentators, such as Risjord, refer to this thought experiment as "the wood-cutters."

202. We may even declare them logically insane, if we stretch the term "logic" far enough, as Wittgenstein seems to do. Even though his thought experiments on pages 202 and 203 of the *Lectures* are illustrations of a clash between practices with different techniques and not with different

logics, he concludes: "We can now see why we should call those who have a different logic contradicting ours mad" (LFM p. 203).

204 For a discussion of this point, see Diamond (1989). For an analysis of how this point figures in Wittgenstein's discussion of the wood sellers, see Cerbone (2000), pp. 302–303.

204. Although Cerbone (2000) seems to appreciate the contextualist point of Wittgenstein's discussion (cf. his remarks in pp. 302–303), he still attributes a *constitutive* view of norms to him: "Wittgenstein has seized upon and articulated more explicitly what I called the 'constitutive strand' of Frege's conception of logic" (p. 306). This interpretation creates an irreconcilable tension in Wittgenstein's view of rules (emphasizing their contextual and fluid character as well as their constitutive and fixed nature); and it makes mysterious why Wittgenstein takes himself to be criticizing Frege in his discussion of the wood sellers. According to Cerbone, the point of this discussion is to elaborate a Fregean thought; namely, that logical aliens do not constitute a genuine possibility because logical laws are constitutive of thought.

205. This may suggest that all we need in order to have an intelligible practice is a regularity. But this is a mistake. On Wittgenstein's view, the bedrock of our normative practices does not consist in empirical regularities but in shared techniques of use. As he puts it, "only through a technique can we *grasp* a regularity" (RFM VI.2). As we shall see in later sections, there is more to a practice and its techniques than mere regularities.

206. Note that Wittgenstein's emphasis on what is "natural" for us constitutes a rejection of his earlier conventionalism. He now underscores that the starting point of a rule-governed practice is not a set of conventions, a list of rules, but a consensus of action. There are indeed rule-governed practices that are established by arbitrarily stipulated conventions; but for these conventions to yield a normative practice, they have to be set in tune with what is "natural" for us (cf. RFM I.116). And, for Wittgenstein, both nature and nurture play a role in setting the "natural limits" of our understanding. For, as we shall see, what is "natural" for us is determined both by our unlearned, automatic responses (e.g., crying out in pain) and by our learned techniques (counting as we do, for instance, is natural for us "though not for everybody in the world"; LFM p. 243).

207. Wittgenstein argues, for instance, that if "there isn't yet a technique" for the use of arithmetical equations, "'. . . times . . . *is* . . .' doesn't yet mean anything," it "isn't yet a mathematical proposition" (LFM p. 107).

208. This will be explained in more detail in the last section of this chapter when I examine the role of community agreement in Wittgenstein's view of normativity.

209. See Williams (1994) and (1998), chapter 7.

210. See Williams (1991), esp. pp. 121–22.

211. And the same is true of more sophisticated mathematical practice. When we say that the result of a proof is necessary, what we express is our "unconditional acceptance" (RFM I.33). "And how does it come out that the proof *compels* me? Well, in the fact that once I have got it I go ahead in such-and-such a way, *and refuse any other path*" (RFM I.34; my emphasis).

212. In fact, for Wittgenstein, those propositions that we regard as necessary are not the objects of our "belief" at all. He argues, for instance, that "13 ¥ 13 = 169" is not something that we truly believe as opposed to other things we might have falsely believed (e.g., "13 ¥ 13 = 0"); rather, this equation is something that we accept blindly (cf. RFM I.109).

213. The importance of self-regulation has been emphasized by D. Pears's interpretation of Wittgenstein's view of rule following in his (1988). Pears emphasizes that it is the regularization of our own behavior that enables us to recognize regularities in the environment: "We discover the regularities in nature's behaviour only by first establishing regularities in our own behaviour" (1988, p. 371).

214. The fixation of standards of similarity by actual practice suggested by Wittgenstein in the case of mathematics has been emphasized by Goodman in the case of inductive practices. Both Wittgenstein and Goodman seem to share the same intuition. As Goodman puts it: "I suspect that rather than similarity providing any guidelines for inductive practices, inductive practice may provide the basis for some canons of similarity" ("Seven Strictures on Similarity," p. 441, in Goodman, 1972). See also Goodman (1979), pp. 121–22.

215. On Wittgenstein's view, there are *three crucial elements* that sustain the consensus of action of the members of a practice: a common physical *environment*, a set of shared, unlearned natural *reactions*, and a set of shared, learned *procedures or techniques*. All these elements must be present for a consensus of action to obtain. The consensus of action required for the mastery of a practice does not spring from our biological makeup *alone* or from our cultural conventions *alone*. One does not participate in a form of life simply by being born with certain biological features or, contractually, by choosing to agree on certain conventions.

216. And, in fact, lacking sensitivity to interpersonal stimulation results in severe learning disorders. In this regard, see, for instance, S. Baron-Cohen's work on autism (1989a and 1989b).

217. Wittgenstein's view of conceptual development has indeed critical force against the model of learning as a process of hypothesis formation and confirmation (e.g., Fodor 1975). According to this model, language learning is a process in which the learner exercises her *autonomous* cognitive

capacities in an independent fashion; that is, a process in which the learner formulates hypotheses about what words mean and confirms or disconfirms them in the light of the evidence available to her. This intellectualist model is closely related to the Augustinian view of language learning by ostensive definition, according to which the learners "have to *guess*" the meaning of words (PI §32; cf. also §33). This view endows the learner with rich intellectual capacities, explaining the acquisition of word meaning on the model of learning a second language: "Augustine describes the learning of human language as if the child came into a strange country and did not understand the language of the country; that is, as if it already had a language, only not this one. Or again: as if the child could already *think*, only not yet speak" (PI §32). An intellectualist account of learning of this sort disregards the crucial significance of the guidance provided by the masters of a practice to the initiate learners, and the way in which this guidance structures the learning process. For a Wittgensteinian critique of the hypothesis-formation model of language learning, see M. Williams (1984).

218. This idea is at the core of the newly emerging paradigm of cultural psychology. See esp. the empirical work of Michael Tomasello (1993) and his colleagues.

219. This is the criterion that Wittgenstein uses to distinguish between rule-following actions and actions resulting from "inspiration": "In the case of inspiration [. . .] I shall not be able to teach anyone else my 'technique' of following the line. [. . .] I cannot require him to follow the line in the same way as I do" (RFM VII.53).

220. In fact, the celebrated "Private Language Argument" of the *Investigations* (cf. §§242ff) could be considered as a corollary of this account of learning. For it is a direct consequence of the indispensability thesis that the radically isolated individual who has not received training into rule-governed practices cannot engage in rule following.

221. As Wittgenstein explains later: "Once you have described the procedure of this teaching and learning, you have said everything that can be said about acting correctly according to a rule. We can go no further. [. . .] what the correct following of a rule consists in cannot be described *more closely* than by describing the *learning* of 'proceeding according to a rule'" (RFM VII.26).

222. For instance, it is because we are oblivious of the decisive influence of past training on our actions that, when we apply a rule, we are likely to think that we are "being guided" by an "ethereal, intangible influence" (PI §175).

223. The accuracy of Kripke's skeptical reading has been repeatedly questioned in the literature, but his reading still remains a highly influential interpretation of Wittgenstein's later philosophy. For critical responses to Kripke's reading, see G. P. Baker and P. M. S. Hacker (1984), esp. pp.

57–97; P. Horwich (1990); C. Diamond (1991), pp. 39ff; Me. Williams (1991), esp. pp. 98–101; and Read (2000).

224. As discussed above, in his later view Wittgenstein holds what Williams (1998) terms a "heterogeneous holism," which contrasts with the "homogeneous holism" he defended until the mid 1930s.

225. The teacher's pointings and utterances cannot be regarded as *definitions* because the requisite capacities for a definition are not yet present, "because the child cannot as yet *ask* what the name is" (PI §6). As it is established later, "only someone who already knows how to do something with it can significantly ask a name" (PI §31).

226. This point has already been argued by Meredith Williams in "Blind Obedience: Rules, Community and the Individual" (1991), pp. 96–97.

227. The Paradox of Interpretation thus appears as the knot that ties together all the arguments of the rule-following discussion. In particular, it provides the nexus that links the negative conclusions of the Regress Argument with the positive conclusions of the Manifestation Argument: building on the Regress, the Paradox establishes that our rule-following actions do not emanate inexorably from interpretations, that it is our *actual* applications of rules, repeated over time and against the background of shared practices, that give normative content to rule formulations, interpretations, and the like.

228. Wittgenstein points out this parallelism when he remarks: "The gesture that means 'go on like this', or 'and so on' has a function comparable to that of pointing to an object or a place" (§208).

229. E.g., Baker and Hacker (1984), Kripke (1982), and Wright (1987).

230. On the other hand, if the pupil copies the series systematically wrong ("for example, he copies every other number"), we are inclined to say that he has misunderstood or "that he has understood *wrong*" (§143). And a misunderstanding can be more pernicious than a mere lack of understanding, for instilling the right regularity in the pupil's behavior then requires an additional task: "to wean him from the systematic mistake (as from a bad habit)" (§143). "And here too our pupil's capacity to learn may come to an end" (§143).

231. Kripke's (1982) community view of rule following suggests that what supports the attribution of competence or understanding is not a behavioral regularity but the conformity with the judgment of others. On Baker and Hacker's (1984) reading, by contrast, behavioral regularities *by themselves* display understanding or lack thereof in virtue of their accord or conflict with rules, independently of the judgment of any community of practitioners, and even if there is no such community. Wittgenstein's discussion of learning makes it clear that the manifestation of understanding or competence requires both a regularity in the learner's behavior and the

checkability of his behavior by other practitioners. As emphasized in the discussion of reading, if we do not consider the subject's behavior over time, there is no way to determine whether his correct performance is indicative of competence, or whether it is, rather, merely "accidental" (cf. §157). On the other hand, as we saw, anything the learner does over time would count as a correct pattern of use if his multiple applications of the rule were not viewed against the background of what competent practitioners regard as "obeying the rule" and "going against it." This strongly suggests that a practice of following a rule requires a regular use of the rule both over time and across individuals.

232. In fact, Wittgenstein's discussion of learning radicalizes the dependence of the understanding of a rule on the correct use of the rule over time. For this discussion establishes that the repeated use of a rule constitutes not only the requisite manifestation but also the *source* of understanding. The practical mastery of a rule arises from multiple applications over time, and the normative attitude peculiar to the competent rule follower arises from the overdetermination of a way of proceeding by repeated use. We acquire the capacity to follow a rule through training: "Following a rule is analogous to obeying an order. We are trained to do so" (PI §206).

233. Some advocates of community interpretations refuse to take up this challenge, arguing that it is indeed unintelligible that the community as a whole could be wrong, for this would involve the collapse of all our normative assessments which are grounded in community agreement. For a defense of this view, see esp. Crispin Wright (1980). However, I don't think that this radical construal of the community view of rule following can provide a satisfactory account of normativity, for it relativizes correctness and curtails the possibility of criticism. I will defend a very different version of the community view in the next section.

234. Of course, one might reply that Wittgenstein's arguments do in fact betray the quietism espoused by his metaphilosophy. It might be argued that Wittgenstein's self-understanding of the significance of his work is not the best account of what his work really achieves. But this claim would have to be substantiated by showing what exactly led Wittgenstein astray in his metaphilosophical reflections; that is, by providing a diagnosis of his metaphilosophy.

235. Minar (1995), p. 446.

236. Minar (1995), p. 445.

237. Minar (1995), p. 446.

238. As Minar puts it: "A distorted understanding of the role that the everyday is to play in Wittgenstein's writings is responsible for the philosophical attraction of community interpretations of his views" (p. 431).

239. Minar (1995), pp. 429–30.

240. "If anyone believes that certain concepts are absolutely the correct ones . . . then let him imagine certain very general facts of nature to be different from what we are used to, and the formation of concepts different from the usual ones will become intelligible to him" (PI p. 230).

241. Minar (1995), p. 430.

242. See B. Williams (1974) and J. Lear (1982, 1984, and 1998). See also D. Bloor (1996).

243. Minar (1995), esp. p. 443.

244. The pluralism of Wittgenstein's philosophy makes room for different pictures or ways of looking at language which can be used in different contexts for different purposes (this seems to be Wittgenstein's point at §132, quoted below). Arguably, Wittgenstein himself makes use of different pictures of language in different argumentative contexts, but all the pictures he uses emphasize, in different ways, the contextualist aspects of language use.

245. Crittenden (1970), p. 39.

246. See Minar (1995), pp. 420–22 and p. 431.

247. Minar (1995), p. 432; my emphasis.

248. This has been argued by a legion of philosophers, but most insistently and from a Wittgensteinian perspective by Hilary Putnam (1987, 1990, 1992). The minimal or pragmatic realism that Putnam has defended in recent years is in fact an elaboration of the contextualist insights of Wittgenstein's later philosophy.

249. Unless, of course, we use a very weak definition of relativism as the rejection of absolute norms whose applicabilitiy is to be viewed *sub specie aeternitatis*. For, as we saw (6.3), the upshot of the rule-following discussion is that norms are always situated in social and historical contexts and embedded in particular practices; and since the more decontextualized a rule is, the less specific its normative content becomes, completely decontextualized norms are radically indeterminate.

250. Crary (2000) has argued forcefully that Wittgenstein's view of meaning does not support a conventionalist and relativist view of norms. This is the view attributed to him by what Crary terms *inviolability interpretations*, according to which the contingent conventions of a linguistic practice *fix* the meanings of the terms employed in it and, therefore, they cannot be violated. Crary argues that the goal of Wittgenstein's discussions of meaning is "to expose as confused the idea that meanings might somehow be 'fixed'" (p. 138), whether by something external to our practices or by something underlying use. I agree with Crary that Wittgenstein's remarks about the lack of fixity of meaning undermine the idea that there are inviolable linguistic norms and that all linguistic moves have to be relativized to autonomous practices, each with its own set of fixed norms.

251. If we had to reserve the term "philosophy" for this kind of theorizing (as Wittgenstein sometimes seems to suggest and Minar clearly does), then the *picture* I have ascribed to Wittgenstein would not be philosophical at all. However, this is a very narrow definition of philosophy; and even if it fits the dominant way of doing philosophy before Wittgenstein, it certainly does not capture all the naturalist, pragmatist, and contextualist ways of doing philosophy available today, after Wittgenstein.

252. As explained in note 249, a defense of this point from the perspective of the quietist reading can be found in Crary (2000). I take the convergence between Crary's interpretation and my own as evidence that my reading is compatible with the antitheoretical spirit of Wittgenstein's philosophy. Others, however, have drawn different conclusions from Wittgenstein's contextualism. In the quietist camp, for instance, Cerbone (2000) takes Wittgenstein's contextualism to be in perfect harmony with a *constitutive* view of norms. I do not think Cerbone fully appreciates the implications of Wittgenstein's contextualist points, which (as argued above; cf. section 6.1 and note 203) contain a powerful critique of the constitutive view. I think Minar (1995) is right that there is no room in Wittgenstein's later philosophy for any kind of constitutivity thesis.

253. It is important to note that philosophical illusions of this kind are not the exclusive property of philosophers. According to Wittgenstein, intellectuals in all fields fall into these illusions when they sever the ties of the concepts they study with the practices that constitute our form of life. In *Remarks on Frazer's Golden Bough* (reprinted in *Philosophical Occasions*, pp. 118–55), Wittgenstein gives examples of how the critical activity of nonphilosophers can become empty and meaningless when the concepts of a practice are assessed without examining the nexus of activities within which these concepts have a home.

254. This is the core of Wittgenstein's critique of radical skepticism and foundationalism, which (I contend) is not based on a priori transcendental considerations but on contextualist grounds. Here again my interpretation converges with that of Crary (2000), rather than with the traditional reading of *On Certainty*. This is how she puts it: "On the prevalent interpretation, Wittgenstein is taken to be arguing that there are aspects of our lives which *cannot* be doubted. The alternative reading I favor claims that [. . .]it is wrong to read him as insisting that there are specific things we cannot doubt. Wittgenstein is drawing our attention to cases in which we have no idea what would count as the realization of a sentence or utterance which we nevertheless confusedly think of as expressing a doubt about an aspect of our lives" (p. 145; note 64).

References

Anscombe, G. E. M. 1959. *Introduction to Wittgenstein's Tractatus.* Harper and Row. New York.

———. 1995. "Ludwig Wittgenstein." *Philosophy* 70, 395–407.

Baker, G. P. 1988. *Wittgenstein, Frege, and the Vienna Circle.* Blackwell, Oxford.

Baker, G. P., and P. M. S. Hacker, 1984. *Scepticism, Rules and Language.* Blackwell, Oxford.

———. 1985. *Wittgenstein. Rules, Grammar and Necessity.* Blackwell, Oxford.

Baron-Cohen, S. 1989a. "Are Autistic Children 'Behaviorists'? An Examination of Their Mental-Physical and Appearance-Reality Distinctions." *Journal of Autism and Developmental Disorders* 19, 579–600.

———. 1989b. "Perceptual Role-Taking and Proto-Declarative Pointing in Autism." *British Journal of Developmental Psychology* 7, 113–27.

Benacerraf, P. 1981. "Frege: The Last Logicist" *Midwest Studies in Philosophy* 6, 17–35.

Black, M. 1964. *A Companion to Wittgenstein's "Tractatus."* Cornell University Press, Ithaca, N.Y.

———. 1986. "Verificationism and Wittgenstein's Reflections on Mathematics." In S. Shankar (ed.), vol. 3, pp. 68–76.

Blackburn, S. 1984. "The Individual Strikes Back." *Synthese* 58, 281–301.

Block, I. (ed.). 1981. *Perspectives on the Philosophy of* Wittgenstein. MIT Press, Cambridge, Mass.

Bloor, D. 1996. "The Question of Linguistic Idealism Revisited." In H. Sluga and D. Stern (eds.), *The Cambridge Companion to Wittgenstein.* Cambridge University Press, Cambridge, pp. 354–82.

Brandom, R. 1994. *Making It Explicit.* Harvard University Press, Cambridge, Mass.

Burge, T. 1992. "Frege on Knowing the Third Realm." *Mind* 101, 633–50.

Cavell, S. 1979. *The Claim of Reason.* Oxford: Oxford University Press.

Cerbone, D. 2000. "How to Do Things with Wood: Wittgenstein, Frege, and the Problem of Illogical Thought." In A. Crary and R. Read (eds.), pp. 293–314.

Chomsky, N. 1972. *Language and Mind.* Harcourt, New York.

Church, A. 1973. "Outline of a Revised Formulation of the Logic of Sense and Denotation (Part I)." *Nous* 7, 24–33.

———. 1974. "Outline of a Revised Formulation of the Logic of Sense and Denotation (Part II)." *Nous* 8, 135–56.

Coffa, J. A. 1991. *The Semantic Tradition from Kant to Carnap.* Cambridge University Press, Cambridge.

Conant, J. 1991a. "The Search for Logically Alien Thought: Descartes, Kant, Frege and the *Tractatus.*" *Philosophical Topics* 20, 115–80.

———. 1991b. "Throwing Away the Top of the Ladder." *Yale Review* 79, 328–64.

———. 2000. "Elucidation and Nonsense in Frege and Early Wittgenstein." In A. Crary and R. Read (eds.), pp. 174–217.

Copi, I., and R. Beard (eds.). 1966. *Essays on Wittgenstein's "Tractatus."* Routledge, London and New York.

Crary, A. 2000. "Wittgenstein's Philosophy in Relation to Political Thought." In A. Crary and R. Read (eds.), pp. 118–45.

Crary, A., and R. Read (eds.). 2000. *The New Wittgenstein.* Routledge, London and New York.

Crittenden, C. 1970. "Wittgenstein on Philosophical Therapy and Understanding." *International Philosophical Quarterly* X.1, 20–43.

Davidson, D. 1984. *Inquiries into Truth and Interpretation.* Oxford University Press, Oxford.

Diamond, C. 1989. "Rule: Looking in the Right Place." In D. Z. Phillips and P. Winch (eds.), pp. 12–34.

———. 1991. *The Realistic Spirit: Wittgenstein, Philosophy, and the Mind.* MIT Press, Cambridge, Mass.

Dummett, M. 1981.*The Interpretation of Frege's Philosophy.* Harvard University Press, Cambridge, Mass.

———. 1991. *Frege. Philosophy of Mathematics.* Harvard University Press, Cambridge, Mass.

Fann, K. T. (ed.). 1967. *Ludwig Wittgenstein: The Man and His Philosophy.* Harvester Press, New York.

Fodor, J. A. 1975. *The Language of Thought.* Harvard University Press, Cambridge, Mass.

Frege, G. 1971. *On the Foundations of Geometry and Formal Theories of Arithmetic.* Yale University Press, New Haven.

———. 1979. *Posthumous Writings*. Blackwell, Oxford.

———. 1984. *Collected Papers on Mathematics, Logic and Philosophy*. Blackwell, Oxford.

Geach, P. 1957. *Mental Acts*. Routledge, London and New York.

Geach, P., and M. Black. 1952. *Translations from the Philosophical Writings of Gottlob Frege*. Blackwell, Oxford.

Gentner, D., and J. Medina. 1998. "Similarity and the Development of Rules." *Cognition* 65, 263–97.

Goodman, N. 1972. *Papers and Projects*. Bobbs-Merrill, New York.

———. 1979. *Fact, Fiction and Forecast*. Harvard University Press, Cambridge, Mass.

Gottlieb, D. F. 1983."Wittgenstein's critique of the *Tractatus* View of Rules." *Synthese* 56, 239–51.

Haaparanta, L., and J. Hintikka. (eds.). 1986. *Frege Synthesized*. Reidel, New York.

Hintikka, J., and M. B. Hintikka. 1983. "Some Remarks on (Wittgensteinian) Logical Form." *Synthese* 56, 155–70.

———. 1986. *Investigating Wittgenstein*. Blackwell, Oxford.

Horwich, P. 1990. "Wittgenstein and Kripke on the Nature of Meaning." *Mind and Language* 5:2, 105–21.

Ishiguro, H. 1969. "Use and Reference of Names." In P. Winch (ed.), *Studies in the Philosophy of Wittgenstein*. Routledge, London and New York, pp. 20–50.

Jacquette, D. 1990. "Wittgenstein and the Color Incompatibility Problem." *History of Philosophy Quarterly*, 353–65.

———. 1998. *Wittgenstein's Thought in Transition*. Purdue University Press, Lafayette, Ind.

Kenny, A. 1972. *Wittgenstein*. Penguin, Harmondsworth.

Kripke, S. 1972. *Naming and Necessity*. Harvard University Press, Cambridge, Mass.

———. 1982. *Wittgenstein on Rules and Private Language*. Harvard University Press, Cambridge, Mass.

Lear, J. 1982. "Leaving the World Alone." *The Journal of Philosophy* 79, 382–403.

———. 1984. "The Disappearing 'We'." *Proceedings of the Aristotelian Society* 58, 219–42.

———. 1998. *Open Minded*. Harvard University Press, Cambridge, Mass.

Lewis, D. 1986. *On the Plurality of Worlds*. Blackwell, Oxford.

McDowell, J. 1984. "Wittgenstein on Following a Rule." *Synthese* 58, 325–63.

McGinn, M. 1997. *Wittgenstein and the Philosophical Investigations*. Routledge, London and New York.

McGuinness, B. 1981."The So-called Realism of the *Tractatus.*" In I. Block (ed.), pp. 60–73.

Medina, J. 2001. "Verificationism and Inferentialism in Wittgenstein's Philosophy." *Philosophical Investigations* 24, 304–13.

Minar, E. 1995. "Feeling at Home in Language (*What Makes Reading* Philosophical Investigations *Possible?*)." *Synthese* 102, 413–52.

Moore, G. E. 1962. *Philosophical Papers.* Collier, London.

Pears, D. 1987. *The False Prison,* vol. 1. Clarendon, Oxford.

———. 1988. *The False Prison,* vol. 2. Clarendon, Oxford.

Phillips, D. Z., and P. Winch (eds.). 1989. *Wittgenstein: Attention to Particulars.* Macmillan, London.

Putnam, H. 1987. *The Many Faces of Realism.* Open Court, La Salle.

———. 1990. *Realism with a Human Face.* Harvard University Press, Cambridge, Mass.

———. 1992. *Renewing Philosophy.* Harvard University Press, Cambridge, Mass.

———. 1994. *Words and Life.* Harvard University Press, Cambridge, Mass.

Ramsey, F. P. 1923. "Critical Notice of the *Tractatus Logico-Philosophicus.*" *Mind* 32, 469–78.

Read, R. 2000. "What 'There Can Be No Such Thing as Meaning Anything by Any Word' Could Possibly Mean." In A. Crary and R. Read (eds.), pp. 74–82.

Reck, E. (ed.). 2000. *From Frege to Wittgenstein: Perspectives on Early Analytic Philosophy.* Oxford University Press, Oxford.

Ricketts, T. G. 1986. "Objectivity and Objecthood: Frege's Metaphysics of Judgment." In L. Haaparanta and J. Hintikka (eds.), pp. 65–95.

Risjord, M. W. 2000. *Woodcutters and Witchcraft: Rationality and Interpretative Change in the Social Sciences.* State University of New York Press, Albany.

Shanker, S. (ed.). 1986. *Ludwig Wittgenstein: Critical Assessments,* vols. 1–5. Croom Helm, London.

———. 1987. *Wittgenstein and the Turning Point in the Philosophy of Mathematics.* State University of New York Press, Albany.

Stern, D. 1995. *Wittgenstein on Mind and Language.* Oxford University Press, Oxford.

Tomasello, M., A. Kruger, and H. Ratner. 1993. "Cultural Learning." *Behavioral and Brain Sciences* 16, 495–552.

Toulmin, S. 1970. "Reasons and Causes." In R. Borger and F. Cioffi (eds.), *Explanation in the Behavioural Sciences.* Cambridge University Press, Cambridge, pp. 1–26.

Weiner, J. 1984. "The Philosopher behind the Last Logicist." *Philosophical Quarterly* 34, 242–64.

———. 1986. "Putting Frege in Perspective." In L. Haaparanta and J. Hintikka (eds.), pp. 9–26.

———. 1990. *Frege in Perspective*. Cornell University Press, Ithaca.

———. 1995. "Realism *Bei* Frege: Reply to Burge." *Synthese* 102, 363–82.

Williams, B. 1974. "Wittgenstein and Idealism." In G. Vesey (ed.), *Understanding Wittgenstein*. St. Martin's, New York, pp. 76–95.

Williams, Me. 1984. "Language Learning and the Representational Theory of Mind." *Synthese* 58, 129–51.

———. 1991. "Blind Obedience: Rules, Community and the Individual." In K. Puhl (ed.), *Meaning Skepticism*. Walter de Gruyter, Berlin, pp. 93–125.

———. 1994. "The Significance of Learning in Wittgenstein's Later Philosophy." *Canadian Journal of Philosophy* 24, 173–204.

———. 1998. *Wittgenstein, Mind, and Meaning: Toward a Social Conception of the Mind*. Routledge, London and New York.

Williams, Mi. 1991.*Unnatural Doubts*. Blackwell, Oxford.

Witherspoon, E. 2000. "Conceptions of Nonsense in Carnap and Wittgenstein." In A. Crary and R. Read (eds.), pp. 315–49.

Wittgenstein, L. 1969. *On Certainty*. Blackwell, Oxford.

———. 1979. *Notebooks 1914–1916*. 2d ed. Blackwell, Oxford.

———. 1993. *Philosophical Occasions 1912–1951*. Hackett, Indianapolis, Ind.

Wright, C. 1980. *Wittgenstein on the Foundations of Mathematics*. Duckworth, London.

———. 1987. *Realism, Meaning and Truth*. Blackwell, Oxford.

INDEX